Frankenstein

Maurice Hindle was born at Great Barr, near Birmingham, in the West Midlands of England. He studied at the universities of Keele and Durham, graduating from Durham in 1972 with an Honours degree in anthropology. From 1976 to 1988 he was a tutor at Tower Hamlets Institute of Adult Education in London. He now divides his time between freelance writing, university teaching and producing programmes for TV. In 1989 he gained a Ph.D. from Essex University for a critical edition of William Godwin's 1794 pioneer novel of politics and pursuit, *Caleb Williams.* As well as editing *Caleb Williams, Frankenstein* and *Dracula* for Penguin Classics, he has edited Godwin's last two novels *Cloudesley* (1830) and *Deloraine* (1833) for Pickering and Chatto's *Collected Novels and Memoirs of William Godwin* (1992). He lives in the Canonbury neighbourhood of Islington, London.

Penguin Critical Studies
Advisory Editor: Bryan Loughrey

Mary Shelley

Frankenstein

Or, the Modern Prometheus

Maurice Hindle

Penguin Books

PENGUIN BOOKS

Published by the Penguin Group
Penguin Books Ltd, 27 Wrights Lane, London W8 5TZ, England
Penguin Books USA Inc., 375 Hudson Street, New York, New York 10014, USA
Penguin Books Australia Ltd, Ringwood, Victoria, Australia
Penguin Books Canada Ltd, 10 Alcorn Avenue, Toronto, Ontario, Canada M4V 3B2
Penguin Books (NZ) Ltd, 182–190 Wairau Road, Auckland 10, New Zealand

Penguin Books Ltd, Registered Offices: Harmondsworth, Middlesex, England

First published 1994
10 9 8 7 6 5 4 3 2 1

Copyright © Maurice Hindle, 1994
All rights reserved

The moral right of the author has been asserted

Filmset by Datix International Limited, Bungay, Suffolk
Printed in England by Clays Ltd, St Ives plc
Set in 9/11 pt Monophoto Times

To the memory of Ruth Macrobbie
and her music

Contents

Contents

Introduction

Frankenstein: A Dream of a Text

To those who have only encountered the extraordinary figures of
Frankenstein and his Creature through films, television or comics –
which is to say, most of us – reading Mary Shelley's novel for the first
time may come as something of a surprise. For although she admitted
to having originally set out to write a ghost story aimed at frightening
the reader – to 'speak to the mysterious fears of our nature and awaken
thrilling horror' (7)* – the novel as written achieved this goal by raising
so many challenging questions about our modern (and perhaps even
'postmodern') human condition that it may be regarded as much a
philosophical novel as it is an English tale of terror. It becomes less of a
surprise once we look into her background and learn that she was
schooled deeply in the writings of her father, radical Enlightenment
philosopher William Godwin, and in those of her mother, innovative
feminist Mary Wollstonecraft, *as well as* being engulfed in the preoccupations of her lover/husband, philosophically-minded poet Percy Bysshe
Shelley (they were married during the composition of *Frankenstein*). In
turn, as we explore the various contexts of production for the book, its
historical genesis, its philosophical implications, and the moral significance it still holds for us, nearly two centuries later, we come to realize
that this really is much more than a tale of terror. Such explorations
form Part Three of this study. Before this, in Part Two, I examine some
of the main themes and literary techniques to be found in the book and
also show how *Frankenstein* needs to be considered in relation to texts
that went before it – principally Milton's *Paradise Lost* and Godwin's
writings.

This concern with the use an author makes of their literary predecessors is a fascinating and valuable part of contextualizing activity in
literary studies. In fact in Chapter 9 I could have gone much further
and explored the sources of names in the novel. For instance, to give
one example it would no doubt be remiss of me to omit: where does the

---

* The bracketed page references to *Frankenstein* given throughout relate to the
  1992 Penguin Classics edition, edited by Maurice Hindle.

name Frankenstein come from? There seems a very good chance indeed that Mary Shelley adapted this from the name of a character she found in P.B. Shelley's early novel *St Irvyne, or The Rosicrucian* (1811). When Wolfstein poisons the bandit chief Cavigni, Ginotti, a witness to the crime, proceeds to harass Wolfstein's life much in the same way that the Creature of Mary Shelley's novel will later in relation to Frankenstein. But why *Franken*stein, rather than Wolfstein? Victor Frankenstein in the novel is a native of Geneva, and thus a French-speaker. Since the language of the Franks was the precursor of modern French, it therefore makes sense for Mary Shelley to reflect this fact in the 'Frankish' name of Victor's old and distinguished family. If we were really keen, and wanted to dig out the source for Shelley's Wolfstein, we would eventually discover that the name crops up in Scott's famous poem, *The Lay of the Last Minstrel* (1805), with which Shelley would almost certainly be familiar. And so on.

But there is a limit to the value of such explorations. In particular, no efforts of contextualization can produce the insights concerning meaning which the close reading of a text can yield. If this is the case with works hitherto more readily accepted as part of the English literary canon studied by English and Humanities students, it is even more necessary a consideration when approaching Mary Shelley's novel. For although there have been many interesting biographical and literary studies written about her and her famous book, especially over the last twenty years, the text has often been selectively plundered to shore up arguments having some ideological axe to grind. This is not to say that some of the text's themes – such as the issues of parenting and gender roles – are not important. They most certainly are of crucial importance, and I am the last person not to give them their full due. But Mary Shelley's novel is too protean and large in its implications to be contained by any one ideological concern, whether focussed upon gender, race or class. *Frankenstein* can be made to address all these concerns, and because it can, perhaps it should be. But it has a great deal more to offer, and only a close reading of the text can deal with this. That is why the bulk of this study in Part One is devoted to that indispensable task.

It should perhaps be enough now to proceed with that reading. Yet because of the book's peculiar status – not because it is yet another of those great unread novel classics of the past, but because it is rather something we *think* we are familiar with, as I said, by crudely conceived film and comic versions producing this effect – I want by way of further introduction to attempt a clarification of how best we might make an initial attempt to 'come at' the text of *Frankenstein*. And in doing so, to show just how difficult that task is. For instance, to start with an old problem connected with this text, how are we to understand and classify the book, to know what genre it belongs to? Is it the first science fiction novel, as many seem to think? Or is it an early work of realism, as critic George Levine has claimed? Many would place it in the genre of Gothic romance, at its height of popularity in late eighteenth and early nineteenth centuries. Yet Northrop Frye, possibly reflecting the values and outlook of the period in which he was writing (the 1960s), has described it as a 'precursor of the existential thriller'. Who is right? Does it matter?

I think it may not matter, ultimately! But in a study such as this, genre is a valuable place to begin. In terms of publication date, to attempt an alignment of *Frankenstein* within the traditional category of 'Gothic romance' would seem to make some sense. Most people would agree that the genre began with Horace Walpole's *The Castle of Otranto* (1764) and more or less came to an end with Charles Maturin's *Melmoth the Wanderer* (1820). This spanned an interval of time not only coinciding with that era of change in Britain we have come to call the Industrial Revolution, but which also saw the rise and fall of the French Revolution. Neither of these upheavals seems to enter into the fictional fabric of the Gothic romances in any obvious way. Rather the opposite in fact, as Jane Lundblad has shown in her *Nathaniel Hawthorne and the Tradition of the Gothic Romance* (1946). She identifies what we might see as the principal 'escapist' features of the tale of terror in the following way:

There is an introductory story in order to produce an old manuscript where the happenings are written down, a Gothic castle forming a gloomy background with its secret corridors and labyrinthine network of subterranean passages, a mysterious crime frequently connected with illicit or incestuous love, and perpetrated by a person in holy orders, a villain (as a rule an Italian or Spaniard) who has pledged himself to the devil, who finally hurls himself into the abyss; ghosts, witches and sorcerers, nature conspiring to effects of terror and wonder, portraits endowed with a mysterious life, statues which are seen to bleed . . .

Although *Frankenstein* doesn't seem to draw on these genre devices in any obvious way, it is possible to offer an account of the novel showing that Mary Shelley adapted them to her own purposes. Instead of the introductory story told to produce an old manuscript, we have an explorer whose encounter with a questing scientist prompts him to write down the stranger's incredible tale. This tells of his devilish decision to father a 'new species' of being, and its consequences. After

3

grovelling in ghostly burial chambers for human parts the stranger has assembled a monstrous creature, not in a subterranean dungeon, but in a remote garret. He is not in holy orders, but this human creator of life has pursued his task 'religiously', finally animating a human-like creature. This is a mysterious crime connected with illicit or incestuous love because he is wholly consumed by what the eighteenth century called 'self-love': 'A new species would bless me as its creator and source [he says] ... No father could claim the gratitude of his child so completely as I should deserve theirs' (52). Abandoned by his 'father', the Creature turns vengeful villain and murderer – 'Evil thenceforth became my good' (212). This provokes a kind of masochistic battle to the death in which the Creature lures his creator to the 'abyss' of the North Pole, where the latter perishes, and the former announces his intended suicide.

Despite its affinities with the Gothic, it is probably a mistake to align *Frankenstein* wholly within this literary genre. That is because Mary Shelley's 'ghost story' breaks with the traditional Gothic tale's medievalism by seeking to engage with affairs and issues of the real world, and of the psychology of real people. It seems the traditional writers of Gothic romance had chosen to ignore the upheavals brought about by Industrial and French Revolutions. Or were they perhaps offering a kind of displaced reference to these by feeding such agitations of the social order into the minds of their wicked protagonists? Whatever the case, Mary Shelley embraced rather than avoided the implications of real technological and political innovations of the period. And she did this by an innovation of her own. Inventing the now common story-writing approach of 'What would happen if ...?', she asked, 'What would happen if one man were physically able to manufacture a living "new man"?'

That *Frankenstein* was concerned with the people, ideas and events of the real world in which it appeared was recognized by some commentators at first publication. In the *Edinburgh Review* of 1818 the reviewer said of it:

There never was a wilder story imagined, yet ... it has an air of reality attached to it, by being connected with the favourite projects and passions of the times. The real events of the world have, in our day, too, been of so wondrous and gigantic a kind, – the shiftings of the scenes in our stupendous drama have been so rapid and various, that Shakespeare himself, in his wildest flights, has been completely distanced by the eccentricities of actual existence.

The writer goes on to say how even Shakespeare would not have dared to write a play based on the rise and fall of the 'private adventurer' Napoleon Bonaparte, implying in a John Bullish way that, despite his political 'adventures' being carried out on an awesome scale, they were in the end still 'eccentric'. But Mary Shelley shows herself to be well in touch with such 'real eccentricities' of the time if we look to the evidence of yet another journal of 1818, the *Edinburgh Magazine*. Here it is told how since 1816 whaling captains had been claiming that the Arctic Sea might now, due to changing climatic conditions, 'become almost open and accessible to the adventurous navigator'. Reviewing several new books on the topic, the writer tells how the project of finding a north-west passage to Asia had now been seriously revived, 'and the more daring scheme of penetrating to the Pole itself has likewise been seriously proposed'. But the reviewer is doubtful about the value of such an attempt, alleging that the facts regarding the new Arctic conditions had given rise on occasion

to much loose reasoning, to wild and random conjectures, and visionary declamation. Glowing anticipations are confidently formed of the future amelioration of climate, which would scarcely be hazarded in the dreams of romance. Every person possessing a slight tincture of physical science, conceives himself qualified to speculate . . .

So here we encounter an interesting conjunction which is at the heart of Mary Shelley's novelistic exploration – the relation between dream and reality. But what of *Frankenstein* as realist novel?

In *The Realistic Imagination: English Fiction from Frankenstein to Lady Chatterley* (1981), George Levine has argued that we should consider *Frankenstein* as an early realist novel because it delivers 'one of the first in a long tradition of over-reachers, of characters who seem to act out the myth of Faust in modern dress', but 'who transport it from the world of mystery and miracle to the commonplace'. The man who 'thoughtlessly' achieves the creation of life is not punished by metaphysical agency, as when God expels Adam from Eden in the Christian creation myth, for in *Frankenstein* God is scarcely alluded to. Instead, Frankenstein is destroyed 'by his own nature and the consequences of living in or rejecting human community'. It is in this sense that Mary Lowe-Evans could be correct in reading *Frankenstein* as a 'complex treatise on situational ethics'. In fact, the only statement of what Mary Shelley had intended to achieve in her book (besides wanting to curdle our blood) is conveyed in very much these terms in a letter she wrote to the poet and essayist Leigh Hunt in 1819. Referring to her novel, she says, 'I have written a book in defence of Polypheme –

have I not?' In Greek mythology Polyphemus was a one-eyed giant of monstrous strength and appearance who fell in love with the sea-nymph Galatea, but was shunned by her. According to the Roman poet Ovid, when Polyphemus saw young Galatea surrender herself to her lover the shepherd Acis, the jealous monster crushed his rival to death with a rock. As with Galatea, the world tends instinctively to hate and reject 'monsters'. But the story of Polyphemus shows that monsters have feelings, which, when they are rejected out of hand, can turn sour and breed violence. Thus at one level of her text at least, Mary Shelley's comment suggests a desire to explore and defend the feelings of those whom the world rejects and betrays. And this would indeed seem to be a 'realist' aim.

But if *Frankenstein* can be considered a realist novel, by one recent definition at least it can equally be regarded as a distinctive work of 'Romantic' writing. In an essay in *The Cambridge Companion to British Romanticism* (1993) Marshall Brown has said that we often make the mistake of linking Romanticism too closely with 'empty dreaming', the kind of reverie that was actually fashionable 'well back before the generation of '98' (i.e. before Wordsworth and Coleridge's *Lyrical Ballads* appeared) and found in writers like Rousseau and William Cowper. 'The writers whom we know as Romantics are distinguished from this earlier generation,' he says, 'by virtue of the fact that they tell their dreams, and, indeed, the more haunted they are . . . the more they try to share and illuminate their hauntings. It is not dreaming that is the distinctive emblem of Romanticism . . . but the moment of awakening in which the dream is preserved.' If this is true, then *Frankenstein* must be the prose Romantic work *par excellence*, for we know from Mary Shelley's detailed account of how she came to write the novel that it arose as the result of a 'waking dream':

I did not sleep, nor could I be said to think. My imagination, unbidden, possessed and guided me, gifting the successive images that arose in my mind with a vividness far beyond the usual bounds of reverie. I saw – with shut eyes, but acute mental vision – I saw the pale student of unhallowed arts kneeling beside the thing he had put together. I saw the hideous phantasm of a man stretched out, and then, on the working of some powerful engine, show signs of life, and stir with an uneasy, half-vital motion. (9)

And the rest is literary history.

So what have we established? If we must categorize *Frankenstein*, it is perhaps best to say it is a work of Romanticism, somehow captured by Brown's definition, but which uses a modified Gothic romance structure to develop its realist concerns. As for it being a 'precursor of the existential thriller', I leave that evaluation for the reader, no doubt familiar to one degree or another with the 'eccentricities of actual existence', to work on.

At the beginning of Chapter 11 I record how when Mary Shelley paid a visit to see the first theatrical dramatization of her novel, Peake's *Presumption* (1823), she expressed delight at seeing the Creature described simply as — in the playbill's list of actors, and wrote that 'this nameless mode of naming the unnameable is rather good'. Unfortunately certain difficulties of naming in this study are not so easily resolved. In what follows, Mary Shelley and Percy Shelley are often referred to close together in the discussion. Many critics and writers have been content to name the author of *Frankenstein* as Mary and call the poet only, Shelley. I could seek to avoid the charge of sexism by using their full names every time, but that seems unnecessarily pedantic. I have thus preferred to mix it: for clarity's sake I never refer to the author of *Frankenstein* as Shelley, but usually name her as Mary Shelley or, occasionally, Mary. I refer to the poet variously as Shelley, P.B. Shelley, or Percy. The context should always make it obvious about whom I am talking. When I refer to the species as 'man', this is sometimes as a matter of convenience, but elsewhere, and especially in Chapter 12, the usage is also tinged with an irony that most should find apparent.

Part One: The Text

1 Robert Walton's Narrative (1)

Letters 1–4

A careful reading of Robert Walton's four letters home to his sister Margaret Saville in England alerts us to many of the key concerns and metaphors of the novel as a whole. Primary among these themes is what happens to human sympathies and relationships when men seek obsessively to satisfy their Promethean longing to 'conquer the unknown' in the service of their fellow humans (I explore what I shall be calling Romantic Prometheanism in Chapter 8, 'Metaphor and Meaning'). Isolation seems necessarily to be a precondition for *and* a consequence of these efforts, which also demand of the questor (here, both Walton and Frankenstein) that he think and organize his reality in terms of a range of binary opposites. For example, the following contrasts are evoked overtly or covertly throughout the text in order to give it meaning and significance:

natural/unnatural
known/unknown
resemblance/difference
masculine/feminine
civilized/savage
beautiful/ugly
good/bad
light/dark
heat/cold

These are not written down in any particular order. Nevertheless we may find that some of the words in the left-hand column are often linked together, as are those on the right. So that what we may regard as 'natural' in our experience of the world would be, generally speaking, what we believe we 'know' about it, and perhaps what we also regard as 'civilized'. Similarly, what we experience as 'unnatural' are often things we know little about and may thus tend to reject as unfamiliar, even 'bad'. But in Mary Shelley's *Frankenstein* we find that our expectations of what can be matched with what, are frequently confounded and undermined. Classifications contradict or start erupting and flowing into each other when we read more closely.

An important instance of this comes at the beginning of the novel, in the second paragraph of Walton's first letter home to his married sister Margaret Saville. He is trying to explain to her his feelings as he advances north on a voyage of exploration to the North Pole:

I am already far north of London; and as I walk in the streets of Petersburgh, I feel a cold northern breeze play upon my cheeks, which braces my nerves, and fills me with delight. Do you understand this feeling? This breeze, which has travelled from the regions towards which I am advancing, gives me a foretaste of those icy climes. (13)

For most of us an icily cold wind blowing down from the North Pole would signal caution concerning the hazardous conditions to come. This is almost certainly how Margaret has seen things, for Walton mentions in passing that she has already had 'evil forebodings' about his 'enterprise'. But Walton is compelled to think otherwise about what the future holds for him. Why should this be? The reason is that the impulse driving him to pursue his quest goes way beyond our ordinary understanding of 'sense'. The cold fills him with delight because, try as he might, he cannot be persuaded that 'the pole is the seat of frost and desolation'. Instead, it 'ever presents itself to my imagination as the region of beauty and delight' (13). Reports of 'preceding navigators' have encouraged him to believe that 'snow and frost are banished' there, so that the perpetually shining sun may sustain a 'land surpassing in wonders and in beauty every region hitherto discovered on the habitable globe' (13). What quickens Walton's pulse is not experiences conveyed to him by his immediate senses, but by an *image* of anticipated future experiences, the vividness of which can only be imparted by the 'light' of his imagination. The warmth of what the imagination can conjure up is not merely sufficient to dispel any immediate discomfort, but in fact transforms for him an icy north wind into a 'wind of promise'.

Right at the outset of her novel, then, we find Mary Shelley doing two things. Firstly she is drawing our attention to a definitive feature of Romantic writing: the importance attached in it to the transforming power of the imagination. But in having Walton state his feelings so explicitly, she also seems to be suggesting that the motives for his enterprise are questionable. There is the implication that women and men may perceive the value of such an enterprise rather differently. We have already noted Margaret's 'evil forebodings' about his voyage, so when he asks his sister, 'Do you understand this feeling?', we might as readers be alert enough to see his question being as much a perplexed plea for help as it is a celebration of the pioneering masculine spirit. The sense of an unstable enthusiasm at work in Walton is confirmed by his later declaration that 'There is something at work in my soul, which I do not understand' (19). He tells Margaret that this expedition of his had been a 'favourite dream' from his early years, when his (self) education had largely been provided by the accounts of attempts to discover a north-west passage to the Pacific Ocean via the North Pole which he had read about in his Uncle Thomas's books of exploratory voyages. These volumes had become his study 'day and night', so that when he learned his father's 'dying injunction' had been to forbid his uncle from allowing him to embark on a seafaring career, he had been bitterly disappointed. His desires had been thwarted, and by a father whose early death meant an 'appeal' was out of the question. It was at this point – at the age of fourteen – that his encounter with the Romantic poets had persuaded him to abandon his 'visions' of being an explorer, and for a year he attempted to become a poet himself. He reminds Margaret how 'well acquainted' she is with his failure at this attempt, but also how his prospects were then altered by the sudden and propitious inheritance of his cousin's fortune. This now enabled him to satisfy the desires of his earlier 'bent' – that of becoming an Arctic explorer – and so he had proceeded with preparations for this task. In so proceeding he seems to have forgotten or ignored his father's dying strictures against a seafaring career. Because this defiance is unremarked upon by Walton, Mary Shelley draws our attention to an important component in the motivation for Walton's Promethean quest – the wilful determination to overcome a desire thwarted by fathers. Such a pattern will be encountered again in Frankenstein's account of his childhood.

As we read on further into Walton's early letters, we find him confessing that although he is now twenty-eight years old and sufficiently equipped in knowledge and experience as a high-seas voyager to attain the 'glory' he seeks, he nevertheless sometimes feels his 'courage and resolution' are insufficient for the task that lies ahead:

... my hopes fluctuate, and my spirits are often depressed. I am about to proceed on a long and difficult voyage, the emergencies of which will demand all my fortitude: I am required not only to raise the spirits of others, but sometimes to sustain my own, when theirs are failing. (15)

The explanation for his periodic lapses of resolution seems to be linked to his earlier experiences. From the scanty account given of his family background, it seems both he and Margaret had grown up orphans, the best years of the youth which he otherwise 'passed in solitude' being spent under her 'gentle and feminine fosterage' (18). It is thus evident that Margaret's kind maternal influence has had a powerful effect upon his character. Not only has it bred in him a repugnance for the 'usual brutality' found among the crews of ships, but on the voyage that might, if he fails, be his last (20), he is desperately aware that she is the person to whom he is emotionally closest. With each mile travelled further north, the greater is the distance put between him and the security and sympathy which she represents. He may find his spirits temporarily raised by being able to write to her, yet he declares that writing for him is 'a poor medium for the communication of feeling'. Human sympathy is what he craves. It is Margaret's feminine nature that has (presumably) won her psychological strength and a husband. But Robert suffers and is companionless. He suffers because his Romantic Prometheanism produces a paradoxical self whose driven, mission-like condition urges him on, for reasons he cannot explain, to the pursuit of wonderful adventures and glory. It seems that such a pursuit can only be carried on at the expense of sacrificing human sympathy. This is why he yearns for

the company of a man who could sympathise with me; whose eyes would reply to mine. You may deem me romantic, my dear sister, but I bitterly feel the want of a friend. I have no one near me, gentle yet courageous, possessed of a cultivated as well as of a capacious mind, whose tastes are like my own, to approve or amend my plans. (17)

The qualities Walton requires for a friend are so like those which he sees in himself that this suggests a strong element of narcissism in his character. But despite his desire to find a friend very much like himself, a man who sympathizes with and will encourage and humour him in his Promethean quest, Walton also recognizes that this person must 'endeavour' to prevent the day dreams that drive him on, from unbalancing his mind (18). This implies he has a measure of insight into his own limitations, just as the earlier statement of his trying '*in vain* to be persuaded that the pole is the seat of frost and desolation' (emphasis added) shows he is at least capable of making attempts at self-analysis. Yet this should not be over-stated, both because these attempts have indeed been 'in vain', and that the advice he requires from his (as yet un-found) friend will only be to 'approve or amend' his plans, not in any way to reject or overturn them. These considerations should be borne in mind for the final pages of the novel, when Walton's decision to turn his ship around and return to England is made only because he feels his crew will mutiny if he refuses to do so. He is a determined voyager, convinced that 'success *shall* crown my endeavours' (21).

He is also gloomily certain that the near-double he seeks as a companion will not be found 'on the wide ocean', nor is this friend likely to be found among the 'merchants and seamen' he encounters recruiting for his ship's crew in Archangel. Here we find the first of what will be many allusions to a key textual influence on the novel, Milton's *Paradise Lost*. Mary Shelley seems to be deliberately linking Walton's dangerous endeavour with the rebellious activities of Milton's 'lost Archangel', Satan. Although he judges the English lieutenant he gets to join him to possess 'some of the noblest endowments of humanity', and learns that the 'noble' master he takes on benevolently sacrificed his lover and his estate to a rival, neither are suitable as friends for him. He finds the former 'unsoftened by cultivation' and the latter to be both 'wholly uneducated' and 'as silent as a Turk' (18, 19). He thus seems destined to remain unsupported in terms of intimate friendship in his endeavours. Despite this, he is defiantly eager to assure Margaret (or himself?) that far from wavering in his resolutions, they are 'as fixed as fate'. Realizing how, to a sister concerned for this same fate, what he has said might seem too obsessive, he quickly adds that he will 'do nothing rashly' on his voyage of discovery, and seeks to remind her of his essentially benevolent nature: 'you know me sufficiently to confide in my prudence and considerateness whenever the safety of others is committed to my care' (19). Is this assurance convincing? In the end we only have Walton's word for it, and what we get in these letters cannot be said to be consistent enough to supply this assurance. Despite his public-spirited motives for making the voyage, his self-confessed psychological instability and desperate pleas for a friend who will correct his mistakes have the effect of undermining his grand declarations, making us uneasy about his bold claims. That we are right to feel this way is amply confirmed by what follows in his defensive gesture at reassuring Margaret. He is simply unable to contain the enthusiasm for his project which his Romantic Prometheanism demands to be given expression, and he now excitedly reveals the hitherto 'secret' source of this zeal. 'I am going to unexplored regions', he says,

to 'the land of mist and snow'; but I shall kill no albatross, therefore do not be alarmed for my safety, or if I should come back to you as worn and woeful as the 'Ancient Mariner'. You will smile at my allusion; but I will disclose a secret. I have often attributed my attachment to, my passionate enthusiasm for, the dangerous mysteries of ocean, to that production of the most imaginative of modern poets. There is something at work in my soul, which I do not understand. (19)

Coleridge was one of the many distinguished personalities who regularly visited the household of Mary's father, the philosopher and novelist William Godwin, in her childhood. On one of his visits she had heard the poet recite *The Rime of the Ancient Mariner* in full, an event which must have imprinted itself indelibly on her nine-year-old mind. We find it initially gratifying that Walton tells Margaret she should not be alarmed for his safety, because he 'will kill no albatross'. It seems to show he has learned the moral of the poem, that we disturb or destroy nature at our peril. But if we look more closely at what he says, we realize he must only have understood the moral in a very limited sense. The 'passionate enthusiasm' he has developed for the 'dangerous mysteries of ocean' described in the poem is not for any real ocean, but for a symbolic one that he mistakes for real. The avenging, uncontrollable forces released in the *Mariner* have been used by Coleridge to show the terrible effects which guilt can visit upon a man whose 'human moral blindness inadvertently introduces evil into the benign systems of nature'.[1]

But what really bewitches Walton – though he does not recognize it – is the enticing prospect of exploring evil. This is probably because he has always been something of an unworldly innocent, brought about by a number of factors. His basic character has been 'refined' early on by the 'feminine fosterage' of Margaret, and he acknowledges his adult views have been the product of a narrow self-education. He has also failed in his dream of becoming a Romantic poet. But above all, he seems not to have had any sexual experience of women. So it is not surprising when we read that he is preparing for his departure with a 'trembling sensation, half pleasurable and half fearful'. For this can be taken to signify that Walton's exploration is really what Freud would have called a 'sublimation' of his sexual drives. That is to say, the immense investment of effort and time he is putting into his exploratory project is a substitute for, a displacement of, untried sexual energies. In a sense, the poem which would fit Walton's 'case' more aptly is Coleridge's *Christabel*, in which the sexual power of the daemonic Geraldine entrances and captivates the innocent Christabel. Knowing this helps us to see more clearly what Walton's statement – 'there is something at work in my soul, which I do not understand' – is really all about. It is the nature of his sexual energy and identity that eludes him.

16

What we are shown in Walton then is an unstable, obsessive, still somewhat adolescent figure of twenty-eight who repeatedly oscillates between two states of mind. On the one hand there is in him a 'love for the marvellous, a belief in the marvellous . . . which hurries me out of the common pathways of men' (20) – his Romantic Promethean quest. But his other mental mode has him solemnly assuring Margaret he will never allow his enthusiasms to do anything transgressively provocative. This sort of assurance is a check he typically puts on himself every time he realizes there are other destinies to be thought of in his quest, besides his own. The problem is that one state of mind always triggers its opposite, in a 'tick-tock' neurotic oscillation that threatens to become, rather like the vacillations of Hamlet in Shakespeare's tragedy, interminable.

In his fourth letter, Walton's repeated swings from enthusiastic dream to self-conscious trepidation are dramatically stilled by the need to deal with external events. First of all, the progress of the voyage is literally halted when ice surrounds them 'on all sides' and a thick fog descends. After the mist clears, the crew is dismayed to see that the ice encircling them seems 'to have no end'. Just as Walton too is beginning to 'grow watchful with anxious thoughts', their attention is attracted towards a dog-drawn sledge being driven across the ice half a mile away by a 'being which had the shape of a man', yet which was of 'gigantic stature' (23). Though no one knows it, they have just seen Frankenstein's Creature. At this first moment of crisis it is worth mentioning just how classically 'gothic' (by one definition of the term, at least) Walton's encounter with this 'strange sight' really is. The assertion of Mario Praz that 'an anxiety with no possibility of escape is the main theme of the Gothic tales'[2] certainly seems borne out by Mary Shelley's text here. For it is when all are trapped, with no way out, and the anxious thoughts of the expedition's leader are multiplying, that the terribleness of the situation is 'resolved' (one might even say 'embodied') by the appearance of what Walton calls an 'apparition'. Against the brilliant white polar landscape the eye perceives the giant figure as real, but the mind, finding what is seen as hardly believable, registers it as ghost-like. That a human of such size could exist, and what is more, be seemingly intent on travelling in a northerly direction hundreds of miles from land, excites 'unqualified wonder' in the crew. Such is the pressing need for the human mind to name and classify all it experiences, that this ghost-like figure (which Frankenstein will similarly denominate a 'monstrous Image' in his narrative) must be fitted in to the conceptual schemes with which the perceivers construct their everyday reality. This

17

construction is elaborated for us the following day, when a half-frozen man is rescued from an ice floe, the ice having now broken up. Upon seeing him Walton says he is 'not as the other traveller seemed to be, a savage inhabitant of some undiscovered island, but an European' (24). The 'European' is Victor Frankenstein (though his name is hardly used in Walton's narrative, an important fact for us to bear in mind).

Walton's characterization of the rescued man as a 'European' and the 'other traveller' as a 'savage' is important to note, not merely for what it tells us about Walton's obsessive frame of mind, but because what lies behind the meaning of this differentiation informs much of the *ordinary* way the remainder of the text and its characters will deal with the 'familiar' and the 'strange'. In giving the meaning of the word 'savage' as 'wild, cruel and uncivilized', the Johnson's dictionary of Mary Shelley's time was not merely evoking the kind of behaviour 'polite' English society would find abhorrent to its social codes. It was also defining a generally shared understanding of what distinguished remote, little-known cultures from the mores of that polite society. Whatever their internal political differences, most Europeans saw their 'polished' nations as having attained to the pinnacle of civilized values and cultural achievement, whereas 'savage' societies, perceived as having a minimum of development in material or intellectual culture, were regarded as uncouthly 'primitive'. (It will be noticed later how the Creature's narrative shows Mary Shelley to have been influenced by Rousseau's view of non-Europeans as of the 'noble savage' type.) Thus the opposing contrast of 'European' and 'savage' in Walton's statement will, for the early nineteenth-century European reader (or for the ethnocentric one of any succeeding period or place), tend to do two things. It will not only implicitly convey corresponding value judgements of, respectively, 'good' and 'evil', but also set up an expectation that the Creature is going to be something irredeemably and dangerously 'other', unassimilable to European cultural values and understanding. Broadly speaking then, the 'savage' individual signals that which is unknown, uncivilized and therefore to be fearfully detested. Conversely, as a European, Frankenstein is meant to stand for that which is known, is civilized and which demands our sympathy and understanding.

It is therefore surprising to Walton that the fellow European he has met should display the peculiar behaviour he does when offered the chance of rescue from the ice. In fact, the newcomer's response to the crew's sympathy for his supposed plight is so strange as to introduce a note of levity into a text not otherwise noted for its jokes:

On perceiving me, the stranger addressed me in English, although with a foreign accent. 'Before I come on board your vessel,' said he, 'will you have the kindness to inform me whither you are bound?'

You may conceive my astonishment on hearing such a question addressed to me from a man on the brink of destruction and to whom I should have supposed that my vessel would have been a resource which he would not have exchanged for the most precious wealth the earth can afford. I replied, however, that we were on a voyage of discovery towards the northern pole. (24)

This satisfies the stranger and he consents to come aboard. Concerned at his having been brought to near collapse by cold and fatigue, Walton now tells how they 'restored him to animation by rubbing him with brandy and forcing him to swallow a small quantity' (24). In a novel where everything ultimately flows from the idea of creating life out of dead matter, such a use of words cannot be accidental, particularly as we know that Walton's frame story was developed after those sections involving the making of the Creature and its sequel of events had been drafted (Author's Introduction, p. 10). Indeed, the 'language of animation' recurs several times in Letter 4, and is each time linked to Frankenstein. When he has recovered a little, for instance, he thanks Walton for rescuing him by saying 'you have benevolently restored me to life' (25). Then, upon learning that the 'one who fled from him might have survived the breaking up of the ice, 'a new spirit of life animated the decaying frame of the stranger' (26). Finally, in a passage where Walton aims to conjure up for Margaret the sympathetic effect that Frankenstein's presence has already had on him (added in the 1831 edition, and revealing a nostalgically evoked Percy Shelley as the model), he tells her how it delights him to hear the sound of his 'full-toned voice', to regard his 'lustrous eyes' dwelling on him 'with all their melancholy sweetness', and to see 'his thin hand raised in animation' (29).[3] It is on a second reading of the novel that this language of animation tends to become noticeable, and as it does so it draws our attention to the way the ebbs and flows of Frankenstein's vitality are intertwined with those of the 'one who fled' from him.

But Walton as yet knows nothing of the part Frankenstein's Creature has played in the decline of the strange, emaciated figure he sees before him. Instead of feeling repelled by the stranger's grudging acceptance of rescue, he finds himself fascinated by the spectacle that the wild-eyed newcomer presents. Despite initially acting as if gestures of social generosity were totally alien to him – or perhaps because of this – Walton feels he has never seen a 'more interesting creature' than the stranger (25). Besides which, while Frankenstein is 'animated' by the prospect of catching up with the 'other traveller', Walton believes himself to have finally encountered the kind of person whose company he has so long craved, and within a few days comes to love him 'as a brother'. Using the phrase twice in one page, Walton says Frankenstein must once have been a 'noble creature', rather than a 'creature destroyed by misery', as he now appears to be (26). (Just as Mary Shelley's language of animation connects Frankenstein with his Creature, so does this repeated use of 'creature' here.) The evidence for this perception is in the 'double existence' Walton observes Frankenstein to be living out. On the one hand he notices how he may 'suffer misery and be overwhelmed by disappointment'. But then he also sees how the man is able to retire into himself 'like a celestial spirit, that has a halo around him, within whose circle no grief or folly ventures' (28). These alternating self-preoccupied states of mind no doubt remind him of his own oscillating moods. Thus in the end the 'sympathy and compassion' which he feels for Frankenstein are based less on his liking for him as a fellow European of his own social class and background *per se*, than on his warming to the man for his personal qualities. As a one-time aspirant to the poet's laurel who failed in words and instead turned to geographical explorations, Walton can now look to the 'cultivated' mind and 'unparalleled eloquence' of Frankenstein for sympathy and support in his Coleridge-inspired quest. Fortunately for him, Frankenstein is not so destroyed by misery that he is unwilling to listen with interest to Walton's dream of reaching a paradisiacal North Pole. As the 'burning ardour' of his soul takes advantage of this new sympathetic ear to enthuse about his project, he makes it clear how far he is willing to go to make it a success:

One man's life or death were but a small price to pay for the acquirement of the knowledge which I sought for the dominion I should acquire and transmit over the elemental foes of our race. (27)

Frankenstein responds to this statement first with gloom and then horror. I say 'horror' because, although the text states that Frankenstein 'placed his hands before his eyes' in an attempt to 'suppress his emotion', this gesture also conveys the secondary suggestion that Walton's assertion has triggered something so monstrous in him that he would rather not 'see' it: 'Unhappy man!' he says finally, 'Do you share my madness? Have you drunk also of the intoxicating draught? Hear me – let me reveal my tale, and you will dash the cup from your lips!' (27)

But the stranger does not proceed immediately with this tale, several hours being required for him to recover from his emotional outburst. Characteristically, Walton seems oblivious of the fact that this outburst has been occasioned by his own passionately 'heated' outpouring and merely notes that Frankenstein 'appeared to despise himself for being the slave of passion' (27). Instead of having his 'strongly excited' curiosity satisfied by hearing the stranger's tale, Frankenstein asks about Walton's past, a tale which 'was quickly told' and which ends when he speaks of his long-standing thirst for the 'intimate sympathy' of an understanding friend. Frankenstein agrees that

'we are unfashioned creatures, but half made up, if one wiser, better, dearer than ourselves – such a friend ought to be – do not lend his aid to perfectionate our weak and faulty natures.' (27–8)

Without saying – significantly, as we shall find out later – that the person was able to serve him in this way, he laments the loss of an old friend who had been (echoing Walton's description of Frankenstein) 'the most noble of human creatures'. His claim to know what the value of friendship really is, is the reason why, having been upset by Walton's wild Promethean proclamations, he decides now to tell his own story. Evidently it is because he has 'lost every thing and cannot begin life anew' that he wishes to 'perfectionate' the 'weak and faulty nature' of Walton, someone he wishes to be allowed to call 'my friend' (29):

'You seek for knowledge and wisdom, as I once did; and I ardently hope that the gratification of your wishes may not be a serpent to sting you, as mine has been.' (28)

He hopes further that Walton 'may deduce an apt moral' from his tale (in the 1818 edition, that his 'faculties and understanding' may be 'enlarged') since he does not wish his new friend to 'lose everything', as he has. The satisfaction of his knowledge-seeking ambitions has left him with a life empty of friends, feeling and hope: but Walton, as yet, has no 'cause for despair'. Yet the explorer seems not to notice that the narrative is being offered as guidance for his own moral welfare. He believes instead that listening to the story will help to 'ameliorate' the fate of Frankenstein (29), having what we would now call a therapeutic effect on him. Frankenstein, who has plumbed the depths of loss, knows more. He politely thanks Walton for his 'sympathy' but says it is 'useless', although he can understand the feeling behind Walton's gesture. His 'fate' is nearly fulfilled and nothing can alter his 'destiny'. But what, we must ask, is behind this 'fate' and 'destiny' such that Frankenstein is able to 'understand' Walton's sympathetic feeling, yet is unable

21

any longer to *experience* or participate in it himself? Why is sympathy 'useless' to him?

These are important questions that the novel both poses and seeks to answer, and which we shall be encountering again in the pages which follow.[4] I started by saying that the novel's plot generates a warning about the price to be paid in loss of sympathy by Promethean questors whose pursuits become obsessive. But as Mary Shelley takes us from Walton's narrative into that of Frankenstein by having the latter say the explorer should prepare to hear 'of occurrences which are usually deemed marvellous' (29), we know that Frankenstein has touched on an acutely sensitive area of Walton's passionate character – the 'marvellous'. In doing so this cleverly arouses both the explorer's self-confessed 'curiosity', and ours too. In a brilliantly sly piece of writing Mary Shelley not only has Frankenstein whetting further Walton's already ample appetite for making strange discoveries in the Arctic of his dreams, but also manages ironically to convey a picture of the Romantic imagination itself at work:

'Were we among the tamer scenes of nature, I might fear to encounter your unbelief, perhaps your ridicule; but many things will appear possible in these wild and mysterious regions, which would provoke the laughter of those unacquainted with the ever-varied powers of nature . . . (29)

Thus in a physically cold and isolated 'wild and mysterious region' we are being asked to listen to a story which has been 'warmed' by the 'wild and mysterious region' of Frankenstein's unruly Romantic imagination, where the 'savage' reality of lived-out dreams is perhaps bound to collide with society's efforts to remain 'civilized'.

2 Victor Frankenstein's Narrative (1)

Geneva (Chapters I–II)

As we enter into a discussion of Frankenstein's narrative, it is as well to bear in mind Mary Shelley's statement that for invention to take place,

> the materials must, in the first place, be afforded: it can give form to dark, shapeless substances, but cannot bring into being the substance itself. (Author's Introduction, p. 8)

The 'substance' behind the form of much of Frankenstein's story derives from the author's own life-experiences and history, and in particular from her relationships to and understanding of her father William Godwin, her dead mother Mary Wollstonecraft, and her lover Percy Shelley. A further important element in the originary substance of the narrative is the use she made of places she had lived in and visited, in order to give a certain symbolic value to the text's meaning. In drawing attention to these facts, I do not want to imply that without detailed knowledge of them the text cannot be properly understood. For it is no more a matter of Frankenstein being constructed to 'represent' the real Percy Shelley (for instance) than it is of Elizabeth being invented to depict the character of the author (even though each fictional character embodies certain characteristics of these people). That is not how good fiction works. Imaginative fiction of enduring value owes its quality to a writing experience that is hard to pin down, a practice inclined more to flow in unpredictable directions, than take directly from life or previous texts. There is certainly something of Percy Shelley in Victor Frankenstein, but so there is in his friend Clerval and in the Creature too, who in turn is also a vehicle for expressing various of the author's strong feelings. When authors incorporate biographical or textual allusions into their writing they do so without clearly knowing the effects this will have on the overall meaning and reception of the text. That is for us as studious readers to determine. Taking into account the allusions produced by an author who emerges from a specific biographical field can only assist us to gain more meaning from the text, especially when one is dealing with so private a person as Mary Shelley. Although I offer a more detailed account of textual and biographical allusions and influences in Parts Two and Three, in what follows I shall also weave into my discussion of the story and its characters some comment on these. Let us start with the author's choice of Geneva for the birthplace of Victor Frankenstein. Why Geneva?

It may seem an obvious choice. In the summer of 1816, when Mary Shelley (then still Mary Godwin) started writing *Frankenstein*, she lived for several months on the outskirts of Geneva with Percy, William her baby boy, her half-sister Claire Clairmont, and their Swiss maidservant Elise. But there is greater significance in Victor Frankenstein's being made a citizen of Geneva than for reasons of mere proximity. For Mary, as for Percy Shelley and Lord Byron, the republican canton of Geneva symbolized freedom in a Europe still dominated by a multiplicity of (largely Catholic) monarchies they would have deemed ruthlessly corrupt. Geneva was where Calvin had pioneered the Franco-Swiss Protestant Reformation. It had been the home and refuge of the protesting (if not conventionally protestant) freethinker Voltaire. But above all for the English Romantic exiles, it was the birthplace of one who was for many years proud to sign himself 'Citoyen de Genève', the philosopher and writer Jean-Jacques Rousseau. Rousseau and his ideas concerning liberty and society enter into the text of *Frankenstein* in many ways. For the moment some preliminary remarks must suffice.

Mary first encountered Rousseau in the works of her parents Godwin and Wollstonecraft, especially in the latter's *The Wrongs of Woman: or, Maria* (1798), where he is called 'the true Prometheus of sentiment'.[1] Then in the period 1815–17 she read, and re-read, his *Confessions* (1782), *La Nouvelle Héloïse* (1761) and *Émile* (1762). In the 1830s she wrote a biographical essay on Rousseau containing (as I shall show later) critical judgements on his life and ideas that reveal acute links with problems of parental responsibility she was concerned to address in *Frankenstein*. Soon after their arrival in Geneva in May 1816, Mary recorded in her journal that she and Percy had twice visited a 'small obelisk erected to the glory of Rousseau' in the Plainpalais. When Percy and Lord Byron went on their famous eight-day boat trip around Lake Geneva the following month, they took with them a copy of *La Nouvelle Héloïse* and visited many of the places where Rousseau had laid the scenes of passion enjoyed by the book's lovers Julie and St Preux. Victor Frankenstein's descriptions of the sublime surroundings of the lake and the Alps also seem to owe something to the landscapes depicted in Rousseau's novel. Of greater significance *vis-à-vis* the pre-occupation with isolation in *Frankenstein* are the five days she spent reading Rousseau's last work, *Reveries of the Solitary Walker* (written

1776–8). She read this upon returning from her visit to Chamonix and the Mer de Glace at the end of July 1816 – an experience she drew on for Frankenstein's momentous encounter with his Creature on the sea of ice. Thus David Marshall's view that we should see Victor Frankenstein as 'a compatriot of Rousseau's' is, at the least, highly persuasive.[2]

At the beginning of his narrative in Chapter I, Victor does seem to recall with pride his belonging to a family which for generations has contributed much to Geneva's republican tradition of justice and social service. Indeed, we learn that his own father had served the canton by filling 'several public situations with honour and reputation', his younger days being spent 'perpetually occupied by the affairs of his country' (31). Such total dedication to public service meant that Alphonse Frankenstein did not marry until the 'decline of life', something which in the first edition of 1818 is explicitly described as being motivated by his desire of 'bestowing on the state sons who might carry his virtues and his name down to posterity'. This phrase implies he married less for reasons of love than to ensure the continuation of a dynastic line dedicated to propagating what one writer has called a masculine 'ethic of justice'.[3] Such a patriarchal ethic is underpinned by unambiguous abstract principles of right and wrong, good and bad, to which Victor's father seems to have strictly adhered. The account of the 'circumstances' of his marriage, which Victor says will 'illustrate his character' more adequately to Walton than a conventional eulogy, confirms this. This report of the train of events leading up to his own birth is also the first of a series of anecdotes – culminating in his own 'marvellous' tale – whose accumulated densities are designed to deliver finally the 'apt moral' he wishes to teach Walton.

Thus he tells how, when the sudden financial ruin of Alphonse's intimate friend Beaufort had driven the latter to retreat shamefacedly from Geneva with his daughter for a life of wretchedness and poverty, his father had been deeply hurt. Alphonse had felt such a departure to be not merely precipitous, but, more seriously, motivated by a 'false pride' which betrayed their long-established friendship. If Beaufort had trusted his friend to help him, his fortunes might have been saved and his self-respect restored. As it was, his 'proud and unbending disposition' compelled him to endure a despairing isolation which ended in sickness and death, before Alphonse was able to locate and help him. The moral seems clear: abandoning established social sympathies for a pride-filled concern with reputation is a miserable and anti-social way out. The evil was exacerbated in this case by his daughter's feeling obligated to undertake menial work in order to sustain him in this wretchedly alienated state. Determined to act as a 'protecting spirit' to the daughter who had been left an 'orphan and a beggar', the principled Alphonse decides to maintain Caroline Beaufort under his protection.

After two years, having gradually shed his public duties in order to devote more time to his charge, he marries her. The words Victor uses to describe his father's purposes in marrying Caroline repay careful study, for he says in effect that Alphonse saw his marriage as an extension of his benevolent work for the state. Before he could 'love strongly', he says, his 'sense of justice' had required that he should 'approve highly'. In other words, his action was dictated by abstract principle rather than desire as such. Thus Alphonse comes to show the young Caroline 'gratitude and worship', he is 'inspired by reverence for her virtues', and he aims to be the means of 'recompensing her for the sorrows she had endured' (32). When we read further that 'He strove to shelter her, as a fair exotic is sheltered by the gardener, from every rougher wind, and to surround her with all that could tend to excite pleasurable emotion in her soft and benevolent mind' (32–3), it is as if we had been transported into a piece of mid-Victorian 'woman-worship' literature, such as Coventry Patmore's poem *The Angel in the House* (1854–62), where the highly- gendered character of Victorian love is captured.

Victor's first memories of his 'mother's tender caresses' and of his father's 'benevolent pleasure while regarding me' subtly underscore the highly differentiated future roles to be played out by the parents. Alphonse may be retired from his job as a magistrate, but the essentially 'public' character of his work still shapes his attitudes at home, determining that he maintain a discreet 'observer's' distance from the baby. Whereas Caroline, operating in the home's private and protected sphere, performs the 'hands-on' nurturing function of a practical mother. Victor says in Chapter II that he feels 'exquisite pleasure' in dwelling on these 'recollections of childhood' (38). Yet the account he gives of how his parents had lovingly raised him is undermined by a brooding tone, suggesting hints of dissatisfaction:

I was their plaything and their idol, and something better – their child, the innocent and helpless creature bestowed on them by Heaven, whom to bring up to good, and whose future lot it was in their hands to direct to happiness or misery, according as they fulfilled their duties towards me. With this deep consciousness of what they owed towards the being to which they had given life, added to the active spirit of tenderness that animated both, it may be imagined that while during every hour of my infant life I received a lesson of patience, of charity, and of self-control, I was so guided by a silken chord that all seemed but one train of enjoyment to me. (33)

Those who have already read through his story once will appreciate the emphasis Victor here puts on the responsibilities parents should feel towards their offspring. For Victor is speaking with the grim authority of one who has himself suffered for neglecting the parental duties he should have fulfilled towards his own unique Creation, the Creature he will later tell of assembling and to which he had 'given life'. But is it really bad conscience that informs Victor's statement? Or is it rather a feeling that the blame for his misery is to be laid at the door of parents who, for all their efforts, somehow failed in fulfilling their duties towards him? Is Victor to blame himself for the train of events which have resulted in his ending up miserably alone, or was there something amiss in his upbringing?

What does seem certain is that Victor's parents endeavoured to 'do good' in the way that a prominent middle-class professional family would have been expected to do in the Genevan republic. So that when the 'benevolent disposition' of Alphonse and Caroline persuades them to 'enter the cottages of the poor' on the shores of Lake Como, Mme Frankenstein feels compelled to act out a role of 'guardian angel to the afflicted'. At this point Mary Shelley 'plants' a link and also a contrast with the Creature who is to appear later, when introducing the figure of Elizabeth. Victor's description of the fair-haired orphan of noble birth, rescued, as was Caroline, from poverty, goes one step further than the portrait he gave of his mother. More than a 'fair exotic', Elizabeth appears 'of a different stock' to the dark-eyed little vagrants who surround her, her whole beauteous mien being 'so expressive of sensibility and sweetness' that she seems to be 'of a distinct species, a being heaven-sent' (34). This is the exact antithesis of what the Creature will be – 'hell-sent' and hideous. Alphonse agrees that this gift of Providence can be adopted by the Frankenstein household, after which she becomes the 'beautiful and adored companion' of Victor, the person he repeatedly refers to as his 'more than sister' (in the 1818 edition she is his cousin). He recalls to Walton how from this time forward he looked upon her as a 'possession' of his own, 'mine to protect, love, and cherish' (35). The bitter irony is that though he may have 'looked upon' Elizabeth in this way (perhaps as baby Victor had been 'regarded' by Alphonse?), Victor will find himself unable, in the end, to meet any of these requirements.

We begin to get hints of why this might be an inevitable outcome, in

Chapter II. Here we learn more about the characters of Victor and Elizabeth, as well as that of their friend Henry Clerval. Most importantly, we are also told about Victor's growing teenage obsession with natural philosophy (science). Victor explains that though he and Elizabeth were brought up together, they were entirely dissimilar in temperament. Whereas the 'calmer and more concentrated' Elizabeth 'busied herself with following the aerial creations of the poets' and enjoyed the varied scenes of nature, Victor, 'capable of a more intense application', was 'more deeply smitten with the thirst for knowledge'. While Elizabeth is content to contemplate the 'magnificent appearances of things', the textures and surfaces of the sensed world, Victor is obsessed with getting below these surfaces and 'investigating their causes'. Above all, the world for him was a 'secret' whose 'hidden laws of nature' he 'desired to divine' (36). These ambitions are clearly parallel to those of Walton, who also excitedly yearns to learn the secrets of 'unexplored regions'. Likè Walton also, Victor had grown up a relatively isolated person, his temper being to 'avoid a crowd' and attach himself 'fervently to a few'. Chief among these few is Henry Clerval, a boy of 'singular talent and fancy' who loved 'enterprise, hardship, and even danger for its own sake' (36). In other words, the qualities Victor looked for in a friend were very much like the active 'masculine' qualities he perceives himself to possess.

In turn, they are also those Robert Walton has long sought for in a sympathetic friend. Had he been able to meet him, Clerval could just as easily have provided Walton with sympathetic images of himself, for like the Arctic explorer his dream had been to be remembered as one of the 'gallant and adventurous benefactors of our species' (37). In fact, it could be said that Robert Walton, Henry Clerval and Victor Frankenstein all share fervently ambitious impulses of a conventionally adventurous and masculine sort. But if received traits of masculinity are being underlined here, the text is also concerned to emphasize these by contrasting them with those of a femininity too. Just as Walton gratefully recalled the fact that his ardent and impatient nature had been modified by Margaret's 'gentle and feminine fosterage', so Victor is pleased to say how Elizabeth's role was not only to 'subdue' him to 'a semblance of her own gentleness', but to reveal to Clerval too the 'real loveliness of beneficence'. This is so that his 'soaring ambition' will produce good rather than evil results (37–8). This corrective, complementary role that the feminine is meant to play to the masculine is one that both glances back to the values projected in Milton's *Paradise Lost* and once again anticipates the Victorian 'angel in the house' attitude:

The saintly soul of Elizabeth shone like a shrine-dedicated lamp in our peaceful home. Her sympathy was ours; her smile, her soft voice, the sweet glance of her celestial eyes, were ever there to bless and animate us. (37)

The essential features of this ethereal depiction of 'feminine virtue' are that it is almost completely other-worldly and passive. Coming from the pen of the daughter of the author of the *Rights of Woman*, it is hard to believe this is not being conveyed for ironic effect. That this actually is a glowing product of Victor's wishful thinking about the past he has lost seems confirmed by his remark that he feels 'exquisite pleasure in dwelling on the recollections of childhood, before misfortune had tainted' his mind (38). Towards the end of the text we will find him saying that his only comfort for months past has been when he can sleep and reunite with his lost friends and family in a dreamy oblivion (197–8). The Elizabeth he portrays is thus an idealized figure, more like the person he hopes to meet in heaven than the one who may actually have attempted to 'soften' his ardour.

Why is this idealizing so necessary? we might ask. Why, if he had the loving attention of parents and the companionship of Elizabeth and Henry to nourish him, did his life result in an 'after tale of misery'? The answer he gives to this question is both unsatisfactory but also telling, largely because of the imagery he uses to account for the 'birth of that passion' which he says afterwards ruled his destiny. He describes this passion as arising, 'like a mountain river, from ignoble and almost forgotten sources', but which accelerated into an unstoppable torrent destroying all his hopes and joys. This is frustratingly unsatisfactory in the way that all metaphors can be, for their explanatory value is limited by the appositeness of the image employed. But the metaphor used by Victor is also significant, for two reasons. When Mary and Percy went to Chamonix in July of 1816, as well as climbing Montenvert mountain to view the spectacular Mer de Glace, they also indulged Percy's passion for pursuing rivers to their source by seeking out the source of the River Arve. This obviously links Victor's desire for 'investigating causes' to the passions of Percy, particularly when he was a student at Oxford (see Chapter 10). But the key phrase 'almost forgotten' also allows us to see, from our post-Freudian vantage point, that the passion which Victor pinpoints as the source of his later miseries has its origin in some deep level of his own being, the 'unfathomable' but also acutely *felt* compulsions of his unconscious mind. It is at this crucial and troubling point of 'investigating causes', both forgotten but also unforgettable, that Victor reveals that 'natural philosophy is the genius that has regulated my fate' (38).

His first contact with natural philosophy had come in early adolescence. The circumstances are a remarkable echo of the chain of events described by Mary Shelley in her 1831 Introduction when the Diodati parties of 1816 retreated indoors from 'incessant rain' to read ghost stories, eventually resulting in her writing of *Frankenstein* (6–7). Victor reports how when he was thirteen on a 'party of pleasure' with his family at the baths near Thonon, the 'inclemency of the weather obliged us to remain a day confined to the inn' (38). Thus confined, he diverts himself, not by reading ghost stories, but by poring over something equally gripping and mysterious, a volume of the writings of the sixteenth-century magician and cabbalist, Cornelius Agrippa. The impact of Agrippa is so powerful that 'a new light seemed to dawn' upon his mind, and with enthusiasm he rushes to tell Alphonse of his discovery. But the father is so carelessly dismissive of the 'sad trash' which has excited his son that Victor assumes he is insufficiently acquainted with the writings of Agrippa to make a proper judgement. As a consequence, Victor goes on not only to read 'with the greatest avidity' the complete works of Agrippa, but also those of the alchemist Paracelsus (who believed alchemy could create a homunculus – a miniature human being) and the unorthodox theologian Albertus Magnus. His determination to persist in the face of his father's contemptuous dismissal offers obvious parallels with Walton's rebellious decision to take up the seafaring life his father had expressly forbidden him to pursue. The 'apt moral' that Walton and we are meant to draw from this part of Victor's tale is very much one informed by Godwinian principles of rational benevolence. If a father wants to avoid provoking the rebellious impulses which thwarted desire produces in a son, he should offer a reasoned explanation for the negative injunctions which he has imposed upon the youth.

Meanwhile, as we read about the obsessive regard Victor's thirteen-year-old mind had for what he later realized were 'exploded systems', we discover in his language how gender and sexuality issues are closely linked to the way he represents nature and science. His infatuation with the alchemists can be seen as a displacement of the surging sexual energies which all adolescents experience in their teenage years. The sexual metaphors he uses to describe the task he understands science – whether fringe or modern – to have set itself, are very explicit. After reminding us of his 'fervent longing to penetrate the secrets of nature', he notes how modern philosophers (i.e. scientists) had 'partially unveiled the face of Nature, but her immortal lineaments were still a wonder and a mystery'. To his youthful mind, the alchemists were superior thinkers because they were 'men who had penetrated deeper and knew more' about the 'citadel of nature' with its 'fortifications and impediments' (39). Yet what is equally important to mention about this portrayal of nature as a female highly resistant to the sexual attentions of probing males, is that it is a language which had been used in science since at least the time of Francis Bacon (1561–1626). Bacon had called upon his fellow men to inaugurate with him 'the truly masculine birth of time' in order that 'the domination of man over the universe' might be achieved.[4] So in that sense, Victor's use of 'masculinist' terminology must be seen in the perspective of a scientific language about the natural and cultural worlds that went back a long way in European history. This identification of woman with 'private' nature and man with 'public' culture is an issue to which we shall find ourselves returning in different ways (see especially Chapter 11).

In following the incidents of Victor's youth as he tells them, it is noticeable that he tends to reject the conventionally 'public' in favour of a preoccupation with 'private' obsessions. This is very like the experience of Walton. Though Victor has had the advantage of a school education in Geneva, this is so 'routine' that, like Walton, he is compelled to be 'self-taught' in his outlawed 'favourite studies'. Walton had felt this self-education to be an 'evil'. But in the case of Victor, whose father was also in effect absent by being 'not scientific' (in the 1818 edition, he had been scientific, which did not fit the needs of the plot, so Mary Shelley changed it), the form which his articulation of regret takes has a certain explanatory value whose significance he seems only vaguely aware of. He says that without his father's guidance he was 'left to struggle with a child's blindness, added to a student's thirst for knowledge' (39). For two key years of his early adolescence, then, Victor is forced to define his intellectual and emotional horizons by what he might have called, if he could have identified them, this 'fatal' combination. Whatever else may happen later, already, at this early stage, Victor's essential life-goals are being set. Driven on by his blind eagerness for the alchemists, he finds himself drawn to the search for the philosopher's stone (the secret of turning base metals into gold) and the elixir of life (the secret of human immortality). Soon it is the secret of immortality that utterly preoccupies him:

Wealth was an inferior object; but what glory would attend the discovery, if I could banish disease from the human frame and render man invulnerable to any but a violent death! (39–40)

This echoes Walton's rejection of 'ease and luxury' in favour of 'glorious' Promethean aspirations. But Victor's Promethean ambitions, linked as they are to a visionary science, are much more potent and spectacular than Walton's. After repeatedly failing to raise the 'ghosts and devils' which his ancient teachers had believed in – nefarious practices Percy Shelley had also pursued well into his late teens – one day in his fifteenth year he witnesses a demonstration of natural power which puts all he has read thus far into the shade. While watching with 'curiosity and delight' the progress of 'a most violent and terrible thunder-storm' at the Frankensteins' lakeside home in Belrive, he suddenly beholds 'a stream of fire issue from an old and beautiful oak'. As soon as the dazzling effects of the lightning bolt have disappeared, he is astonished to find the tree reduced to a 'blasted stump'. When the 'man of great research in natural philosophy' whom Mary Shelley has placed conveniently nearby explains to Victor his theories on galvanism and electricity, he finds them so 'new and astonishing' that the alchemical 'lords' of his imagination are completely overthrown. But although disinclined to return to his old studies, neither is he inspired to pursue new ones by what he has witnessed and been told. Rather he experiences a kind of neutralizing effect brought on by a feeling of dismay before the scale of the powers with which he has to contend. Disgusted with 'a would-be science which could never even step within the threshold of real knowledge' he turns to the more safe and secure subject of Cartesian mathematics. To some extent this move resembles the swing from enthusiastic dream to self-conscious caution we saw in Walton's narrative. There it was Walton's 'feminine tutored' conscience which kept putting a check on his more extravagant Promethean outbursts. Here the 'almost miraculous change of inclination and will' which leads Victor to renounce his alchemical studies is attributed by him to the 'victory' of a feminine 'guardian angel' in his soul. However, he says, this 'strong effort of the spirit of good' was not to be sustained, for 'destiny was too potent, and her immutable laws had decreed my utter and terrible destruction' (41). We now have two aspects of 'feminine nature' battling it out for the prize of Victor's soul, it seems – one constraining and protective, the other alluring and corrosive.

Knowing as we do that his fascination for penetrating an 'electric' female nature will win out in the end, it is interesting to note that Mary Shelley borrowed the image of the lightning-shattered tree from the third canto of Byron's *Childe Harold's Pilgrimage*. Byron is celebrating the departed spirit of 'the self-torturing sophist, wild Rousseau', whose 'love', he says:

> . . . was passion's essence – as a tree
> On fire by lightning; with ethereal flame

> Kindled he was, and blasted; for to be
> Thus, and enamoured, were in him the same.

So self-tortured is Victor in telling Walton the story of where his dreadful 'amour' led him, that he does not seem to notice how the immediate 'destiny' awaiting him in the next phase of his history was to be determined less by female deities, than by the actions of a real man – his father.

Ingolstadt (Chapters III–IV)

Alphonse has decided that Victor must attend the German University of Ingolstadt in order to complete his education and to experience the customs of another (European) country. But before he can depart, tragedy strikes the Frankenstein household when his mother Caroline dies of a scarlet fever caught when she selflessly nurses Elizabeth back to health from the disease. In this heroic gesture, we can perhaps detect something of the nostalgic regard Mary Shelley felt (and had long been taught to feel by her father Godwin) for the mother who had brought her into the world, only to die ten days later. We should bear in mind too that the 'void to the soul' felt by Victor upon his mother's death was one that Mary had experienced herself when she heard in October 1816 of the suicide of her older half-sister Fanny. Fanny herself had been a product of the same fondly remembered Wollstonecraft womb, conceived in the heat of the French Revolution yet finally left without the kind of companionship Mary had been able to find in the figure of Percy Shelley.

The explanation for Victor's gloomy mood of resignation in the face of feminine destiny may well be linked with the statements concerning him and Elizabeth that Caroline makes on her death-bed. Although she dies 'calmly' with a countenance expressing 'affection even in death' (just as an angel in the house should), the heartfelt dying wishes which may seem benign to unquestioning devotees of filial duty could also be seen as a complicating web of potential confinement for one of Victor's Promethean predilections. Victor has indeed described Elizabeth as his close childhood companion, his 'more than sister'. But Caroline's death-bed 'expectation' that their future marriage must now become the 'consolation' of Alphonse instead of herself contains within it the germ of an injunction, as powerful in its way as the paternal death-bed command had been for Robert Walton, and which he had therefore resentfully seen fit to break. That Victor does welcome his escape from the familial scene is conveyed by the thoughts going through his mind as he journeys to Ingolstadt. At first he feels sad about having to leave behind his 'amiable companions', forced to shift for himself in a new situation where he will know no one. The problem is particularly acute because his life had 'hitherto been remarkably secluded and domestic', leaving him 'totally unfitted for the company of strangers'. He is leaving the familiar – defined, literally, by the family – for the unfamiliar, the unknown. Yet his 'spirits and hopes' rise as he begins looking at the situation in a positive light:

I ardently desired the acquisition of knowledge. I had often, when at home, thought it hard to remain during my youth cooped up in one place, and had longed to enter the world, and take my station among other human beings. Now my desires were complied with, and it would, indeed, have been folly to repent. (44)

Thus does he come to terms with his lot by the time he has reached Ingolstadt and ascended to his 'solitary apartment'.

Having turned from his father's door with 'reluctant steps', he is initially repelled by the man who might temporarily function as his replacement, the 'uncouth' professor of natural philosophy, M. Krempe. Although acknowledging Krempe to be 'deeply imbued in the secrets of his science', Victor finds him repugnant. Primarily this is because Krempe regards the alchemical studies Victor pursued for so long with such contempt that the new student feels deeply humiliated. He conceives an antipathy for the 'repulsive countenance' of this 'little squat man', positively refusing 'to go and hear that little conceited fellow deliver sentences out of a pulpit' (45, 46). This reaction to Krempe tells us two important things about Frankenstein. Despite his partiality for uncovering the 'secret' causes of things rather than admiring their outward appearances, in regard to Krempe he demonstrates a distinct sensitivity to physical appearance, and at a moment when he feels degraded by another's superior knowledge. This should be borne in mind for the events occurring in the aftermath of the Creature's creation. Secondly, his remarks about the pulpit suggest a young man not only out of sympathy with the Church, but perhaps, given his previous obsession with alchemy, out of sympathy with the idea of a God altogether. In other words, he could be an atheist, just as Percy Shelley was so proud of being. (Shelley was expelled from Oxford University in 1812, along with his friend Hogg, for publishing a pamphlet provocatively entitled 'The Necessity of Atheism'.) The problem for Victor is that on the one hand he has thrown over his attachment to the theories of the 'forgotten alchymists' as 'dreams', but on the other he finds the 'uses of modern natural philosophy' equally useless, because so seemingly mundane. If the gestures of the original 'masters of the science' had been futile in their grasping after immortality and power, at least these had been *grand* gestures. So that Victor now feels he is 'required to exchange chimeras of boundless grandeur for realities of little worth' (46).

However, when Victor attends the chemistry lectures of Krempe's fellow-professor, M. Waldman, his whole view of modern science is changed. To begin with, the appearance of Waldman is 'very unlike' that of his colleague (even though they are both short). Waldman's person is 'remarkably erect', he has 'an aspect expressive of the greatest benevolence', and his voice is the 'sweetest' Victor had ever heard. This description shows Mary Shelley to have modelled Waldman on her father Godwin. The 'panegyric upon modern chemistry, the terms of which', Victor says, he will 'never forget', was based upon material she had studied in 'Davy's Chemistry', as she calls it. A brilliant innovator in and popularizer of chemistry, Davy embodied all that was most exciting about early nineteenth-century science. Echoing the words of another distinguished visitor to the Godwin household in her childhood, the panegyric is worth repeating in full:

The ancient teachers of this science . . . promised impossibilities, and performed nothing. The modern masters promise very little; they know that metals cannot be transmuted, and that the elixir of life is a chimera. But these philosophers, whose hands seem only made to dabble in dirt, and their eyes to pore over the microscope and crucible, have indeed performed miracles. They penetrate into the recesses of nature, and show how she works in her hiding-places. They ascend into the heavens: they have discovered how the blood circulates, and the nature of the air we breathe. They have acquired new and almost unlimited powers; they can command the thunders of heaven, mimic the earthquake, and even mock the invisible world with its own shadows. (46–7)

Read carefully, nothing could be less 'gothic' than this writing. True to her 'substantial' aims, Mary Shelley is reflecting some of the attitudes she had found in Davy's enthusiastic 'Romantic Science'. Science by the early 1800s had indeed made ascent 'into the heavens' possible with air balloons, just as electricity had begun to be harnessed (commanding the 'thunders of heaven'); explosives invented (mimicking the earthquake); and the Zoetrope had made the creation of visual illusions possible (mocking the invisible world with its shadows). What attracts Victor Frankenstein to Waldman's panegyric on science is the language the lecturer deploys to show that with the development of modern scientific techniques, the grand *vision*, rather than the theories of the alchemists, was now actually realizable. It is no wonder that when he hears of the 'new and almost unlimited powers' which modern science can wield in 'penetrating' the recesses of Mother Nature, Victor feels the 'various keys' forming the 'mechanism' of his being touched into fiery life. In retrospect he realizes that the effect of the lecture had been to trigger a succession of self-regarding impulses and motives into motion. But the younger, idealistic and socially inexperienced Victor had been able only to think in terms which saw his 'one thought, one conception, one purpose' as a magnificent liberation for himself and for the world.

Moreover, when Victor pays Waldman a private visit the following day, he receives every encouragement to pursue his studies. Whereas Alphonse and Krempe had poured scorn on his alchemical interests, the 'mild and attractive' professor is tolerant enough to show no contempt. On the contrary, he begins by telling him (in a long passage written by Percy Shelley) that the alchemists were 'men to whose indefatigable zeal modern philosophers were indebted for most of the foundations of their knowledge' (47). Converted to the gospel of modern chemistry on this 'memorable' day, the professor's latest disciple leaves clutching a reading-list. This encounter between Waldman and Frankenstein is very reminiscent of the way Percy Shelley responded so enthusiastically in 1812 when William Godwin replied to the nineteen-year-old fledgling poet's pleas for intellectual guidance, a role the veteran of 1790s philosophical radicalism had played for many an idealistic youth over the years. Shelley had long been a worshipper at the shrine of Godwin's *An Enquiry into Political Justice* (1793), a work which had argued for the 'perfectibility' of man in a world which would have to shed itself of all forms of government and 'positive institution' if it were to be free. Much of Godwin's Enlightenment optimism had been inspired by Rousseau and other radical French *philosophes*. When the 'luminary too dazzling for the darkness that surrounds him' (as Shelley described Godwin) had agreed not only to be his intellectual mentor, but also suggested he become the chief instrument of transmitting the ideas of *Political Justice* to the next generation, Shelley was overwhelmed, writing that the friendship the middle-aged philosopher had offered him was 'more valuable than the gifts of Princes'.[5] (It will be remembered how Walton told Margaret that his life might have been passed 'in ease and luxury' but that he 'preferred glory to every enticement' of wealth.) It is unnecessary to pursue very much further the significance of Mary Shelley's use of Percy's disciple status *vis-à-vis*

Godwin for the Waldman–Frankenstein relationship. But it should be noted that when Victor is encouraged and accepted by Waldman, his declaration that in the chemist he has found sympathy and 'a true friend' does show significant parallels with the Percy Shelley case. Like P.B. Shelley, Frankenstein is thrilled by the attentions of his new guru because he facilitates rather than thwarts his desires, instructing him with an admirable 'air of frankness and good nature, that banished every idea of pedantry' (49). Though respectful of their fathers, neither Percy nor Victor had been inspired by them. Mary Shelley in depicting Waldman is representing the kind of ideal father for whom English male Romantics, disenchanted with the 'Moloch of legitimacy' (as Hazlitt called the corrupt system of government) which their real fathers had condoned, were seeking. It will be as the ideal father that Waldman expresses the 'most heartfelt exultation' at Victor's rapid progress in his studies.

With this sort of stimulation it is not surprising that someone of Victor's Promethean impulses should become so 'engaged, heart and soul' in the pursuit of scientific discoveries, that two whole years pass by without him paying a single visit to his parents. In a passage which provides the exact note of irony Mary Shelley was evidently wishing to achieve, it is Percy Shelley who himself underwrote (so to speak) Victor's preoccupation with scientific inquiry, by adding the following to the manuscript of the novel:

None but those who have experienced them can conceive of the enticements of science. In other studies you go as far as others have gone before you, and there is nothing more to know; but in a scientific pursuit there is continual food for discovery and wonder. (49)

At this mention of the 'endless' allure which science now holds for Victor, it is a timely moment to pause and ask why the author chose Ingolstadt as the place where the 'one thought, one conception, one purpose', which ends in a human-like Creature being built and animated, was triggered. Again the answer is linked to Percy Shelley. By sending Victor to the University of Ingolstadt, Mary was signalling his 'association with the radical politics advocated by Percy Shelley in *Queen Mab* (1813), 'Feelings of a Republican on the Fall of Bonaparte' (1816), and *Laon and Cythna* (1817)'.[6] Ingolstadt was where a secret revolutionary society called the Illuminati – as William St Clair has aptly noted, so neatly cognate with 'Enlightenment' – had been founded in 1776 by the university's professor of law, Adam Weishaupt. It was the Illuminati who had masterminded international Jacobinism, according to the Abbé Barruel's influential *Memoirs of Jacobinism*, published in a late 1790s Europe whose monarchs were terrified of revolutionary France's expansionist ambitions. That a conspiracy to overthrow established political and religious institutions had been fomented in Ingolstadt thrilled one of Barruel's most avid readers, the young Percy Shelley, who believed (as Mary Shelley says in a note to his 1817 poems) that he 'possessed the power of operating an immediate change in the minds of men and the state of society'.[7] It is with an insider's knowledge of how the force of this kind of enthusiasm could manifest itself that Mary proceeds to have Victor Frankenstein outshine his teachers in scientific accomplishment after only two years at university, after which he embarks on a single-handed programme of exploration for the source of the 'principle of life'. It is this 'bold question' which makes Victor delay his return to family and friends in Geneva, a decision which will ultimately lead to his utter inability to deal honestly and sympathetically with the needs of others.

The theme of sacrificing social values for what soon becomes an obsessive personal quest was one that Mary Shelley had found in Percy's 1816 poem, *Alastor, or, The Spirit of Solitude*. Or rather, it is more accurate to say she found it in his Preface to the poem, rather than in the poem itself. 'The picture is not barren of instruction to actual men,' explains Percy in the Preface. 'The Poet's self-centred seclusion was avenged by the furies of an irresistible passion pursuing him to speedy ruin.' As Richard Holmes has pointed out, the actual text of the poem fails either to endorse this judgement, or Percy's claim that 'Among those who attempt to exist without human sympathy, the pure and tender-hearted perish through the intensity and passion of their search after its communities, when the vacancy of their spirit suddenly makes itself felt.'[8] The youthful Poet does indeed die after a long and lonely search for the beauteous secret of life. But the 'irresistible passion pursuing him to speedy ruin' misrepresents the source, mechanism and effects of the poem's jagged flows of linguistic power. As Mary Shelley noted, *Alastor* was the occasion for 'an outpouring of [Percy's] own emotions',[9] so that it is his enthusiastic passion for the pursuit of ideal beauty that energizes its frantic pace and imagery, his craving for the secret of life that produces a gripping celebration of an approach to life which he had in fact wished to censure. He had wanted to explore and perhaps exorcise those elements of his own psychology and sexuality he felt ran counter to the vision of 'social beauty' implied by the revolutionary doctrines of *Queen Mab*. (*Alastor* is loosely structured around the myth of Narcissus and Echo, and traces the pursuit of a youth – 'the Poet' – for an ideal vision of beauty, which ends in death.) Thus we find Shelley using memories of one particular preoccupation – the idea that the 'principle of life' is to be found by exploring death and decay. He addresses his beloved Mother Nature:

> . . . I have watched
> Thy shadow, and the darkness of thy steps,
> And my heart ever gazes on the depth
> Of thy deep mysteries. I have made my bed
> In charnels and on coffins, where black death
> Keeps record of the trophies won from thee,
> Hoping to still these obstinate questionings
> Of thee and thine, by forcing some lone ghost,
> Thy messenger, to render up the tale
> Of what we are. In lone and silent hours,
> When night makes a weird sound of its own stillness,
> Like an inspired and desperate alchymist
> Staking his very life on some dark hope,
> Have I mixed awful talk and asking looks
> With my most innocent love . . .

It is this self-same 'mixture' which we see Victor bringing to bear when he starts out on his 'innocent' scientific quest for the secret of animation. When logic tells him that: 'To examine the causes of life, we must first have recourse to death', he is content to spend 'days and nights in vaults and charnel houses' in pursuit of his goal. Or is he *really* so content to do this? He claims that darkness had no effect on his fancy, that his father's education had ensured his 'mind should be impressed with no supernatural horrors'. However, he also says that the application to his studies 'would have been irksome, and almost intolerable' if he had not been 'animated by an almost supernatural enthusiasm' to pursue the task (50). It is because he *himself* is the agent of supernatural energies that he is able to avoid the terrors of the supernatural. He is 'Enlightenment man' *par excellence* – yet with a difference. The Enlightenment man mainly reasons, but the Romantic feels, rationalizes and, above all, imagines. It is the element of 'supernatural enthusiasm' intent on imagining the unimaginable which so takes possession of Victor. It is this which produces the 'brilliant and wondrous' light, making him 'dizzy with the immensity of the prospect which it illustrated' (51). It is perhaps no surprise to learn that Percy Shelley wrote these words, which parallel in their intensity one of the most imagistically vivid passages of *Alastor*, and which appear to be key for our understanding of Victor's 'creative' aims.

The passage comes where the searching Poet of the poem, spurning the attentions of a real 'Arab maiden', falls asleep and finds himself dreaming of a 'veiled maid' who talks in 'low solemn tones' to him of the things closest to his (and Percy Shelley's) heart – 'lofty hopes of divine liberty'. Having begun to make music on a 'strange harp', the maiden now becomes so emotionally overwrought that she suddenly rises up and the Poet sees

> . . . by the warm light of their own life
> Her glowing limbs beneath the sinuous veil
> Of woven wind, her outspread arms now bare,
> Her dark locks floating in the breath of night,
> Her beamy bending eyes, her parted lips
> Outstretched, and pale, and quivering eagerly.

Confronted with such an enticing vision the dreaming Poet cannot contain himself:

> . . . He reared his shuddering limbs and quelled
> His gasping breath, and spread his arms to meet
> Her panting bosom: – she drew back a while,
> Then, yielding to the irresistible joy,
> With frantic gesture and short breathless cry
> Folded his frame in her dissolving arms.
> Now blackness veiled his dizzy eyes, and night
> Involved and swallowed up the vision; sleep,
> Like a dark flood suspended in its course,
> Rolled back its impulse on his vacant brain.
>
> Roused by the shock he started from his trance –
> The cold white light of morning, the blue moon
> Low in the west, the clear and garish hills,
> The distinct valley and the vacant woods,
> Spread round him where he stood.

This is probably the finest representation we have in Romantic poetry of what we now sometimes call a 'wet dream'. In this masturbatory sequence, there are a number of elements relevant to our discussion of *Frankenstein*. The most striking is the theme of masturbation itself. In seeking to challenge the claim of Sandra Gilbert and Susan Gubar that Frankenstein's Creature represents Mary Shelley's 'Eve', David Musselwhite has pointed out how the account Victor Frankenstein gives of his Creature's creation depicts the atmosphere and labours of masturbation far more than it does anything resembling 'birth'.[10] A close reading of the text tends to confirm this. Victor talks of carrying out his

obsessive task in a 'solitary chamber', in his 'workshop of filthy creation'. (Interestingly, Peter Conrad has taken this description to stand
for 'the romantic brain' itself[11].) The 'secret toil' he engages in urges
him forward with an 'almost frantic impulse' in which he seems 'to
have lost all soul or sensation but for this one pursuit', and he
considers the whole period of his eager activity as a 'passing trance'
motivated by an 'unnatural stimulus'. Above all, the 'vital' erotic
imagery which we have already noticed both Frankenstein and Waldman using for the scientific process is again deployed when Victor says
the moon gazed on his 'midnight labours' as he, 'with unrelaxed and
breathless eagerness . . . pursued nature to her hiding-places' (53). A few
pages on, following the animation of the Creature, he further describes
how the moon's 'dim and yellow light . . . forced its way through the
window shutters' (57). This is far from being the last time the moon's
appearance will be linked with that of the Creature. As we shall see, at
key points of the novel the moon will again and again signal and
accompany the Creature as his companion of the night, a 'watching
over' function strongly suggesting the presence of the author (who, as I
shall explain, was identified with the moon as traditional 'female
principle' by Percy Shelley).

Animation and After (Chapters V–VI)

The events following Frankenstein's animation of his Creature tend to
confirm the masturbation hypothesis and also tell us something about
the nature of the transgression he has committed. In words that
continue to describe the kind of frenzied activity associated with masturbation, he says that he had desired to infuse life into an inanimate body
'with an ardour that far exceeded moderation'. The process 'had finished', but instead of realizing his vision, 'the beauty of the dream
vanished and breathless horror and disgust filled my heart' (56). He
could not 'endure the aspect of the being' he had created, he says, so
retreated to his bedchamber seeking 'a few moments of forgetfulness' in
sleep. Instead of forgetfulness he has a nightmare which confirms the
fact that his transgressive act has entailed an irrecoverable sacrifice of
fundamental social sympathies. The nightmare which replaces his hideous living dream involves his wish to meet Elizabeth. Delighted and
surprised to see her 'in the bloom of health, walking in the streets of
Ingolstadt', his attempt to embrace and kiss her transforms her into the
figure of his dead mother, in whose shroud he sees grave-worms
crawling. This makes him start from his sleep, his teeth chattering. His

transgressive act of creation has involved a violation of Mother Nature, and he is now forced to suffer the alienating consequences of this.

This 'sacrificial' creation having taken place, it is important to read carefully what happens when the Creature appears at Victor's bedside, for it is far from being the kind of threatening situation that the Frankenstein movie tradition has suggested. Victor tells how his now living creation

held up the curtain of the bed; and his eyes, if eyes they may be called, were fixed on me. His jaws opened, and he muttered some inarticulate sounds, while a grin wrinkled his cheeks. He might have spoken, but I did not hear; one hand was stretched out, seemingly to detain me, but I escaped, and rushed downstairs. (57)

The Creature is, in effect, experiencing the first hours of his life after birth, and like a baby is seeking its parent for solace and nurture. Thoughts of meeting such inoffensive demands could not be further from the mind of Frankenstein, who is so horrified he does not know whether the Creature has spoken or not. All he can see before him is a 'thing such as even Dante could not have conceived', and interprets its friendly gesture of recognition as a threateningly aggressive move from which he must escape at all costs. He runs away and spends the night pacing the courtyard below in terror. When the morning, 'dismal and wet, at length dawned' (the influence of *Alastor* lingers on), Victor flees from what he calls the 'asylum' of the courtyard into the streets. Although he seems to be using the word in its general sense, as a refuge, there is also the implication that through the activities of the past two years, he may have been sheltering in the grounds of a madhouse – of his own making. In Chapter IV, he had after all without prompting been induced to say to Walton: 'Remember, I am not recording the vision of a madman' (51). (Interestingly, the manuscript shows at this point an insertion of the word 'not', originally missed out by Mary Shelley.) Once out into the Ingolstadt streets, he wanders about aimlessly, his heart palpitating with such 'sickness of fear' that he is inspired to quote from the *Ancient Mariner* to describe his feelings, a move calculated to endear the Coleridge-loving Walton to him even more than before. When he finally stops, he does so, he 'knew not why', at the town's coaching terminus. If he is hoping to meet Elizabeth there, to make amends for his neglect of her, he will be disappointed. Instead he bumps into his old friend Clerval, whose narrow-minded merchant father has finally relented, and permitted him, in a phrase Mary Shelley clearly meant to be ironically loaded, 'to undertake a voyage of discovery to the land of knowledge'. (59)

After breezily upbraiding his friend for neglecting to contact his family and friends, Henry notices his worn condition. But Victor is careful not to disclose any facts about the solitary undertaking which has caused this. On their return to his rooms, he is so in dread of allowing his friend to see the Creature he fears to find there that he makes him wait at the bottom of the stairs. Victor tells how he first 'recollected' himself before having the courage to fling open the door of his apartment. The use of the word is significant, implying that the price he has paid for putting together and animating the disparate parts of the Creature's body has been the shattering and dispersal of his own personality. This is confirmed by his report that he became 'lifeless' following a nervous collapse caused by his hallucination of the Creature attacking him, and he failed to recover his senses 'for a long, long time'. Indeed, in an echo of terms we have already encountered, he says that it was only through the conscientious attentions of Clerval that his friend 'could have restored me to life' (60). Not until the spring, four months later, does he feel renewed to the state he was in before he was 'attacked by the fatal passion'. Much of his recovery is aided by his rediscovery of the charms of nature, shunned for so long, but now providing a revivifying force within him. Yet nature's healing effects, which we shall find appealed to more and more as the text goes on, are insufficient to quell Victor's anxiety when Henry demands to speak to him 'on one subject'. This is Alphonse's and Elizabeth's request that Victor write to them after his long absence from home. Clerval may be satisfied with his friend's reply, but as readers we are aware of the deep irony underlying Victor's nervously glib response:

'Is that all, my dear Henry? How could you suppose that my first thought would not fly towards those dear, dear friends whom I love, and who are so deserving of my love?' (61)

As a close friend who has sacrificed his time and own unbegun studies to nurse Victor back to health, Henry is clearly willing to overlook the ambiguity of his remark under the circumstances, and hands Victor a letter from Elizabeth which has arrived for him.

The letter from Elizabeth starts Chapter VI. This chapter provides some light relief after one of horror, and at the same time it creates suspense in the reader, who has been left wondering about the whereabouts of the Creature. Victor now decides to join Henry in his study of Oriental languages to soothe his troubled mind, and they undertake a local walking tour prior to Victor's long-delayed return to Geneva. The chapter is also of lighter tone because we find ourselves involved with more characters, and so are deflected away for the moment from Victor's entrapping obsessions. Yet even Elizabeth's offerings of news from Geneva 'innocently' carry reproaches that are bound to sting Victor's conscience. She tells how Alphonse is decidedly unpleased that Victor's sixteen-year-old brother Ernest wants a 'military career in a distant country', and is reluctant to see a second son desert the family until his first returns. Victor has now been away from Geneva for nearly six years. When Elizabeth talks of 'the growth of our dear children', likening their 'placid home' to the unchanging blue lake and snow-clad mountains, both regulated by 'immutable laws' (63), this must arouse anxiety in Victor, whose own vanished progeny will before long disrupt the happy home. Her phrase 'our dear children' has in addition the peculiar effect of further confusing the kinship structure of a family where the roles are already quite muddled. That is to say, firstly, that Alphonse's adopted daughter has taken the place of his dead wife Caroline in mothering his remaining younger children. Secondly, although she and Victor are not blood-related, they have grown up so like brother and sister that the fear of incest must be a factor in the way we are meant to read their relationship thus far. Elizabeth's use of the phrase 'our dear children', as well as signalling that her role as Caroline's maternal substitute is now fully established, implicates Victor as her future husband, but also – oddly – as 'father' of his own brothers.

This slippage of functions and meanings in the domain of kinship is complicated even more by some of Elizabeth's remarks concerning Justine Moritz, the Frankenstein household's servant whose history she recapitulates for Victor's benefit. Elizabeth reports on Caroline's observation that the twelve-year-old Justine was always 'the favourite of her father; but, through a strange perversity, her mother could not endure her, and after the death of M. Moritz, treated her very ill' (63). Caroline succeeds in persuading Mme Moritz to allow her daughter to live with her. (This is a bitterly powerful echo of Mary Shelley's own situation at the age of twelve, when as a result of the hostility shown towards her by her stepmother Mrs Clairmont, she was sent away by a reluctant Godwin to live near Dundee with the Baxter family for nearly two years.) So impressed had Justine become with her rescuer Caroline Frankenstein that she had modelled herself on her, and to the extent that now 'her mien and her expressions' continually remind Elizabeth of Victor's mother (64). Thus in a sense Caroline lives on, her mothering function performed by Elizabeth, and her 'phraseology and manners' preserved in the character of Justine, one 'frank-hearted and happy' glance from whom had ever been enough in Victor's youth to dissipate his bad moods (63). As well as these resemblances and substitutions having the effect of blurring the identities of Justine, Elizabeth and the dead Caroline, we need to note how this is in some sense a repetition of what we have read before in the text. Walton has wanted a friend resembling himself to share his lonely adventure, and hopes Victor Frankenstein will fill the role. In turn, the somewhat more ambitious Victor, having left his family and friends behind, has been intent on creating a whole new species of beings, 'like myself'. However, far from producing resemblance, he has manufactured a creature looking so repulsively different from himself that he cannot bear to look at him, let alone be responsible for him.

Victor's inability to accept responsibility for this gigantic assemblage of 'difference' is perhaps why he cannot bring himself to confide this 'secret' even to his best friend, Henry Clerval: he is ashamed of where his 'over-reaching' Promethean ambitions have led him. That is why he suffers so badly when in Clerval's presence Professors Waldman and Krempe enthusiastically praise his scientific achievements in the university. Especially ironic is Krempe's interpretation of the suffering expressed in Victor's face when receiving such fulsome praise: 'Ay, ay . . . M. Frankenstein is modest, an excellent quality in a young man. Young men should be diffident of themselves, you know, M. Clerval . . .' (66). Of course, the last thing Victor has been is modest or diffident, having broken through the laws of nature by creating life! Yet the abandonment of his feelings for that same nature and of his social impulses – both of which had made his 'penetration' of nature possible – is a process he soon attempts to reverse. Out of gratitude to his friend, and 'an unwillingness to leave Clerval in a strange place before he had become acquainted with any of its inhabitants' (the irony being that the anti-social Frankenstein seems hardly equipped to help in this quarter), he delays his planned return to Geneva by many months. When the impassable wintry roads make this delay even greater, he is compelled to spend much more time in Ingolstadt than he had planned. Finally, eighteen months after building and abandoning his Creature, as Victor waits for the letter fixing his final travel arrangements, Clerval proposes they go on a two-week 'pedestrian tour in the environs of Ingolstadt' (68).

For someone who had originally lectured Victor on the need to restore intimate contact with his family, this seems an odd proposal for Clerval to make, just when he knows Victor is awaiting his letter 'daily' (67). It is almost as if Henry were seducing him away from his familial commitments. The eagerness with which Victor accedes to Henry's proposal shows that he is perhaps keener to remain with his friend than return home, in spite (or perhaps because?) of having already spent eighteen months in intimate contact with him. He says he longs to see his 'native town' and 'beloved friends' again, but fails to mention any specific desire to see Elizabeth. On the other hand, the praise and love he expresses for Henry is unbounded. Study has secluded him from 'the intercourse of my fellow-creatures', says Victor, but Clerval called forth the 'better feelings' of his heart, teaching him to love nature once more, and 'the cheerful faces of children':

Excellent friend! how sincerely did you love me and endeavour to elevate my mind until it was on a level with your own! A selfish pursuit had cramped and narrowed me, until your gentleness and affection warmed and opened my senses; I became the same happy creature who, a few years ago, loved and beloved by all, had no sorrow or care. When happy, inanimate nature had the power of bestowing on me the most delightful sensations. A serene sky and verdant fields filled me with ecstasy. The present season was indeed divine; the flowers of spring bloomed in the hedges, while those of summer were already in bud . . .

Henry rejoiced in my gaiety, and sincerely sympathised in my feelings: he exerted himself to amuse me, while he expressed the sensations that filled his soul. The resources of his mind on this occasion were truly astonishing: his conversation was full of imagination; and very often, in imitation of the Persian and Arabic writers, he invented tales of wonderful fancy and passion. At other times, he repeated my favourite poems, or drew me out into arguments, which he supported with great ingenuity. (68)

A number of important points emerge from a close reading of this passage. First of all Frankenstein is offering Walton some serious misrepresentations of himself and his actions in order to preserve a self-image of 'civilized' innocence. He plays down the gravity of his creative experiment by merely observing that study and a 'selfish pursuit' had made him an unsocial being. Then, in a deeply ironic statement, he says that Clerval had taught him to love the cheerful faces of children and the aspect of 'inanimate nature' once more. There are clearly some faces of society and nature that prove natural and acceptable to Frankenstein, and others that do not. Though he is happy to bestow loving glances upon the somewhat idealized smiling children encountered on their walking tour, we cannot help but remember what Victor chooses to forget – how he had run away in horror from the grin that had 'wrinkled' the cheeks of his own gigantic 'son'. What he also seems to forget is the fact that from his childhood he had much preferred investigating the causes behind the 'magnificent appearances of things', rather than celebrating the 'majestic and wondrous scenes' surrounding his Genevan home (36). In an effort to rid his memory of the ghastly being he animated into life, it is no wonder he has now decided to embrace the acceptable face of 'inanimate' nature that had once been the province of Elizabeth.

A final major point to be made about this quotation concerns the role that Clerval plays in 'warming and opening' Victor's senses. At one important level, the preference that Victor shows for male rather than female company simply repeats that of his Promethean pupil, Walton. But male camaraderie – as ever – tends not to promote the sharing of sensitive feelings or confidences. Victor says that Clerval 'sincerely sympathised' in his feelings, and in attempting to amuse him, 'expressed the sensations that filled his soul'. Yet the degree to which Clerval *can* sympathize – i.e. 'agree in his feelings' with Victor – is severely limited by what the latter is able to convey to his friend. Since Victor refuses to reveal his dark secret, the sympathy achieved must in the end be a somewhat shallow affair. This probably explains why Clerval's offer of sympathy is really less important than the cheering display of his 'truly astonishing' talents. If Victor has been preoccupied with narcissistically demonstrating his own omnipotence, then Henry is more concerned with the pursuit of skills that are essentially entertaining. We have already observed that the demonic side of Percy Shelley's personality had provided the stimulus for Victor's portrayal. But now we have to acknowledge that the source for Clerval was Percy Shelley as well. William Veeder has offered the two most relevant comments to be made here, observing how 'Many readers have noted that Mary locates in Henry all the best of her husband', and that, 'Ultimately, woman does not exist for the narcissistic Shelley'.[12]

Geneva and the Trial of Justine (Chapters VII–VIII)

Upon his return amidst the dancing peasants and happy, gay people of Ingolstadt, Victor receives a letter from his father which kills his joy stone dead. The (by now not unexpected) authorial irony comes with Alphonse Frankenstein's remark to Victor that 'Absence cannot have rendered you callous to our joys and griefs; and how shall I inflict pain on my long-absent son?'. Of course, Victor's prolonged absence from his family and friends *had* produced callousness in him: or rather, the price of pursuing his production of the Creature had been a complete abandonment of everyday social sympathies. (There is also the implication here of the novel's existence as a revenge-commentary on the man who once called *Frankenstein* 'fruits of my absence' – Percy Shelley.) Alphonse has written to say that Victor's young brother William is dead, found murdered in Plainpalais on 7 May. Victor records that the walking tour was begun at the beginning of May. This citing of times and dates can only be meant to convey to the reader the fact that had Victor returned to Geneva as planned instead of absenting himself once more for his own purposes, the death of his brother may have been prevented. Elizabeth feels responsible for the death, since the motive for the murder seems to have been the theft of a miniature of Caroline Frankenstein that William had been pestering her to let him wear. After seeing the murderer's mark on William's throat,

She fainted, and was restored with extreme difficulty. When she again lived, it was only to weep and sigh. (70)

Here we find Mary Shelley again pointedly deploying what I earlier called the 'language of animation' to powerful effect. Given a brilliantly obsessive, socially disregarding attitude towards nature, it has seemed relatively easy for Victor to bring an artificial being to life. But it is with great difficulty in this story that humans are themselves restored to life. Victor's response to the letter is the same as when he hallucinated seeing the 'dreaded spectre' of his Creature approach him – he covers his face with his hands (71). The good Clerval endeavours to be as encouraging as possible, and expresses his 'heartfelt sympathy', which is, of course, as 'useless' to Victor now as it will be when Walton offers it to him after the conclusion of his tale. The moral damage has been done.

Victor hurriedly departs for Geneva, anxious to 'console and sympathise' with his 'loved and sorrowing friends'. Yet as he approaches the home he has not seen for nearly six years, the dread of 'a thousand nameless evils' brings him to a halt, and he delays the final confrontation with his family by remaining in Lausanne for two days in a 'painful state of mind' (72). We are not told the reason for this, but it is clear that he is suffering from a conflict-ridden guilty conscience. For a while his newly-acquired love of nature acts as a diverting restorative. Content now with the 'surfaces' instead of the inside workings of nature, he sees a 'calm and heavenly scene' when he looks on Lake Geneva and the surrounding snowy mountains, the 'palaces of nature'. He embraces his 'dear mountains' and his 'own beautiful lake' as long-lost friends:

'How do you welcome your wanderer? Your summits are clear; the sky and lake are blue and placid. Is this to prognosticate peace, or to mock at my unhappiness?' (72)

Frankenstein knows it is the latter, for it is his own lapses, his own interference with nature's processes that have driven him to reflect in this fashion. His rhetorical questions offer a classic demonstration of Romantic thinking at work, where the outward scene is exploited to project an inward emotional state. This interior state is murky and in turmoil, compared with the bright, clear and placid scene he sees around him. That he is experiencing a kind of moral vacuum within is shown when darkness begins to fall, for as he nears his home and the mysterious challenge of his brother's death, the scenes which had so recently cheered him are now no longer visible, and cannot be relied upon to orientate his spirit. Instead, when he looks around, the 'picture' appears to him as 'a vast and dim scene of evil, and I foresaw obscurely that I was destined to become the most wretched of human beings' (72). We should notice two things at this point. In seeing himself as a future 'wretch', he is evoking the first of many identifications to be made between his own destiny and that of his Creature. But what is evoked here once again, as Frankenstein hints at the experience of a 'fall' from light into darkness, is the imagery and tone of Milton's *Paradise Lost*. The use Mary Shelley makes of this epic poem to image the frustrations and dilemmas of Frankenstein and his Creature is extensive (see Chapter 9). In this she follows very much in the footsteps of her father, whose novels are pervaded by Miltonic allusions. At the same time, writing in the dawning age of electricity, she is able to imbue the traditional, symbolic imagery of light and dark with an astounding psychological acuteness. Thus when Victor arrives so late at Geneva that the gates are closed, his prohibition from entering the city can be seen as a symbolic banishment from Paradise – it is 'completely dark' (72). However, as he takes a boat across the lake to visit the scene of William's murder at Plainpalais, what he does see in the midst of this hellish 'darkness visible' is 'the lightnings playing on the summit of Mont Blanc in the most beautiful figures' (73). This heralds not only the coming of a storm, but also the arrival of Frankenstein's Creature. As the electrical 'spark of life' brought the Creature into being, so does the text make the electrical storm produce the Creature. The latter's Satanic nature is spelled out in an allusion to the 'arch-fiend' of *Paradise Lost*, whose domain was the 'lake of liquid fire:'[13] 'vivid flashes of lightning dazzled my eyes, illuminating the lake, making it appear like a vast sheet of fire' (73). Victor is entranced by the 'beautiful yet terrific' tempest over the lake, just as Mary Shelley was in the summer of 1816 when she '*enjoyed* a finer storm than I had ever before beheld'. But in making his oxymoronic statements about the 'noble war in the sky', Victor is also unwittingly referring, not to the 'battle in heaven' so graphically depicted in Milton's epic, but to the psychomachia now going on in his own mind – the 'battle within'. So identified has his internal state become with the storm that he finds his spirits 'elevated', and he calls out, 'William, dear angel! this is thy funeral, this thy dirge!', a dramatic appeal answered by the fleeting appearance of the being who will later describe himself as 'the fallen angel' – Frankenstein's creation.

As soon as he sees the 'filthy daemon' whose appearance he regards significantly as being 'more hideous than belongs to humanity' – for it means he sees his creation as non-human and thus 'other' – he is convinced that this Other is the murderer of William: 'The mere presence of the idea was an irresistible proof of the fact.' This is hardly a sound method for ascribing guilt, we may think, but then, as Victor himself tells us, it was not merely an idea but his *imagination* which had convinced him: 'No sooner did that idea cross my imagination, than I became convinced of its truth' (73). It had been the 'spark' of his obsessive Romantic imagination – what Peter Conrad (as I have said) calls his 'filthy workshop of creation' – which had been the essential ingredient in bringing forth the reality of his Being.

After the Creature's swift departure to the heights of Mont Salêve, it is this same faculty which Victor deploys in thinking back over the events of the past two years. During the wretched night he has spent out of doors – parallel in many ways to the night of the Creature's animation – his imagination, 'busy in scenes of evil and despair', begins to suggest something like the truth to him:

I considered the being whom I had cast among mankind . . . nearly in the light of my own vampire, my own spirit let loose from the grave, and forced to destroy all that was dear to me. (74)

This is so like images Edmund Burke had used to describe the spirit of evil he felt had been released into Europe during the course of the French Revolution that one is tempted to suppose Mary Shelley was here thinking of specific passages from his *Reflections on the Revolution in France* (1790), a book which both she and Percy Shelley had indeed studied. Throughout history, argues Burke, good and evil are the inherent principles of human nature animating the leaders of society to one degree or another. When French revolutionary idealists felt they had once and for all replaced a corrupt regime with an honest one, they were bound to fail, for in such a situation vice simply

assumes a new body. The spirit transmigrates; and, far from losing its principle of life by the change of its appearance, it is renovated in its new organs with the fresh vigour of a juvenile activity. It walks abroad; it continues its ravages.[14]

But the problem with Victor's insight, that he had, through his thoughtlessness, created a being which embodied his 'vampire ... spirit', his capacity to do evil, is that it is too 'essentialist', and too simplistically self-serving. It allows him to see his abandonment of the Creature as fully justified, on the grounds that an ugly exterior signals an ugly, 'evil' intention. In what is clearly emerging as a metaphorical narrative arguing against this view – for the Creature is going to be given the opportunity of showing that his character and intentions are good – no such assumption is supportable that does not take into account the real existence and experiences of the supposedly 'evil Other'. While he continues to label that which he is unwilling to confront courageously and responsibly in this way, Victor is always going to be able to find excuses about what he has done, 'not to tell': and he does. Hence his excuse that his story would be received as the 'ravings of insanity' by the authorities, and that it would be useless to attempt pursuit of the Creature because of its 'strange nature' and its superhuman capacities. Interestingly, when he finally and in desperation takes his story to a magistrate, the judge does give this predictable response. The point that Mary Shelley seems to be making, however, is that it is Victor Frankenstein's own misplaced sense of idealism that 'created' the problem, and it is for him to attempt its correction. But while his self-deceiving excuses persuade him to 'remain silent', no correction of the situation can be effected; far from it, for his inaction now will guarantee that others suffer both for his earlier actions and for his lapses.

In such a mood of inaction it is unsurprising to find him indulging in nostalgic grief at the portraits of his dead mother and little brother. The portrait of Caroline Beaufort kneeling by the coffin of her dead father 'in an agony of despair' should be a grim reminder to Victor of the follies of stubborn pride, but ever the aesthete, he is only able to see in it 'an air of dignity and beauty, that hardly permitted the sentiment of pity' (75). He persists in his decision to keep silent about the Creature, cocooning himself in a false sense of confidence about the fate of Justine, who has now been accused of William's murder. Again he delivers himself up to the same self-deluding Romantic imagination whose extreme Prometheanism had resulted in the creation and abandonment of a botched 'new man'. 'I was firmly convinced in my own mind that Justine, and indeed every human being, was guiltless of this murder', says Victor, who is 'calmed' by Alphonse's hope for her acquittal and his assurance to a weeping Elizabeth that she should 'rely on the justice of our laws, and the activity with which I shall prevent the slightest shadow of partiality' (78).

Of course, in Chapter VIII we find that this confident trust in the laws of the land to bring justice to the case is entirely misplaced. But Justine's trial becomes a 'wretched mockery of justice' not because the legal process is evil or malicious – though this had been the Godwinian drift of a passage in the 1818 edition that Mary Shelley modified in 1831.[15] It is because the kind of justice appropriate to the solution of the case is beyond the capacity of a regular judiciary to exact. As Victor privately confesses, the murder and the conviction of Justine are both the ultimate results of his 'curiosity and lawless devices', his 'unhallowed arts' (79, 86). As a trangressor of natural and divine laws, Victor is confusedly coming to realize that his actions have deprived him of all recourse to God, or access to conscience, in order to achieve some kind of forgiveness. This is the meaning behind Justine's futile attempt to gain absolution by confessing to a crime she did not commit. Her failure to gain absolution is a kind of warning of the fate which awaits both Victor and the Creature, the living embodiment of Frankenstein's transgressions. Victor says that he would have willingly confessed to the crime ascribed to Justine, but being 'absent' at the time 'such a declaration would have been considered the ravings of a madman, and would not have exculpated her who suffered through me' (79). This clever use of the word 'absent' does not merely trigger our thoughts concerning Victor's persistently truant disposition, but implies a much more profound vacancy, the loss of God. With God absent in him, and his 'first hapless victims' destroyed, it is little wonder that Victor feels a hell within him which 'nothing could extinguish' (85). (Yet another allusion to *Paradise Lost*, IV.75.)

3 Frankenstein's Narrative (1) (continued)

Towards the Sea of Ice (Chapters I–II)

With little William and Justine *both* dead, Victor is seized by guilt and remorse, 'which hurried me away to a hell of intense tortures, such as no language can describe'. It seems appropriate that no language can describe these feelings, for the source of the problem has been in his having 'committed deeds of mischief beyond description horrible' (87). Nowadays such 'gothic' forms of expression have become so familiar through sensational newspaper reports and horror films that they may seem clichéd. But if we take what Victor says seriously – that he really *can* find no adequate language to convey either his feelings now, or to articulate his remembrance of the making of his Creature – how are we to explain this 'loss for words'? A clue to what is going on comes with the suspect comments he makes immediately following the last quotation:

Yet my heart overflowed with kindness, and the love of virtue. I had begun life with benevolent intentions, and thirsted for the moment when I should put them in practice and make myself useful to my fellow beings. Now all was blasted . . . (87)

For a start, the wise old saying 'the road to hell is paved with good intentions' seems fully applicable here. As we have already observed, Victor's own account has offered little evidence of a genuine desire to serve people. Rather the opposite. Despite his good intentions, he has been waylaid into seeking personal glory as the father of a new race of beings whom he expects to look gratefully upon him as their deliverer. Rationalizing his purposes as philanthropic, he has pursued one 'creative thought' so obsessively that all other thought for the living world of people around him has been discarded in the process.

This is neatly captured in the remark he makes when he realizes the Creature has begun to seek revenge for his rejected condition. All would be solved if only he could 'extinguish that life which I had so *thoughtlessly* bestowed', he says (89, emphasis added). But when his thoughts then quickly spiral towards an 'immoderate' desire to avenge the deaths of William and Justine, and Elizabeth demands that he should banish these 'dark passions' from himself and instead count the blessings that remain to him in their 'land of peace and beauty', this only serves to remind him just how much he has to fear from the Creature. Whereas the Creature has nothing to lose by his revenge, Victor stands to lose a lot. Nevertheless, the words which Mary Shelley uses to frame Victor's frightened judgement on this score reveal once again how he still only really 'values' Elizabeth in terms of a possession:

And could not such words from her whom I fondly prized before every other gift of fortune, suffice to chase away the fiend that lurked in my heart? Even as she spoke I drew near to her, as if in terror; lest at that very moment the destroyer had been near to rob me of her. (90)

Now defined only by the alternating 'fiends' of revenge and remorse, Victor is without resource, able neither to respond to the warmth of Elizabeth nor to the beauty of his surroundings. In a cruel parody of the isolation in which he had chosen to build his Creature, he now feels condemned to avoid everyone, for 'all sound of joy or complacency was torture to me; solitude was my only consolation . . .' (87).

It seems fitting that the effort he now makes to 'forget myself and my ephemeral, because human, sorrows' should take him up into the cold and isolated regions of the Alps (91). There he hopes to extinguish the burning hell of guilt tormenting him by worshipping at the great shrine of 'a power mighty as Omnipotence' which he senses among the towering peaks. Though he feels he has changed in the six years since he last visited the valley of Chamounix, he is convinced the 'mighty Alps' have not; that they are the 'habitations of another race of beings' not subject to the painfully fluctuating passions of men. Though this phrase prepares us for an encounter with the Creature, Victor seems oblivious of the prospect he has himself invoked, reflecting instead how a 'tingling long-lost sense of pleasure' often came across him during the journey. The 'maternal nature' he finds around him is soothing rather than threatening, bidding him to 'weep no more'. When he retires weary to his rest that night, he is lulled into sleep by the rushing sounds of the River Arve passing beneath his window.

For one who has so single-mindedly abused and exploited this 'maternal nature' (another phrase Mary Shelley borrowed from Canto 3 of *Childe Harold*), these boons to the soul cannot be lasting. In Chapter II the author has the compulsive Frankenstein move inexorably towards a confrontation with – in the most literal double sense – his own Being. On the way, it is no surprise to find him arriving at the source of the Arve, for had he not earlier described his predilection for probing the cosmos as arising 'like a mountain river, from ignoble and almost forgotten sources' (38)? And yet he feels pleasantly 'subdued and tranquillised' in what he calls the 'glorious presence-chamber of imperial Nature'. He is fascinated by the awesome effects of the 'silent working of immutable laws' that rend and tear the ice of the enormous glaciers 'as if it had been but a plaything in their hands' (93). We should notice the most exquisite effect of irony at work here. Whereas in the 1818 edition Victor had been content simply to celebrate the calming influences of the 'awful and majestic in nature', in 1831 Mary Shelley makes the scientist utter words which reveal his (unconscious) omnipotent identification with the 'immutable laws' underlying this nature. For he too has manipulated power in an arbitrary way, creating an assemblage of dead human parts and animating it as if it had been a 'plaything' in his hands. The concept of power deployed here was that which Percy Shelley had evoked as 'untameable wildness' in his 1816 poem 'Mont Blanc'. Mary Shelley seems to deploy this in order to make a comment on the 'unruly' way in which Percy Shelley had in his life so often indulged his impulses, often without regard to the consequences. The once wielder of omnipotent power, unaware that the Creature who is its product inhabits these frozen regions, retires once more into sleep, feeling at ease when the 'sublime and magnificent scenes' which have so elevated his spirit during the day 'gather round' him once more in his dreams.

But when he wakes the following morning, he finds 'the faces of those mighty friends', the mountains, obscured by rain and thick mist, and as a result falls into a 'dark melancholy' (93). Night had deprived Victor of a sight of these friends when first he returned home from Ingolstadt; this time it is the weather that does this. But the Promethean Frankenstein is not so easily beaten. He determines – and let us note with some alarm the words he uses – to 'penetrate their misty veil and seek them in their cloudy retreats'. His wish is to recapture the 'sublime ecstasy' which viewing the 'terrifically desolate' scene presented by the Mer de Glace at the summit of Montanvert had once given him. As he ascends, the thick mist and driving rain create in him a 'melancholy impression', which Mary Shelley points up by having Victor quote from Percy Shelley's poem *Mutability*:

> We rest; a dream has power to poison sleep.
> We rise; one wand'ring thought pollutes the day.
> We feel, conceive, or reason; laugh or weep,
> Embrace fond woe, or cast our cares away:

> It is the same: for, be it joy or sorrow,
>   The path of its departure still is free:
> Man's yesterday may ne'er be like his morrow;
>   Nought may endure but mutability!

This is Frankenstein's way of cursing the waywardness of the human imagination that has been his downfall: if only men were more like 'immutable' nature, they might be free. Again this provides a deeply ironic comment on the god-like act of creation which he had actually achieved, but which he fails to recognize, though he suffers its effects.

Having attained the summit of Montanvert he crosses the sea of ice, which he describes in terms that symbolize his own disordered condition. It is 'very uneven', he says, 'rising like the waves of a troubled sea, descending low, and interspersed by rifts that sink deep' (95). Once across the glacier of frozen turbulence he stations himself in a recess of the rock, where he is able to gaze on the 'wonderful and stupendous scene' of Mont Blanc in its 'awful majesty'. His heart swelling with 'something like joy' he feels moved to call aloud to the 'wandering spirits' of the mountains either to allow him his 'faint happiness', or to take him as their companion 'away from the joys of life'. As if providing an instant reply, his own creation suddenly appears running towards him with 'superhuman speed': the daemonic 'spirit of solitude' has manifested itself. Victor had wished simply to gaze upon the faces of his mighty friends, but is forced now to confront the 'unearthly ugliness' of his own Being, 'almost too horrible for human eyes' (95). Since Victor regards his creation as a savage 'wretch' who has been the evil perpetrator of his brother's murder, it is little wonder that the first outraged word he utters to him is 'Devil'. This is in a sense appropriate, since we are soon to learn that the Creature sees his dilemma very much in the light of Milton's devil Satan, whom he has learned about from a copy of *Paradise Lost* he fortuitously found. Thus when Frankenstein explodes with violent fury and accusation, the Creature is not surprised.

In fact, despite his grotesque appearance, he demonstrates himself to be a thoughtful, experienced being – ironically, since it is supposed to be Frankenstein who is the 'civilized' one. Also, if only Frankenstein will listen – the very last thing of which he is capable, at present – he will find explained in the first speech made by his 'progeny' both the essentials of his deplorable situation and what he proposes to do should his maker refuse to comply with his wishes. With the Creature's explanation of the situation, we as readers are also supplied with a summary of the remainder of the story's plot:

'I expected this reception,' said the daemon. 'All men hate the wretched; how, then, must I be hated, who am miserable beyond all living things! Yet you, my creator, detest and spurn me, thy creature, to whom thou art bound by ties only dissoluble by the annihilation of one of us. You purpose to kill me. How dare you sport thus with life? Do your duty towards me, and I will do mine towards you and the rest of mankind. If you will comply with my conditions, I will leave them and you at peace; but if you refuse, I will glut the maw of death, until it be satiated with the blood of your remaining friends.' (96)

'How dare you sport thus with life?' As well as providing what might serve as a pithily insightful epigraph to the whole book, this question shows the Creature has special intelligence of Frankenstein's omnipotent mode of thinking. Victor has marvelled half admiringly at the monstrous way in which the 'immutable' laws governing nature treat the world as a 'plaything' in their hands. Now the Creature observes with uncanny accuracy how Frankenstein also presumes to sport – to play – with his own creature's life and death. Yet this is not intuition on the Creature's part. As well as drawing on Milton's version of the Christian story in *Paradise Lost*, he had also discovered in the pocket of a garment taken from Frankenstein's laboratory a journal detailing the 'series of disgusting circumstances' which led over a four-month period to his own 'accursed origin' (126).

Frankenstein's angry impulse upon seeing the Creature now is to grapple with him in 'mortal combat'. Then, when he hears the Creature reproach him for his creation, he springs at him with greater fury, aiming to 'extinguish the spark which I so negligently bestowed' (96). But the Creature easily deflects this feeble attempt, and Victor is once more forced to listen to a Creature who shows himself, amazingly, to be educated both in the ways of the world and in literature. In words that remind us that the Creature addresses Frankenstein standing beneath the 'awful majesty' of Mont Blanc, he says that despite the superior physical abilities that his maker has given him, he is nevertheless prepared to be 'mild and docile to my natural lord and king' if only Victor will show him 'clemency and affection' (96). Adapting his knowledge of *Paradise Lost* for his petition, he asks Frankenstein to

'Remember, that I am thy creature; I ought to be thy Adam, but I am rather the fallen angel, whom thou drivest from joy for no misdeed. Everywhere I see bliss, from which I alone am irrevocably excluded. I was benevolent and good; misery made me a fiend. Make me happy, and I shall again be virtuous.' (96–7)

Ironically, complaints similar to some of these have already been voiced by Frankenstein concerning his *own* condition, although he has become socially marooned for reasons of guilt rather than for reasons of social rejection. Alas, Frankenstein speaks only too symptomatically of his own shrunken moral state when he refuses to hear the Creature's pleas, asserting that there can be 'no community' between them. This is because, as we have already observed, by his actions Victor has lost the capacity for sympathy – fellow-feeling – the very quality essential for maintaining any human community worthy of the name.

Despite his inability to move Frankenstein, the Creature continues to plead for 'goodness and compassion', since he has no one else to turn to for help. Victor's 'fellow-creatures', he says (acknowledging that there is indeed a 'species difference' between them), offer him no hope, as they 'owe' him nothing. But Victor does. In a clever echo of the Lord's Prayer, he says it remains in his 'creator's' power to 'deliver [the world] from an evil' so potentially vast that not only he and his family, but 'thousands of others' are in danger of being 'swallowed up in the whirlwinds of its rage' (97). The Creature had learned from Victor's brother William before he killed him that their father was a magistrate, so it is with a certain shrewdness that he makes his last request for compassion by appealing to the system of law. Even the guilty 'are allowed, by human laws, bloody as they are, to speak in their own defence before they are condemned', he says (97). A serious political point is being made by Mary Shelley here, whether Godwinian or not, for in 1818 the laws of England remained bloody indeed. As William St Clair has stated, 'Between 1800 and 1820 there were between seven and eight hundred executions a year in Great Britain, the highest ever recorded.'[1] This was largely because the nation then faced 'the most widespread, persistent and dangerous disturbances, short of actual revolution and civil war, [that] England has known in modern times.'[2] (See Chapter 11 for the political context.)

At first Frankenstein does not respond to the Creature's 'legalistic' appeal, for he is unable to shake off the disturbing influence his horrid appearance is having upon his senses. When he becomes so affected by this that he demands the Creature relieve him of the sight of his 'detested form', the Creature ingeniously facilitates this by covering up Victor's eyes, saying: 'thus I take from thee a sight which you abhor'. The full significance of his half-playful action only becomes apparent when he adds, 'Still thou canst listen to me and grant me thy compassion.' This has a powerful effect upon Frankenstein. His visually aesthetic sense now suspended, he is forced into moral reflection.

Perhaps physical appearance is not the basis for making a just estimate of a person's worth, after all. This for the moment seems to provide an unanswerable argument, for when the Creature insists that Frankenstein hear his tale in 'the hut upon the mountain' and starts to walk off on to the glacier, his creator follows him. Frankenstein is partly motivated in this by his curiosity to find out whether his Creature really is the murderer of William. But more importantly, the Creature's words have had the effect of re-creating a tiny glimmer of sympathy in Frankenstein's breast. For the first time, says Victor,

I felt what the duties of a creator towards his creature were, and that I ought to render him happy before I complained of his wickedness. (98)

He feels he does 'owe' his creation something, after all.

4 The Creature's Narrative

The Pleasure and Pain of It All (Chapters III–IV)

In his hilarious picaresque novel *Candide, or, Optimism* (1759), the French *philosophe* Voltaire used the adventures of his young hero satirically to challenge the sacred cows of religious and philosophical belief prevailing in eighteenth-century Europe, and particularly in France. In many ways, the various reactions to the world delivered in the Creature's narrative to Frankenstein have a similar function. From the account he gives of his initial puzzlements and delights at nature, then the yearning admiration he develops for the de Lacey family's 'civilized' values, to his final disenchantment with the deeply prejudiced ways of men, we are provoked to reflect on some of the basic assumptions and values we carry with us in dealing with one other.

Much of the narrative is built on Mary Shelley's reading of John Locke's *An Essay Concerning Human Understanding* (1690). She read Locke from 16 November 1816 to 8 January 1817, the most sustained period of continuous study of a single work undertaken during the composition of *Frankenstein*. The effects of her reading are especially evident in Chapters III and IV, where the monster's account of his earliest memories after 'birth' illustrate the arguments put forward by Locke; in particular, his keystone empirical conviction that 'All ideas come from Sensation or Reflection', that is to say, from experience, or 'testing'. It is important to bear in mind that for Locke 'ideas' are a somewhat protean category. He tells us they could equally be described as 'phantasms', 'notions' or 'species': all 'objects' of the mind's thinking. He also says his understanding of 'idea' is signified by 'conception' – a word with interesting implications for this study, of course. We are probably safest in our search for a working equivalent of 'idea' to think in terms of 'impression', since this avoids for the moment having to choose between signifiers denoting 'abstract' rather than 'felt' evaluations.

The debt to Locke's central argument that all impressions come from sensation or reflection is apparent from the outset. When the Creature seeks to describe his earliest experiences, he explains that a 'strange multiplicity of sensations seized me, and I saw, felt, heard, and smelt at the same time' (99).[1] The most overwhelming of these first sensations is the experience of light, which obliges him to shut his eyes after a while because it 'pressed' upon his nerves. Closing his eyes helps, but darkness troubles him, so he opens them, whereupon 'the light poured in upon me again'. From being merely 'pressing' the light finally becomes so 'oppressive' that he is compelled to seek shade in the forest near Ingolstadt, where he also rests from his exertions. Having recovered his strength a little, the sensations of hunger and thirst now overtake him. He satisfies these by drinking from a stream and eating berries, and then sleeps. But when he wakes he feels cold, despite having clothed himself in some garments he had found when leaving the laboratory. Chilled and frightened, a feeling of desolation now overcomes him:

'I was a poor, helpless, miserable wretch; I knew, and could distinguish, nothing; but feeling pain invade me on all sides, I sat down and wept.' (99)

Locke divides all experiences into those producing pleasure and those producing pain. At no point so far in his narrative has the Creature been able to report any experience of pleasure. On the contrary, with his ironic comments no doubt retrospectively informed by Frankenstein's detailed notes on his manufacture, the Creature observes that the light which had 'poured in' upon him was far from providing the kind of 'enlightenment' that his maker had so dizzyingly envisaged. The 'torrent of light' which the natural philosopher had wished to 'pour into our dark world' (52) has so far brought his creation nothing but pain. That the Creature's use of this parallel imagery has the ironic purpose of attacking Frankenstein's 'thoughtless' Enlightenment conception seems confirmed by the fact that the animation had taken place on a 'dreary night' when there was only a 'half-extinguished' candle to illuminate the nativity scene. This could hardly have provided the blaze of light which the Creature claims to have been so pained by, following his 'birth'. The Creature may be using Lockean terms to open his story, but when it comes to describing the subjective effects of Frankenstein's experiment, Mary Shelley's careful use of language shows that the Creature is far from merely commenting upon his physical apprehensions. He is also intent upon developing a moral critique of his creator's blindingly brilliant thinking.

This is shown in the Creature's response to the rising of the moon. The moon, he tells Frankenstein, provided his first experience of pleasure, and it also helped him to solve the problem of feeling cold:

'Soon a gentle light stole over the heavens, and gave me a sensation of pleasure. I started up and beheld a radiant form rise from among the trees. I gazed with a kind of wonder. It moved slowly, but it enlightened my path, and I again went out in search of berries. I was still cold when under one of the trees I found a huge cloak, with which I covered myself, and sat down upon the ground . . . the only object that I could distinguish was the bright moon, and I fixed my eyes on that with pleasure.' (99–100)

It is not surprising that the Creature's first pleasurable sensation should be occasioned by the moon's appearance. In contrast to the fierce light that Frankenstein had through his creation 'poured' into the world, the illumination which usefully enlightens the Creature's path towards the cloak and warmth is 'gentle' and moves 'slowly'. In Romantic literature the moon is frequently used as a feminine symbol denoting gentleness and fecundity, while the sun represents more aggressive, masculine traits. More particularly, both in Shelley's poetry and in their letters, the moon was frequently used as an 'agreed' sign for Mary, with Percy designated as the sun, whose beams make her gently visible, (This deployment is most evident in Shelley's poem *Epipsychidion*.) I have already pointed out that in *Frankenstein* the seemingly unobtrusive moon does in fact play a far from passive role. We must now recognize that from the first it is of major importance to the novel, for it represents the active and watchful presence of Mary Shelley herself in the text. From the moment that the moon gazes on Frankenstein's 'midnight labours' to 'animate the lifeless clay' (53), this presence comes to be identified with, and a companion of, the Creature. When Frankenstein woke from his nightmare after the Creature's animation, it was by the light of the 'dim and yellow' moon – which had most *ungently* 'forced its way through the window shutters' – that Frankenstein was directed to see the 'dull yellow eye' of his creation. Compelled to look upon the product of his inglorious efforts, Frankenstein had then made good his second escape. From this moment on, the 'radiant form' takes on a protective role towards the abandoned Creature. It remains to light his way, standing guard over his efforts to survive in the forest until his faculties are improved enough for him to enjoy and explore the world with more confidence.

The Creature discovers a second source of pleasure in the singing of the forest birds. His touching efforts to imitate them, perhaps in the hope of communicating with living beings other than himself, only produces 'uncouth and inarticulate sounds'. Yet his Lockean sensations develop so rapidly, his mind receiving every day 'additional ideas', that he is ever on the alert for new and valuable experiences. A major discovery comes when he finds a smouldering fire left by travellers. At first he is 'overcome with delight' at the warmth it offers him, but the pain which follows his attempt to touch it produces a profound philosophical response: 'How strange, I thought, that the same cause should produce such opposite effects!' (101). The innocent response is acute, because even at this early stage of his existence it implies a certain awareness in him of the ambiguous nature both of his own origins and of his prospects. He has been endowed with the 'spark' of life, but will it be a life of pleasure or of pain? For the moment, he is intrigued enough by his discovery to want to find out more, so that in his further explorations he becomes something of an empirical scientist – like Frankenstein! He notices, for instance, that when wet wood dries, the fire will burn it:

I reflected on this; and by touching the various branches, I discovered the cause, and busied myself in collecting a great quantity of wood . . . (101)

As well as finding out that fire gives light as well as heat, he makes the accidental (yet momentous) discovery that it improves the taste of offals left by travellers (but ruins the taste of berries). This simple preference for cooked over raw food establishes his status as a being of human culture, for only humans cook their food.[2] As an aspirer after culture rather than nature, one would now expect him to move towards the company of humans rather than birds, and Mary Shelley ensures that this happens. But his motives are still mostly appetite-led and he only meets his first human being since leaving Frankenstein's laboratory because he has been forced to abandon his fire and to forage further afield for scarce supplies of food.

Eager to satisfy his curiosity about the interior of a hut he stumbles upon in this search, his effect on the old shepherd who breakfasts within does not bode well for his future relations with humans. When the old man (like Frankenstein before him) flees in terror at his monstrous appearance, the unsocialized Creature is merely 'somewhat surprised' by such a hasty departure, and gratefully falls to eating the bread, milk and cheese left behind. Having eaten and slept to his satisfaction, he decides to continue his travels, not to find food – he still has some – but presumably to discover human society. This he does, but his next encounter with humans is less fortunate than the last. After a long trek across fields, he is even more amazed at the 'miraculous' appearance of the neat houses and gardens of a village he arrives at than he was with the dry and 'divine' retreat from the elements that the shepherd's hut had provided. His admiration increases when he spots the tempting foods on the window ledges of cottages. When his inquiring nature induces him to enter 'one of the best of these' (his discriminatory powers improve apace!) children scream, a woman faints, and it is not long before he is attacked so viciously by villagers that he is forced to retreat to open country, having been 'grievously bruised by stones' (102). Fortunately, he is soon lucky enough to find refuge in a bare 'low hovel.' This adjoins an isolated cottage, which he finds to be 'an agreeable asylum from the snow and rain' (103).

The Creature being driven into hiding by human society marks an important but not unexpected moment in his narrative, a moment that is of interest to us for several reasons. Firstly, we know what he does not: that he is repulsive to the eyes of men. After animating his Creature, Frankenstein had escaped from the horror of his own folly to find 'asylum' in a dark and rainy courtyard. As events unfold, he finds the society he had studiously avoided in order to build the Creature now makes him feel so guilty that he turns to nature to find solace. Conversely, when the Creature 'innocently' seeks to extend the transition he is making from nature to culture (he enters the village), he is driven, by what he is entitled through a 'dearly bought experience' to denominate 'the barbarity of man', into an asylum which shelters him from the rain. Moreover, whereas it was Frankenstein's offended aesthetic sense which had driven him away from the ugliness of his Creature, that same Creature, in judging the abode of his new neighbours to be of 'a neat and pleasant appearance', shows himself to be developing his own aesthetic sensibilities more and more. He may look monstrously unhuman, but his sensations and emotions are fully human.

Yet there is a further aspect to the Creature's being driven away from society that we should note. This involves the figure of Rousseau. I stated at the beginning of my discussion of Frankenstein's narrative that Rousseau's ideas concerning liberty and society were important sources for the formation of Mary Shelley's novel. When the Creature is stoned and chased away by the villagers, this echoes the treatment Rousseau had had to endure at Neuchâtel in France after the publication of his two books *The Social Contract* and *Émile* in 1762. In *The Social Contract* he had argued for a political system guaranteeing the members of a community their individual rights and freedoms. In *Émile* he had taken this further by arguing that every individual 'child of nature' should be brought up to be the 'natural man' in society, learning to live with other people, to love and be loved, and to contribute to the common good. His ideas were not merely seen as impious and politically threatening, but, as he says in his *Confessions*, 'I saw myself suddenly misrepresented as a frightful Creature, such as had never existed.' Worse, as Mary Shelley recounts in her essay on Rousseau, from execration the peasantry of Neuchâtel 'proceeded to personal attack; stones were thrown at him during his walks'.[3] As Milton Millhauser has argued, Mary Shelley really does seem to want Frankenstein's Creature to be read as a Noble Savage of the Rousseauan type.

Established in the hovel that will be his sanctuary for months to come, it is now that the Creature's education truly begins. From his hidden location adjoining the cottage, he will learn to speak, to read and to understand something of the values and abuses of society. He does this by observing and listening to the family inhabiting the cottage, the De Laceys. As we have come to expect, the observations he begins to offer of the life he sees going on inside the cottage reveal a creature of fine Rousseauan sensations and sympathy, someone who quickly develops a yearning to become part of this intimate human group. The picture Mary Shelley paints of the De Laceys is very much based on the type of patriarchal idyll portrayed in Rousseau's *La Nouvelle Héloïse*, 'where a household lives in relative isolation from the wicked cities and provides a model of loving interdependence'.[4] This is also the kind of romantic rural idyll which Godwin had painted in his novel *St Leon* (1799). The Creature is adept at conveying his first impressions of this close-knit family, whose inexplicable gloom he is pleased to find lifts a little when the old man starts playing his guitar, producing 'sounds sweeter than the voice of the thrush or the nightingale' (104). His capacity for careful observation is now becoming very keen. When the playing produces tears in the girl, and old De Lacey responds only when she begins to sob 'audibly', this proves to the Creature that the man must be blind. The old man's reaction to her distress has a sensible effect on the secret observer, for when he

raised her, and smiled with such kindness and affection . . . I felt sensations of a peculiar and overpowering nature: they were a mixture of pain and pleasure, such as I had never before experienced, either from hunger or cold, warmth or food; and I withdrew from the window, unable to bear these emotions. (104)

The Creature has pleasurably identified with the sentiments of the scene, but in doing so he also feels the first painful pangs of emotion related to his own parental deprivation. He yearns to 'belong' and to be comforted himself. Abandoned, he has no one to care for him, and he dare not declare himself to the cottagers for fear of encountering, once more, the kind of rejection he has already experienced.

Yet when he compares his own isolated lot with the conditions enjoyed by his neighbours, the Creature is puzzled at the silent tears shed so frequently by the young man and woman. Why were these gentle beings unhappy? he innocently asks. They had a house to live in, fire for warmth, food, clothing, the boon of each others' company and conversation, and, above all, the opportunity to exchange each day together 'looks of affection and kindness' (107). Like a true eighteenth-century empirical philosopher – again, ironic reminders of Frankenstein's own efforts never seem far away – he is moved to wonder about the causes for the phenomena he sees: 'What did their tears imply? Did they really express pain?' He is baffled. As with most experiments where the investigator has first to become really acquainted with his data before making a breakthrough, a 'considerable period' must elapse before the Creature discovers 'the causes of the uneasiness of this amiable family' (108). Eventually he finds out: the cause of the 'evil' is poverty. This condition sometimes prompts the young man and woman to sacrifice their portion of food to the unsuspecting old man, a 'trait of kindness' which jolts the Creature into making another discovery: his conscience (another vital regulator of the moral life for Rousseau). For some time he has been regularly stealing some of the cottagers' food for himself. As soon as he realizes this has 'inflicted pain' on them, he is not merely content to return to a diet of berries, nuts and roots, but tries to make amends by providing the cottagers with a frequent supply of firewood. Noticing that this enables the young man to pursue other vital tasks, he is rewarded with feelings of pleasure. If tracing effects to their causes can satisfy the investigator's curious mind, then employing knowledge of such causes in order to perform actions that will benefit a person are so much more satisfying. This 'applied' approach to scientific endeavour is one that the more 'pure' scientist Frankenstein would do well to take heed of. Unfortunately, he seems constitutionally incapable of bestowing gifts in the way the Creature does, forced, like the De Laceys, to think in terms of some 'good spirit' ameliorating their respective plights (111, 197).

He feels he has found a worthwhile way of entering into the lives of the cottagers, albeit anonymously. But the inquisitive Creature now makes a discovery that will take him to the very heart of social and cultural experience – human language. He reports having made this discovery by his typically empirical way of proceeding. He has noticed how the 'articulate sounds' made by the cottagers to each other 'produced pleasure or pain, smiles or sadness, in the minds and countenances of the hearers' (108). As a being who feels defined by pains and pleasures over which he has little or no control, he now greatly desires to become acquainted with this 'godlike science' of speech for reasons which would today come under the heading of 'empowerment'. The power of making speech seems to be a prerequisite for becoming part of society. As a student of John Locke, it is not surprising to find Mary Shelley developing the Creature's impulses in this direction, for in the *Essay Concerning Human Understanding*, which she had carefully studied, Locke writes under the heading of 'Man fitted to form articulate sounds' the following:

God, having designed man for a sociable creature, made him not only with an inclination and under a necessity to have fellowship with those of his own kind, but furnished him also with language, which was to be the great instrument and common tie of society. Man, therefore, had by nature his organs so fashioned as to be fit to frame articulate sounds, which we call words.[5]

There are two problems for Mary Shelley to overcome in adopting this account for the development of the living Creature:

(1) God did not 'design' the Creature, Frankenstein did.
(2) Whereas Locke could assume everyone is born into a nurturing and sociable society and so acquires language 'naturally', the Creature is not born into society. Yet he is nevertheless required somehow to learn human language.

On the first point, because Frankenstein created the person of his dreams in his own (imperfect) image, the Creature has been rejected both from his creator's society and subsequently from the society of others; therefore his destiny is bound to be 'unnatural'. Secondly, and following on from this, although Locke is correct to say that language is 'the great instrument and common tie of society', it is one thing to possess the capacities for society and speech, but quite another to say *how* these powers are actually acquired and made workable. Not surprisingly, given that Locke's is the earliest modern attempt to construct a philosophy based on experience, this is nowhere explained in his *Essay*. So that Mary Shelley is compelled, in her explanation of how the Creature learned the meaning and use of the cottagers' basic vocabulary, to confine herself merely to describing the effort taken to effect the breakthrough. Hence the Creature manages to learn and apply words 'by great application' over a period of several months (109), just as it took Frankenstein 'days and nights of incredible labour and fatigue' to create life where none had existed before (51). Language acquisition is almost as difficult to explain as 'life' itself. (The attempt to explain 'life' was very much on the agenda in the period in which Mary Shelley was writing, as I explain in Chapter 11.)

At one level these lacunae in the textual fabric may seem like deficiencies threatening to undermine our confidence in the novel. Jerome Bruner has explained that our initial mastery of language 'can come only from participation in language as an instrument of communication ... It is only *after* some language has been acquired in the formal sense that one can acquire *further* language as a "bystander".'[6] In other words, it is impossible for the Creature to learn language by eavesdropping on the conversation of the cottagers. Such learning could only be facilitated by his *participation* in the family's social interactions, where the meanings of words are actively focussed by the subjective *experience* of what they signify for each person. Criticizing the novel on this technical level brings out how important active participation in a shared and active language community is. Within such a language community we gain and master the arts of being social human beings; without it we become asocial and unstable isolates. In addition we must not fall into the trap of making *Frankenstein*'s technical deficiencies a reason for neglecting the moral questions it raises. Perhaps this is why Sir Walter Scott, one of the few early admirers of *Frankenstein*, said in his discussion of this problem that 'as we have consented to admit the leading incident of the work, perhaps some of our readers may be of opinion, that to stickle upon lesser improbabilities, is to incur the censure bestowed by the Scottish proverb on those who "start at straws after/swallowing *windlings*"'.[7] It is far more important to understand the book's power as a profoundly *ethical* work than to notice its several 'improbabilities' (though there are points about the language issue to which I return in Chapter 8). Regardless of the technique by which the Creature has been created and the method by which it gains its education, the central deficiency conveyed in the novel is the one that Frankenstein ensures will inhabit (and inhibit) his Creature. In the months when he was 'thoughtlessly' engaged upon its construction, Frankenstein had thereby 'built into' his creation the very factor he was neglecting to recognize in his own life. The appalling ugliness of the Creature will ensure that he will be rejected by the society that Frankenstein himself has turned his back on in order to create his 'son'. It is this 'thoughtless' (and thus language-less) exclusion of society that will finally make the experiences of Frankenstein and his Creature maddeningly inseparable mirror-images of each other.

The Creature has yet to learn of the ugliness that Frankenstein's wayward delirium has produced, and is still preoccupied with discovering the world around him. His admiration for the 'gentle manners and beauty' of the cottagers, whose names he now knows, becomes so great that he begins to see himself as one of their number, unhappy when they are dejected, and 'when they rejoiced, I sympathised in their joys' (109). This introduces another curious variant on the theme of 'likeness' which we find in the novel. Frankenstein had aimed to create 'a being like myself' and the result was a ludicrous pastiche. The Creature himself, unaware as yet of his hideousness, achieves in a sense what his creator cannot, in as much as he now 'feels like' one of the family which is so constantly under his loving surveillance. Even when he does discover his monstrous appearance in the reflection of a pool, though he is initially 'filled with the bitterest sensations of despondence and mortification' (110), he soon bounces back and becomes an eager optimist once more. The experience of natural growth going on around him, and of educational growth within him, ensures this. As spring advances and budding nature brings forth food aplenty for the cottagers, he is inspired to 'bright rays of hope, and anticipations of joy' (112). He fondly conjectures that when he has learned the arts of speech and reading, he will be ready to declare himself to the family. Once facing them he will by his 'gentle demeanour and conciliating words' persuade them to overlook his appearance and win their hearts and minds to his cause (111). Of course, he is in for a rude shock.

The 'strange system of human society' (Chapter V)

For the moment, the Creature's senses are intoxicated with the 'thousand scents of delight' and the 'thousand sights of beauty' brought by the spring. These pleasures are added to when Safie, the 'sweet Arabian', arrives. Identified as he is with the characters he absorbedly watches, he cannot but be as thrilled as Felix is by her ravishing looks. Yet the 'ecstatic joy' and excitement displayed by Felix at his lover's arrival also enthrals him: 'at that moment I thought him as beautiful as the stranger' (113–14). This recognition of passion and beauty by one who is hideously ugly is so pathetic that it has the effect of awakening our sympathy for the Creature's plight. Though used a great deal by Walton, and especially by Frankenstein, the word 'sympathy' has remained little more than a word, an empty cipher, until now. Approaching the centre of the text, we sense that Mary Shelley is bringing us to the heart of her book's concerns. With Safie's 'musical' voice and her 'countenance of angelic beauty and expression' (113), one is irresistibly reminded of the effect the 'angelic' orphans Caroline and Elizabeth had respectively had upon Alphonse and Victor Frankenstein. But the strength of *our* growing identification with the Creature's multiplying desires and hopes, in the way we begin to feel uncomfortably implicated in his destiny, makes us realize just how bloodless and superficial these attractions really had been for father and son.

In turn, we are led to an awareness of the parodic parallels Mary Shelley is setting up between the adolescent situation of Victor and that of his rapidly developing Creature. Victor, despite loving his family, had felt 'cooped up in one place' (44). Leaving domesticity behind, he had opted for the glory of a solitary career in science for six years. The Creature is also 'cooped up', but desperately wishes to exchange his lone condition in the hovel for a domestic scene where he can feel accepted as an equal. The only 'experiment' in which *he* wishes to indulge is one that will accord him the privilege of gaining access to those very social sympathies which Frankenstein had turned his back on by his presumptuous 'probings'.

He finds a ready method of moving towards this goal when he discovers that Safie, ignorant of the language the De Laceys use to converse with each other, is to be taught to speak and write French by her lover Felix. These lessons afford the Creature a great chance of improving his Lockean understanding, and after two months he can 'comprehend most of the words' spoken by the cottagers (115). As well as expanding his French vocabulary, he also learns the 'science of letters' by way of the 'very minute explanations' which Felix gives to Safie using Volney's *Ruins of Empires* (115). For several reasons, it is significant that the beginning of his crash course in Western civilization begins with the Comte de Volney's *Les Ruines, ou Méditations sur les Révolutions des Empires* (1791). As a French Revolutionary text announcing what one writer has called an imminent 'rationalist apocalypse',[8] its teaching is to be felt deeply both in Percy Shelley's *Queen Mab* and his *Revolt of Islam*, the latter written as Mary was completing *Frankenstein* at Marlow in 1817. But whereas Volney is a source of inspiration for P.B. Shelley's atheistic revolutionary enthusiasm, the Creature's reception of the text results in an outcome far more complicatedly 'radical' than anything the poet could have envisaged. The 'cursory knowledge of history' he gains from Volney seems completely at odds with what he has observed in the De Lacey household. Though it is perhaps unsurprising that he should weep along with Safie over the 'hapless fate' of the American Indians – for is he not a rejected 'savage' too? – he is astonished that the historical narrative could reveal man as 'at once so powerful, so virtuous, and magnificent', but also 'so vicious and base'. It is only when he hears 'details of vice and bloodshed' that he ceases to wonder at the reason why laws and governments are necessary. And then he learns about the 'strange system of human society' that imposes these governments and laws upon itself, and begins to speculate about his own place in the world:

'I heard of the division of property, of immense wealth and squalid poverty; of rank, descent, and noble blood.

'. . . I learned that the possessions most esteemed by your fellow creatures were, high and unsullied descent united with riches. A man might be respected with only one of these advantages; but without either he was considered, except in very rare instances, as a vagabond and a slave, doomed to waste his powers for the profits of the chosen few! And what was I? Of my creation and creator I was absolutely ignorant, but I knew that I possessed no money, no friends, no kind of property. I was, besides, endued with a figure hideously deformed and loathsome; I was not even of the same nature as man . . . When I looked around I saw and heard of none like me. Was I, then, a monster, a blot upon the earth, from which all men fled and whom all men disowned?

'. . . Oh, that I had forever remained in my native wood, nor known nor felt beyond the sensations of hunger, thirst and heat!' (116–17)

These last words are a distinct echo of statements Frankenstein has already made. When Walton had sought to extract the 'secret of life' from him, he was given this warning:

Learn from me, if not by my precepts, at least by my example, how dangerous is the acquirement of knowledge and how much happier that man is who believes his native town to be the world, than he who aspires to become greater than his nature will allow. (52)

Again, in his lone ascent into the Alps, Frankenstein had lamented the condition of man, observing how he 'might be nearly free', were his impulses 'confined to hunger, thirst, and desire' (94). Yet as we know, human impulses are *not* so confined, and it is this that sometimes makes thinking and knowledge such torments.

In their different circumstances then, both creator and created, Frankenstein and his Creature, deplore the impact that 'knowledge' has had upon them. Knowledge of the secret of creating life has robbed Frankenstein of his capacity for social sympathy. Knowledge that his unique and uncared-for condition makes a mockery of his aspirations to engage the sympathies of human beings leads the Creature to feel a 'miserable, unhappy wretch'. Only death can rid the mind of knowledge it would rather not have; only death – the Creature learns – can cancel completely 'the sensation of pain' (117). Yet, like Hamlet, who was also tempted to thoughts of self-annihilation by the pain of existence (as was Adam in *Paradise Lost*), Frankenstein's noble savage is still full enough of life for death to seem an option best avoided for the moment. He has been deprived of the care of a mother and father – indeed, of 'all the various relationships which bind one human being to another in mutual bonds' (117). And this has led him to ask, not for the last time, 'What was I?' Yet despite all this seeming hopelessness, the 'various feelings of indignation, delight, and wonder' produced in him by witnessing the living story of the people he has innocently and self-deceivingly come to regard as his 'protectors' so buoy him up that 'all terminated in additional love and reverence' for them (118).

Safie's Story (Chapter VI)

Chapter VI is as much a vehicle for ventilating Mary Shelley's abhorrence of injustice as it is an opportunity for us to discover the histories of the De Laceys and of Safie. It is also an opportunity for her to celebrate the kind of determination under conditions of adversity which had been such a feature of her mother's writing. Although the story is in some ways a repetition of the various social disasters with which we are becoming so familiar, for both of these reasons the story is worth rehearsing.

Until a few months prior to the Creature's arrival at the cottage, De Lacey, like Alphonse Frankenstein a man of 'good family', had been living with his son and daughter in Paris for many years, affluent and surrounded by friends. Safie's father had been the cause of the family's ruin and removal from France to the lonely exile of their isolated German cottage. A successful Turkish merchant living in Paris, this man had fallen foul of the French authorities. Jailed for alleged criminal activity, the real reason for his incarceration was prejudice against his religion and resentment of his financial success. Felix De Lacey was present at the trial and became so indignant at the injustice of the death sentence imposed that he resolved to help the merchant escape. The grateful Mahometan is willing to give Felix anything for this service, and when he sees the young man has fallen in love with his daughter, offers him her hand in marriage. Safie has fallen in love with Felix too, and with the help of her father's old servant, writes to him in French about her own life and dilemmas. (Attracted by their subject-matter, the Creature somehow manages to make copies of these letters and promises to show them to Frankenstein as proof that his story is true.)

Safie's letters explain that her mother had been a Christian Arab, seized and enslaved by the Turks. Her father, struck with the mother's beauty, had married her. But the woman strove against the unfamiliar bondage which she now found imposed upon her as a Muslim wife. In time she communicated to her daughter Safie the tenets of Christianity, teaching her to aspire to 'higher powers of intellect and an independence of spirit forbidden to the female followers of Mahomet' (120). The mother dies, but 'her lessons were indelibly impressed on the mind of Safie', who, when she meets Felix, finds the prospect of living in a Christian rather than a Muslim country 'enchanting' since there she will be 'allowed to take a rank in society' (121). As well as finding a way of showing how 'indelible' the lessons of Mary Wollstonecraft had been upon her, in choosing Islam as an emblematic substitute for the 'tyranny' of European prejudices, Mary Shelley was here using a satirical device long established among French eighteenth-century writers, like Voltaire, who had even written a play called *Mahommed*.

Felix's father and sister aid in the escape plan by allowing the Turk and his daughter to impersonate them, departing for Italy with passports procured by Felix. While the Turk, Safie and Felix are hiding out at Leghorn, Felix's plot is discovered and De Lacey and Agatha are thrown into prison. When he discovers this, Felix returns to Paris but fails to secure the freedom of his family. Instead their fortune is confiscated and they are banished from France, ending up in the 'miserable asylum' of the German cottage. Learning of Felix's defeat, the Turk treacherously returns to Constantinople, arranging for Safie to follow him along with the 'greater part of his property' when it arrives at Leghorn (123): yet another Wollstonecraftian jab concerning the contemporary inferior social status of women. Safie, her 'generous nature' outraged by the Turk's 'tyrannical mandate', resolves to escape. With help, she eventually finds her way to the exiles and their isolated cottage.

The Creature as Reader – and More Rejections (Chapters VII–VIII)

The Creature says that the 'views of social life' he found in Safie's story made him admire the virtues of the cottagers even more and 'to deprecate the vices of mankind' (124). But it has had a much more profound effect than this: by showing him that the cottagers are exiles, strangers in a strange land, he is encouraged to think of himself – also an 'outsider' figure – as someone who might well prove acceptable in their eyes, someone qualified 'to become an actor in the busy scene where so many admirable qualities were called forth and displayed' (124). Indeed, in this chapter he will make a bid to enter the domain of his 'protectors' – and fail. But before this is attempted, his 'education' is to be completed by reading the three books Peter Brooks describes as constituting 'a possible Romantic *cyclopaedia universalis*'[9]: a volume of Plutarch's *Lives*, *The Sorrows of Young Werther* and *Paradise Lost*. Covering the 'public, the private, and the cosmic realms, and three modes of love',[10] these not only expand greatly the Creature's knowledge, but also stimulate him to think further on his place in the order of things. In the case of Goethe's sentimental novel *The Sorrows of Young Werther* (1774), his experience of the cottagers' lives has prepared him for the book's 'gentle and domestic manners' and its 'lofty sentiments and feelings, which had for their object something out of self' (124). His sympathies lie, above all, with the frustrations and final 'extinction' of the 'divine being' Werther, the hero whose unrequited passion for Charlotte drives him to suicide. (The story was actually based upon Goethe's own hopeless love for his friend's fiancée, Charlotte Buff.) The Creature 'inclines towards the opinions of the hero' because, like him, his desires are madly frustrated. When he weeps for Werther's death by suicide 'without precisely understanding it', this is a touching portent of his own ultimate destiny. The desolate outcome of Goethe's book leads him to reflect on his own perplexing and unfortunate state:

'I found myself similar, yet at the same time strangely unlike to the beings concerning whom I read, and to whose conversation I was a listener. I sympathised with and partly understood them, but I was unformed in mind; I was dependent on none, and related to none. "The path of my departure was free," and there was none to lament my annihilation. My person was hideous and my stature gigantic. What did this mean? Who was I? What was I? Whence did I come? What was my destination? These questions continually recurred, but I was unable to solve them.' (125)

As well as providing a succinct statement of the Creature's dilemmas, this passage captures well the self-conscious and perplexed cultural condition attending what Michel Foucault has called the emergence of 'man in his finitude' at the end of the eighteenth century in Europe.[11] Mary Shelley was living in an epoch when the 'twin revolutions'[12] – French and Industrial – were having their most turbulent social and psychological effects, in particular the challenge to God's existence. This situation, argues Foucault, throws man back on to himself, forcing him to become newly and acutely aware of his capacity for exorbitant desires of various sorts, but also of his limited capacities to satisfy and understand these, deprived of a framework of Divinity in which to 'place' himself. The difficulty of constructing new modes of knowledge in such a situation, when the available language is inadequate to the task, is a problem evident in Godwin's fiction (see Chapter 9). The effects of the 'death of God' is something which ultimately underlay the concerns of Percy Shelley's poetry, and the reason perhaps why Mary Shelley again offers here a further quotation from his poem 'Mutability'.

The Creature is raised from the 'despondency' and 'gloom' of Werther's 'imaginations' by Plutarch's accounts of the heroes of the past. These provide far 'mightier scenes of action' than any he has encountered in observing the 'patriarchal lives' of the tranquil cottagers, the 'only school' he says, 'in which I had studied human nature'. Without direct experience of large cities, masses of people, or 'men concerned in public affairs, governing or massacring their species', he is thus confined to registering the 'ardour for virtue' and the 'abhorrence for vice' which pleasurably rise within him as he reads. Lockean 'learning theory' is being flaunted here once again, with some challenging effects. He conjectures what his response to Plutarch might have been, had he been introduced to humanity by a young soldier 'burning for glory and slaughter', rather than by the people he persists in calling his 'protectors' (125–6). A certain ominous tone is produced by this thought. Perhaps he might actually have *preferred* a 'warlike' upbringing?

These mute rebellious stirrings are partly satisfied by *Paradise Lost*, where 'the picture of an omnipotent God warring with his creatures' excites feelings of 'wonder and awe' in him. He begins to see similarities between his own situation and that of Adam, both having been created as original entities 'united by no link to any other being in existence'. But there the similarity ends. God has fashioned Adam as a 'perfect creature, happy and prosperous, guarded by the especial care of his Creator' and even allowed to converse and gain knowledge from 'beings of a superior nature' (i.e. the angel Raphael). He, in contrast, is 'wretched, helpless, and alone', but a 'filthy type' of the normal human being, and 'more horrid even from the very resemblance' (126–7). This leads him to identify more closely with God's chief antagonist, Satan, rather than Adam, he being a 'fitter emblem' of his condition. Like the fallen angel Satan, who resents being subject to the ordinances of God and his Son, when the Creature sees the 'bliss' enjoyed by his 'protectors' the 'bitter gall of envy' rises within him (126). The Creature bitterly reproaches Frankenstein with the observation that even Satan had his 'fellow-devils to admire and encourage him'. He has read Milton's work as a 'true history', as he has the other books, and this compounds

75

his misery the more. He, a Creature without companions, is utterly alone, 'solitary and abhorred'.

These feelings of degradation are unfortunately only reinforced when he reads a fourth 'true history' – his own. The laboratory notes of Frankenstein reveal in minute, even pornographic detail (given the masturbatory nature of Frankenstein's fantasies) 'that series of disgusting circumstances' resulting in his 'accursed origin'. He was 'sickened', he tells his maker, when he read the journal kept by him over the four months of the creative experiment. His anger well and justifiably established, he bursts out with bitter recriminations against him (though still taking his cue from Milton):

'Hateful day when I received life!' I exclaimed in agony. 'Accursed creator! Why did you form a monster so hideous that even *you* turned from me in disgust?' (126)

That, as they say, is the million-dollar question – and the unanswerable key to the book. Who *can*, after all, satisfactorily explain this desire of Frankenstein's, that 'far exceeded moderation' (56)? The nearest we get to an answer is Walton's mystified evaluation that 'There is something at work in my soul, which I do not understand' (19).

Despite recalling how the books he had found and read served finally only to aggravate his feelings of resentment and loneliness, the Creature also demonstrates that he was still 'noble savage' enough to regard these as constituting but a part of his responses to the world. Despite 'hours of despondency', he was still sufficiently enamoured of the 'amiable and benevolent dispositions' of the cottagers to persuade himself that they would sympathize with his feelings and cheer his gloom if he could but summon up the courage to solicit openly their 'compassion and friendship' (127). Although they may share many psychological similarities, the Creature differs from his creator in resolving 'not to despair'. He is an optimist. At the same time, despite the 'angelic countenances' of the De Laceys, he sometimes realizes his hopes are 'all a dream', and he wakes often enough only to find that 'no Eve soothed my sorrows nor shared my thoughts' (127). This realization bears an uncanny resemblance to the recognition experienced by Victor after he had animated his Creature. Not only had the 'beauty of the dream' vanished with the Creature's 'coming' to life, but when he attempted to escape the consequences of this in sleep, he was denied the comfort of embracing his future wife Elizabeth by his punishing unconscious guilt, something which will continue to torment him, preventing him from sharing his true thoughts with her.

As the Creature's first 'birthday' approaches, he resolves on a plan to claim the 'protection and kindness' of the cottagers. In order to maximize his chances of social success – for he cannot bear to think of failure – he decides to capitalize on two factors he has noticed about the De Laceys: their refusal to turn the poor away empty-handed from their door, and the fact of old De Lacey's blindness. Having learned that 'the unnatural hideousness of my person was the chief object of horror' for those who have seen him, he has 'sagacity enough' to make his application for help at the cottage in the guise of a poor traveller only when the blind De Lacey is at home alone. When this meeting finally takes place, after months and months of preparation on the part of the Creature, it is arguably the most dramatically moving encounter of the whole novel. Because he cannot see his physical ugliness, the 'patriarchal' De Lacey's responses to the Creature's hesitant, and then more desperate pleas for assistance are all that the latter could have wished for. 'Do not despair', says the old man,

'To be friendless is indeed to be unfortunate; but the hearts of men, when unprejudiced by any obvious self-interest, are full of brotherly love and charity.'
(130)

De Lacey shows himself to be just such a man:

'I am blind and cannot judge of your countenance, but there is something in your words which persuades me that you are sincere. I am poor and an exile, but it will afford me true pleasure to be in any way serviceable to a human creature.'
(130)

Perhaps adapting to her purpose the discussion of a blind man's perceptions and 'judgement' she had read in Locke's *Essay*, Mary Shelley is here offering one of the key arguments of her father Godwin's optimistic philosophy of 'universal benevolence'. The Creature is overjoyed to be welcomed as a poverty-stricken fellow exile by De Lacey, especially as he hears from the old man's own lips that he and his family have been 'unfortunate' enough to have been 'condemned, although innocent'. This is a Godwinian situation of injustice with which not only the Creature can fully identify; one should also remember its effect upon the vexed conscience of the listening Frankenstein, 'helpless' witness as he had been to the miserable execution of Justine. For the first time in his life, the Creature has heard 'the voice of kindness' directed towards him, by a man he now considers his 'best and only benefactor'.

But this warming encounter with 'humanity' – that favourably loaded

Enlightenment term – is to prove all too short. It is cut short in a way that reminds us that the blind De Lacey's offer 'to be in any way serviceable to a *human* creature' was actually made quite ambiguous by the author (emphasis added). At the moment when the Creature is about to disclose how the 'friends' from whom he seeks help and protection are none other than De Lacey himself and his family, Felix, Agatha and Safie all return from their walk and are horrified to see an eight-foot Creature clinging to the knees of the bewildered cottage patriarch. Without the 'advantages' of his father's blindness, the sight that Felix sees is hardly calculated to fill him with the credo of 'brotherly love and charity' enunciated by his father. What he does rather 'see' is the 'obvious self-interest' of his father under threat – of his life – from something Other. Felix therefore responds in the 'prejudiced' way that humans so often do when confronted by the perturbing and unfamiliar – he lashes out. As the Creature tells Victor, he could have torn Felix 'limb from limb' in response to his attack. But he does not, for he is a noble savage. The gentle bid of a monstrous-looking giant to join the ranks of human society has failed, yet the pain and anguish he feels when he retreats to his hovel show him to have been all too poignantly human in his feelings.

In Chapter VIII, concluding the Creature's narrative, this sadness soon turns to anger. The frightened departure of the cottagers effects his second major abandonment by humans, and when he is finally shot for saving a human life he decides that Frankenstein must either help him to be happy, or otherwise endure his bloody revenge, already begun with the unpremeditated murder of little William.

On the night of the attack on him by Felix, the Creature gives vent to his anger and anguish in 'fearful howlings' while he rampages through the wood, smashing all in his path. Likening himself to the 'arch-fiend' – Satan in *Paradise Lost*, who also found himself 'unsympathised with' – he bears a 'hell within' whose fury he decides can only be appeased by declaring an 'ever-lasting war against the species' of man (132). Yet when exhaustion sets in and the pleasantness of the following sunny day restores him to 'some degree of tranquillity', he has a brief respite from these inclinations. This mirrors the relief Frankenstein felt when his grief over the deaths of William and Justine was 'subdued and tranquillised' by scenes of nature in the Arve valley (93). But the Creature does not merely display a Romantic capacity for experiencing nature as a restorative. With time to reflect, he decides his conclusions have been 'too hasty', that he had 'acted imprudently' in expecting to gain acceptance by so suddenly presenting himself to De Lacey. In concluding that he should have found ways of familiarising the family to himself gradually, he reveals an essential humanity and good sense that has been quite beyond the reach of his creator, whose capacity for reflection was eaten up by his monomaniacally 'creative' impulses. It is with these 'gradualist' Godwinian thoughts in mind that he resolves to return to the cottage to attempt a meliorating audience with the old De Lacey. Alas, the humanity and reasonableness with which he has returned to his problem is not to be found in the fearful precincts of the cottage, from which the occupants have fled. The Creature soon discovers that Felix is willing to sacrifice three months' rent and the garden produce rather than risk the life of his father. In a violent tremble, Felix tells the landlord, who tries to persuade him to stay, how the old man is in the gravest danger – 'I intreat you not to reason with me any more' (134). Of course, in a sense Felix is right: reason is of no avail when what is all too humanly perceived as unreason has been encountered.

Unfortunately, the departure of the De Laceys, by making the Creature again feel 'spurned and deserted', does for a time encourage him to become a willing victim of unreason. This is shown by his decision to wait for the moon to sink below the horizon before putting the cottage to the torch, the furious but useless act of revenge he exacts upon his withdrawn 'protectors'. It is only when the moon is out of sight that he yields to the 'insanity' of his spirits, committing acts which require not only a symbolic total darkness for their performance, but which are also out of the presence of the object which, in the absence of a doting parent, had first given pleasure to him: the symbol of the wise, comforting and rational spirit of Mary Shelley herself.

Deciding that his only recourse for 'justice' is to seek out Victor Frankenstein, the man he now designates not merely as his creator, but also his 'father', he sets off towards Geneva to gain 'pity and redress' from him (135). As he travels, his heart becomes as hard as the wintry ground upon which he treads. Not until the warmth of spring comes along to offer the restorative effects we have come to associate with Frankenstein and his Creature, does the latter feel 'emotions of gentleness and pleasure' revive within him. Momentarily, as he makes his way through a deep wood in the sunshine, he forgets his 'solitude and deformity' and 'dared to be happy'. But, as so often happens in this text, every prospect of joy is shadowed by threat, thwarted by evil, so that any happiness is invariably short-lived. For instance, when he emerges from the wood, and sees a young laughing girl stumble into the 'deep and rapid river', his first generous instinct is to rescue her. This is of course another vulnerable being in distress who requires help, a situation with which he has become only too familiar through his own experiences and those of the De Laceys. In the joyous and happy mood which nature has generated in him, to rescue the girl's senseless body and be able 'to restore animation' in her – which he does – is simply to return to nature one of nature's own, maintaining the sanctity of life at all costs. Prejudiced society has a different attitude. The girl's father gladly accepts the revived infant snatched from the jaws of death, but damns the re-animated being who has delivered her. When he snatches away his daughter and dashes off into the wood, the Creature says that he 'followed speedily, I hardly knew why' (136). But *we* know why. It is because he feels a responsibility towards the child in whom he has 'restored animation', unlike the creator who had 'animated' *him*. It is in such twists of irony that Mary Shelley displays her precocious writing ability.

The reward for his benevolence in saving a human being from destruction is to be shot and badly injured by the father. This marks a decisive turning-point in the Creature's experiences, for the 'feelings of kindness and gentleness' which had buoyed him up but a few moments before now give way to 'hellish rage and gnashing of teeth' (137).

This time there is to be no remission of his hatred. Rather, with the constant soreness of his bullet wound to remind him of this latest humiliation at the hands of man, such negative feelings intensify:

'My daily vows rose for revenge – a deep and deadly revenge, such as would alone compensate for the outrages and anguish I had endured.

'. . . The labours I endured were no longer to be alleviated by the bright sun or gentle breezes of spring; all joy was but a mockery which insulted my desolate state, and made me feel more painfully that I was not made for the enjoyment of pleasure.' (137)

When he arrives fatigued and hungry on the outskirts of Geneva, neither the sight of the setting sun nor the 'stupendous mountains of Jura' are capable of imparting joy. Yet when he is woken from a shallow sleep in the bushes by the 'sportive' approach of a 'beautiful child', his Lockean imagination is miraculously re-inspired. Having constantly been denied human sympathy because of his horrific ugliness, the thought strikes him that 'this little creature was unprejudiced, and had lived too short a time to have imbibed a horror of deformity. If, therefore, I could seize him and educate him as my companion and friend, I should not be so desolate in this peopled earth' (137-8). But this boy is no Wordsworthian innocent, like himself; he is William, brother of the aesthete-scientist Victor Frankenstein, and son of

Alphonse Frankenstein, distinguished elder of the respectable Protestant canton of Geneva. As such, he has been deeply socialized into the well-bred proprieties of Genevan upper middle-class life. Thus when the Creature seizes him to carry out his pedagogical intentions, just as his older brother before him had 'placed his hands before his eyes' when seeing him, so does the horrified young boy. Efforts to make a friend of him are met with a stream of abuse wherein William reveals that his father is M. Frankenstein, the syndic. The Creature's response is immediate:

'Frankenstein! you belong then to my enemy – to him towards whom I have sworn eternal revenge; you shall be my first victim.' (138)

The tide which he had hoped might carry him to social success has now finally turned for the Creature, and he claps his hands with 'exultation and hellish triumph' following William's murder. This gesture seems so characteristically Shelleyan it is hard to avoid thinking the author did not have the poet mischievously in mind here. Evil has now overcome the Creature, so much so that it enables him to turn the 'enlightening' education he got from Volney to vengeful effect. Coming across the sleeping form of Justine, he conceals upon her the 'portrait of a most lovely woman' – Caroline Frankenstein – which he had found hanging around William's neck. 'Thanks to the lessons of Felix and the sanguinary laws of man, I had learned how to work mischief,' he says.

These encounters with Caroline's portrait and the Frankensteins' female servant do not serve Mary Shelley merely as a plot device enabling the Creature to manipulate a second vengeful punishment on someone close to Frankenstein. They also serve to foreground an element of the story as yet unstressed, the dimension of sexuality. In gazing upon both the miniature of Caroline and upon Justine, the Creature's sexual desires are aroused. However, he sourly realizes that the 'joy-imparting smiles' of these women will never be for the likes of him, and begins to rationalize the murder he has committed in terms of his own sexual deprivation and thwarting: '[for] the murder I have committed because I am robbed forever of all that she could give me, she shall atone' (139).

Yet however much revenge for his rejected condition he may be able to wreak, it will do nothing to satisfy the awakened sexual desire which the Creature, defining his predicament in this radically new way, now feels. And it does not go away. This 'burning passion' continues to consume him as he wanders aimlessly through the mountains, and finally encounters the preoccupied and disoriented Frankenstein (139).

81

The whole of his story, the reader now realizes, has served to bring him to a point where he can make the request of Frankenstein that will satisfy his sexual desires:

'I am alone, and miserable; man will not associate with me; but one as deformed and horrible as myself would not deny herself to me. My companion must be of the same species, and have the same defects. This being you must create.' (139)

5 Frankenstein's Narrative (2)

A Monstrous Suggestion (Chapter IX)

At first Frankenstein meets the Creature's request for a female companion with an absolute refusal. He had allowed his anger to subside when listening to the earlier part of his narrative, impressed (rather as Leigh Hunt would be) to hear about the peaceful, bucolic existence he enjoyed in the 'company' of the De Laceys. However, when it strikes him that the manufacture of a female companion has the potential of unleashing a 'joint wickedness' that 'might desolate the world', he finds such a prospect utterly 'base', and will not comply. But the Creature, ever alert to all that might be of advantage to him in his plight, cleverly counters the charge that he is attempting to force his maker's hand. On the contrary, he says, he is 'content to reason' with Victor, desirous of persuading his master that his demand for a wife should be seen 'as a right', a matter of simple justice (140). In saying this the Creature probably has in mind God's granting of Adam's wish for a wife in *Paradise Lost* (VIII.444–57). But as we have noticed before, Frankenstein is not God, and the Creature is not Adam. Although Victor agrees to manufacture a partner for him by the end of the chapter, it is not without a struggle. A father who disdains to admit kinship with his son will feel little responsibility for him.

The Creature explains that he never wanted to be violent, and had always 'intended to reason'. He has done his best to find a way of living with man 'in the interchange of kindness', but, repulsed at every turn, he now realizes that 'the human senses are insurmountable barriers to our union' (140). There are multiple ironies in these words. His whole story has demonstrated how he too actually possesses 'human senses', so much so that even Frankenstein has to admit he is 'a creature of fine sensations' (141). Yet his attempt at bringing about an 'interchange of kindness' has failed for the very reason that he has been consistently perceived as *not* belonging to human 'kind'. (The extraordinarily clever and poignant play on words here seems to echo Hamlet's sharp response to the regicide Claudius's greeting of him as 'my cousin' and 'my son': 'A little more than kin, and less than kind.' *Hamlet*, I.ii.65.) It is this situation of his *feeling* all the possibilities of being human while having at the same time to endure constant rejection *by* humans which has reduced him to violence. 'I am malicious because I am miserable,' he says, repeating the formula which aggrieved apologists of violent revolution have ever found so convenient to their pragmatic needs. He is fully prepared to continue being malicious unless the prospect of 'abject slavery' is removed by compliance with his wishes. If no accommodation can be made for his 'injuries', he is determined to 'desolate' Frankenstein's heart '. . . so that you shall curse the hour of your birth' (141). Just as, in fact, *he* has been compelled to do, for some time.

When bitter reflections on this 'crime' well up in him, the Creature blames Frankenstein's hard-hearted refusals for his own passionate 'excess', and reiterates how this makes his demands 'reasonable and moderate'. 'Oh! my creator, make me happy,' he pleads,

'. . . let me feel gratitude towards you for one benefit! Let me see that I excite the sympathy of some existing thing; do not deny me my request!' (141)

Victor begins to be persuaded that as his maker he is perhaps morally obliged to provide for his happiness. (Unlike his Creature, the atheistic Frankenstein seems to have read neither the Bible nor Milton.) But when the Creature promises that he and his Creature-wife will seek a peaceful, isolated and even vegetarian existence far away from human beings, the sceptical Victor still remains suspicious. Having tasted the love and sympathy of another, he argues, will he not in the end desire the company of humans once more? And having been repulsed, will he not again turn to violence, this time with a fellow-Creature to aid in the destruction? The Creature disagrees, repeating the 'rational' formula that once provided with a companion, he will be satisfied: 'My evil passions will have fled, for I shall meet with sympathy! my life will flow quietly away, and in my dying moments I shall not curse my maker' (142).

Frankenstein's immediate response to this is to feel flattered at being compared to a beneficent god. The 'strange effects' he feels are perhaps a vaguely pleasing reminder of his original desire to create a new species which would bless him 'as its creator and source' (52). Such reflections now serve to arouse his compassion and 'a wish to console him'. Yet they do not, it is important to note, excite Frankenstein's own sympathy. Rather, when he finally turns from his godlike imagination to the 'filthy mass' confronting him, he is again filled with 'horror and hatred', concluding that 'as I could not sympathise with him, I had no right to withhold from him the small portion of happiness which was yet in my power to bestow' (142). The usage given to 'sympathy' here may appear strange. Surely Frankenstein would comply with the Creature's request because he *did* sympathize with his plight, not because he didn't? But as I have already asserted, one of the key disclosures this text has made possible is that where human sociability is set aside by a man obsessed by the pursuit of a 'beautiful idea', that man risks sacrificing his capacity for sympathy, risks a corruption of his moral fibre by indulging his over-reaching and selfish fixation. Frankenstein has indeed lost this capacity, able only to understand the Creature's dilemma in the narrowest of terms. Yet it is certainly understandable that he should be suspicious of a creature who has murdered once and manipulated the legal death of another: that he may well be set upon further revenge.

However, when he hears the Creature's final imploring speech, he is won over. It is worth repeating that this does not involve the activating of sympathy on Frankenstein's part. Instead, the Creature cleverly uses his rhetorical powers to appeal to Victor's vanity, saying that

'My vices are the children of a forced solitude that I abhor; and my virtues will necessarily arise when I live in communion with an equal.' (142)

Frankenstein is no doubt reminded of his own 'forced solitude' here. Providing his Creature with a female companion should thus enable him, absolved of his guilt, to return to the ranks of his own 'kind' and become once more 'linked to the chain of existence and events' (143), the goal too of the Creature of whom he hopes he will finally be rid. So he concludes that for reasons both of justice to the latter, and to his own 'fellow-creatures', he will look charitably upon the Creature's situation. He acknowledges that the eight-foot Creature's early promise had been blighted by the 'loathing and scorn' of society (characteristically, his own primary rejection is here overlooked), but, more importantly, that humanity will remain at risk so long as the demands of his Creature are unmet. He will make him a 'wife'.

Yet as Victor makes his way back down the mountain and journeys on without pause to the family home in Geneva, the prospect of his being able to enter into society once more feels as distant as ever to him. When he built and animated his Creature, his heightened sensations of enthusiasm were accompanied by a stifling of all social sympathies, though he seemed hardly aware of this destructive side at the time. On the occasion of this second attempt to create life, he needs must avoid the company and confidence of others once again. On the other hand, the situation this time is quite different. Before, the compulsive motive to father a being whose creation was supposedly aimed at promoting the cause of society had come from him alone. This time the compulsion comes from 'without', from the Creature he created. And the dominant motive for his actions now is the defence of his own nuclear family rather than the dizzy promotion of society's interests. This is not a situation he feels comfortable with:

I felt as if I were placed under a ban – as if I had no right to claim their sympathies – as if never more might I enjoy companionship with them. (144)

Victor's ominous feeling is well-founded, and it signals a radical shift in the direction which the story will now take. If it started out with the high hopes of an 'artist' enthusiastic for the regeneration of man and society through science, convinced of his masterly powers, 'society' will now more and more recede in significance, the focus turning towards and upon a struggle between Creature and creator in which the power roles are reversed.

6 Frankenstein's Narrative (2) (continued)

To England and the Orkneys (Chapters I–II)

Days pass into weeks as Victor delays launching into a task he views with the utmost 'repugnance'. He takes refuge in 'the most perfect solitude', watching the clouds from his boat on the lake for days at a time. He looks to nature once again as a spiritual restorative, and, as ever in this Romantic text, it works (145). Alphonse is delighted at Victor's lighter mood, and unconsciously alludes to the disintegrating effects his son's Promethean scientific debauch had had on his selfhood:

'I am happy to remark, my dear son, that you have resumed your former pleasures, and seem to be returning to yourself.' (146)

Yet Alphonse remains troubled. Victor may be returning to himself, but he studiously avoids contact with his family and shows little sign of wanting to marry Elizabeth. Alphonse has looked forward to this marriage as the 'tie of our domestic comfort, and the stay of my declining years' and is clearly perplexed to find his eldest son showing no interest whatever in perpetuating the distinguished Frankenstein family line (146). In trying to get to the bottom of this, he entertains three possible reasons for the delay:

(1) that Victor had always regarded Elizabeth as a sister rather than as a potential wife;
(2) that Victor may have found another lover;
(3) that he, Alphonse, in sending Victor away to Ingolstadt, may have helped destroy his own long-held wish: 'so blind is the experience of man, that what I conceived to be the best assistants to my plan may have entirely destroyed it' (146).

In fact, all three factors have contributed to preventing Victor's marriage to Elizabeth. By sending Victor to Ingolstadt, Alphonse did indeed enable the whole process of Victor's scientific 'mission' to be initiated. As regards the young man's love for Elizabeth, I have noted before how a genuine passion for his 'more than sister' seemed somewhat lacking. By his own reckoning, in fact, his two great loves have been his 'dream beauty', the rejected Creature, and his bosom pal Clerval, with whom Victor has spent far more time than anyone else in this story (and with whom he is about to spend even more time). Despite this, and a narrative told to Walton in which no indication whatever has been given of his having even met, let alone had eyes for, any other woman, he assures Alphonse that no woman excites his 'warmest admiration and affection' as Elizabeth does. We as readers remain to be convinced.

Victor tells Walton that the 'real' reason why 'the idea of an immediate union' with Elizabeth had filled him with 'horror and dismay' was his inability to indulge his own sexual gratification while that of his Creature was being denied, this constituting a debilitating 'deadly weight' which hung around his neck (147). The allusion to the *Ancient Mariner* is of course appropriate to his guilt-ridden case, and suitably chosen for the ears of the Coleridge-loving Walton. But Victor cannot delay his efforts any longer, if he is to satisfy the desires of his father, his Creature and his future spouse. Therefore he announces his intention to travel to England on a journey of recuperation. He imagines that, having consulted an 'English philosopher' for his second experiment, a successful outcome 'would quickly be achieved', enabling him to be restored to his family 'in peace and happiness', and in turn to 'claim' the 'reward' of Elizabeth (147, 148). When Alphonse and Elizabeth arrange for Clerval to keep him company on the trip, he is irritated that this 'interfered with the solitude I coveted' in order to complete his task. Yet it provides a welcome diversion for him, initially at least, and it enables Mary Shelley to draw heavily on her own travel experiences in taking the story forward.

Victor and Henry travel north to Holland down the Rhine, a 'vagabond' voyage Mary had undertaken in 1814 upon her youthful elopement with Percy Shelley. Passing between the picturesque scenes on each riverbank, Frankenstein, *à la* Rousseau[1] and his disciple Percy Shelley, once more drinks in the refreshing boons of nature. Yet it is the 'poor unsuspecting' Clerval who now shows himself even more attached to the 'scenery of external nature', which 'he loved with ardour', than his friend. In what the author clearly means to be an ironical allusion to that wayward pair of isolated souls, Frankenstein and his Creature, Clerval reflects that the spirit of the Rhine has 'more in harmony with man than those who pile the glacier, or retire to the inaccessible peaks of the mountains of our own country'. And yet, quoting from *Tintern Abbey*, Mary Shelley also attributes to Clerval agitating nature-reveries: like Wordsworth, 'The sounding cataract/Haunted him like a passion . . .' (151).

By the time they reach London, Victor is utterly miserable, feeling there is 'an insurmountable barrier placed between me and my fellowmen'. This echoes his Creature's earlier lament (140), reminding us of the dilemma of isolation they both feel. Meanwhile, Clerval is in great spirits, 'inquisitive and anxious to gain experience and instruction' that will enable him to assist 'the progress of European colonisation and trade'. But such enthusiastic entrepreneurial ambitions only serve to depress Victor further, revealing him as 'the image of my former self' (153).

As they travel towards Perth, Scotland, and the banks of the River Tay that had provided Mary Shelley with an 'eyry of freedom' in her younger teenage years (Author's Introduction, 6), Frankenstein and Clerval follow a route taking in places where Mary and Percy had previously lived or visited: Windsor, Oxford, Matlock, the Cumberland lakes, Edinburgh. Henry is keen to meet 'men of talent' (156), but Victor, unwilling perhaps to be reminded too much of Professors Waldman and Krempe, tells how he 'abhorred society', preferring to view the 'wondrous works' of nature (154). When he reflects that discontent had never visited his mind as a youth, we as readers must wonder again at the reliability of this narrator, especially when he ambiguously claims that 'the study of what is excellent and sublime in the productions of man' had always served to dispel any *ennui* he might have suffered. Really? And what of the 'scientific productions' of man? Intriguingly, he now sees himself as a 'blasted tree' whose soul has been invaded by 'the bolt'. This allusion to the tree he had seen destroyed by a bolt of electrical lightning at Geneva when he was fifteen is presumably meant to suggest that whatever goodness his soul had contained has now been obliterated. For the first time he admits that the act of creating his Creature has visited a curse upon his head 'as mortal as that of crime'. Yet despite feeling 'haunted' by this crime he nevertheless feels 'guiltless' (157).

This is strange, since having left Henry at Perth in order to assemble a female Creature in the isolation afforded by 'one of the remotest of the Orkneys', the description of the solitary 'labours' he now embarks upon recalls those guilt-ridden 'masturbatory' terms he had used earlier when relating the construction of a being which, as it were, was made to 'come to life':

During my first experiment, a kind of enthusiastic frenzy had blinded me to the horror of my employment; my mind was intently fixed on the consummation of my labour, and my eyes shut to the horror of my proceedings. But now I went to it in cold blood, and my heart often sickened at the work of my hands. (159)

The dream that enabled life to 'come' to him before is well and truly over.

'I shall be with you on your wedding-night' (Chapter III)

When Victor pauses in his labours one evening to indulge in sombre reflections on the possible outcome of his actions, it is no accident that this moment occurs as 'the moon was just rising from the sea' (160). As we have already seen, the presence of the moon in the text is no 'passive' event; rather it gives out a signal that we are in the company of the active if covert gaze of the author. What it also signals is the imminent arrival of Frankenstein's Creature. Certainly the Creature is in Victor's thoughts as he entertains a series of increasingly wild speculations about what 'might' happen after the Creature-wife has been created. The female Creature *might* 'become ten thousand times more malignant than her mate, and delight, for its own sake, in murder and wretchedness'; she *might* 'refuse to comply with a compact made before her creation'; they *might* 'hate each other'; she *might* 'turn with disgust from him to the superior form of man'; she *might* then 'quit him, and he be again alone, exasperated by the fresh provocation of being deserted by one of his own species'. But Frankenstein's worst fear is not that the two Creatures will separate: rather that they will together breed a 'race of devils' who *might* 'make the very existence of the species of man a condition precarious and full of terror' (160).

Is Victor Frankenstein right to entertain such fears? In a general sense, of course, there are always elements of uncertainty and unpredictability in the events of life, so that it can be sensible to err on the side of caution when entertaining high hopes or expectations of things. But this is no ordinary 'life' dilemma. We are dealing here with a literary text written by an author acutely concerned to show how the consequences of rash, ill-considered, self-centred, Promethean-driven actions can result in disaster for the initiators of those actions. Frankenstein's rash 'idealistic' act was to create a living creature that looks monstrous but which feels, thinks, imagines, and – most importantly – *desires*, as a fully human being. But Frankenstein and everyone else who encounters the Creature (except blind De Lacey) rejects the possibility of its being understood *as* human. Instead, unable to accept that the Creature's resentful actions are in any way linked to his lived and learned experiences, Frankenstein prefers to perceive his unwanted 'son' as an alien 'other', motivated by frighteningly unpredictable impulses. This 'uneducated' attitude is clearly exposed to us when we hear him telling Walton

about the dangers of creating 'another being, of whose dis
was alike ignorant' (160). Such an 'essentialist' view of motiv
character not only explains why Victor Frankenstein is preven
understanding that his Creature's actions have been determined
by environmental and social experiences; it also suggests once
that he might be unable to feel the normal desires of a human being
himself. In modern parlance, he not only refuses to 'open' to another
person's wants and needs, but also as a consequence (perhaps of his
own unmet emotional needs) projects his own fears on to this horrific
'other'.

That this does indeed seem to be the case is confirmed when Victor,
his mind full of monstrous imaginings, looks up and sees 'by the light
of the moon, the daemon at the casement'. The Creature now appears,
as he had when he first beheld his creator, with a grin 'wrinkling' his
face. But this time, Frankenstein's fearful frame of mind makes this
grin seem 'ghastly', compelling him to read the Creature's face as
expressing 'the utmost extent of malice and treachery' (161). It is
possible of course that the Creature is experiencing some degree of
triumphalism in having persuaded his creator to do his bidding. Yet
what motive could he have for showing himself as a malicious and
treacherous being in this way? His grin is much more likely to signal
pleasure and gratitude for the near prospect of having a partner of his
own 'species' with whom to commune. So far as he knows, he is about
to be blessed with a wife who should bring him happiness!

In fact, it is Frankenstein who is now driven by malice and treachery,
his evil preoccupations compelling him to go back on his promise, to
tear 'to pieces the thing on which I was engaged' (161). He seems partly
to have understood the implications of this destructive act for his
Creature: 'The wretch saw me destroy the creature on whose future
existence he depended for happiness'. But his further remark that the
Creature withdrew 'with a howl of devilish despair and revenge',
reveals both his inability to *feel* for his plight, and his consequent
compulsion to 'demonize' him. Frankenstein's choice of language shows
this. 'Revenge' is not an emotion but an action, suggesting it is Frankenstein himself who is at this point bent upon revenge, not the Creature.
It is no wonder that Victor is left to experience 'the most terrible
reveries', an oxymoron neatly describing his divided psychological
state. (Reveries are normally the product of a benign, musing and
dreamy state.)

There is now an interlude of several hours during which 'the winds
were hushed, and all nature reposed under the eye of the quiet moon'.

As Victor gazes out on the 'motionless' sea, we sense that the cool, controlling (and possibly vengeful?) authorial presence (in the guise of the moon) is overseeing some unnamed evil act; that this interval is merely the calm before the storm. In fact, the Creature is now enacting a 'tit for tat' revenge for Frankenstein's actions, and has left to murder his best friend Clerval. When Victor hears a boat land, and, shortly afterwards, his cottage door creaking open, he is 'rooted to the spot' by a sickening 'sensation of helplessness', the kind 'so often felt in frightful dreams, when you in vain, endeavour to fly from an impending danger' (161–2). Of course, this echoes the experience when first he had fled from his own creation, quoting from the *Ancient Mariner* to describe how he'd walked 'in fear and dread', terrified that 'a frightful fiend' did 'close behind him tread' (58). But this time there is no escape, the defining essence of the truly 'gothic' experience. The phenomenon which functions as his swingeing conscience, the Creature, now appears, responding to Frankenstein's categorical refusal to create him a Creature-wife with an announcement on the situation which is to govern the downward spiralling of events that remain of the story:

'Slave, I before reasoned with you, but you have proved yourself unworthy of my condescension . . . You are my creator, but I am your master – obey!' (162)

Victor is forced to agree: 'The hour of my irresolution is past, and the period of your power is arrived.' Nevertheless it is a power from which he will not flinch: 'I am firm, and your words will only exasperate my rage.' For now, the Creature is able only to respond 'in the impotence of anger', repeating the lament that his scorned affections have resulted in misery. But when Victor tells him to leave, the Creature utters the threat which is to cast the deepest shadow yet upon his creator's mind:

'It is well. I go; but remember, I shall be with you on your wedding-night.' (163)

Frankenstein's first response to this threat, which will preoccupy him for the next three chapters, is characteristic: 'Before you sign my death-warrant, be sure that you are yourself safe.' He has perceived the threat as something that concerns him only, and this is shown again when he reflects on the fact that his wedding-night

was the period fixed for the fulfilment of my destiny. In that hour I should die, and at once satisfy and extinguish his malice . . . [but] . . . when I thought of my beloved Elizabeth, – of her tears and endless sorrow, when she should find her lover so barbarously snatched from her ... I resolved not to fall before my enemy without a bitter struggle. (163)

Frankenstein is again guilty of the grossest of paralogisms. Although he seems to understand that what will satisfy the Creature's desires is a female mate of his own 'species' who can genuinely sympathize with him, he can only see the Creature's threat in terms of himself. ('Had I a right, *for my own benefit*, to inflict this curse upon everlasting generations?' (emphasis added) he had asked himself when manically mulling over the consequences of creating a wife for his Creature.) Although he has heard from the Creature himself how it was sexual frustration which motivated him in manipulating the downfall of Justine ('because I am forever robbed of all that she could give me, she shall atone' – 139), Frankenstein seems incapable of seeing that it is actually Elizabeth who now stands in the greatest danger. This obsessiveness with his Creature could hint at a homoerotic element in Victor's make-up. But the text has already 'defined' the way he perceives his own Creature, as something 'nearly in the light of my own vampire, my own spirit let loose from the grave' (74).

The Creature having departed, this avenging ghost nevertheless remains 'in' Frankenstein, 'it' being identified with him: 'I walked about the isle like a restless spectre, separated from all it loved, and miserable in the separation' (164). Only after sleeping does he feel 'as if I belonged to a race of human beings like myself'. Sleep offers the possibility of forgetfulness and hope, and not for the last time (197–8). But this is only a brief respite from renewed feelings of disintegration. Having construed himself as a restless spectre, he is now forced to confront the remains of his 'half-finished creature' which lie 'scattered on the floor': 'I paused to collect myself, and then entered the chamber' (165). He is determined to dispose of the mangled limbs at sea, but as he sails out in the early hours of the morning to do this, guilt assails him once again when he sees other small boats, forcing him to avoid 'any encounter with my fellow-creatures' with a 'shuddering anxiety' (165). Of course, the 'dreadful crime' which he feels he is about to commit is the final denial of his Creature's 'rights', a withdrawal of good sense and justice which can only result in more revenge-motivated deaths.

Just as his Creature waited for the moon to disappear before putting the De Lacey cottage to the torch, so does Frankenstein now take the opportunity of its being 'overspread by a thick cloud' to cast the weighted basket of human remains into the sea. In deepest darkness, he 'listened to the gurgling sound as it sunk, and then sailed away from the spot'. Having disposed of his guilty burden, his spirits rise. Clouds still cover the moon, so he decides to enjoy his dark triumph by subsiding Shelley-style into the bottom of the boat, and falls asleep. When the following day comes, the discovery that he has been driven far out to sea convinces him he will drown, and the thought that this will leave his family at the mercy of the Creature plunges him into another 'despairing and frightful' reverie (166). Yet when after some hours he sees land, his joy at having cheated death leads him to say, 'how strange is that clinging love we have of life even in the excess of misery' (166) – an echo of his Creature's earlier remarks (96).

As ever in this text, no joy lasts long. Almost immediately after he has landed, he is arrested and accused of the murder of a man whose body had been washed up on the beach of this Irish port, the night before.

Ireland, a Murder, and Victor's 'Trial' (Chapter IV)

From the moment that Victor animated his Creature, he has been beset by psychological torments, but now he will be faced with the incredible prospect of being put on trial for the murder of his best friend. As yet unaware that the dead man is Clerval, he nevertheless exhibits 'extreme agitation' (170) when he learns that the only sign of violence on the body had been 'the black mark of fingers on his neck' (169). Despite being met with the horrific charge of murder, Victor's prospects seem auspicious. Whereas the lower-class Justine had had little hope of acquittal, well-born Victor is lucky to have fallen into the hands of the magistrate Mr Kirwin, 'an old benevolent man, with calm and mild manners' (169), another version of the Percy Shelley ideal-father types (Godwin in real life, and, as we have seen, Professor Waldman in this text). Nevertheless Kirwin is efficient at his job. Regarding Victor with some degree of 'severity', he proceeds to call witnesses whose stories seem to incriminate him as Clerval's murderer. Its discoverers tell how they found the dead body still warm, so had 'put it into a bed and rubbed it', trying, 'in vain, to restore it to life' (169–70). Once again Mary Shelley is ironically 'reviving' the whole issue of life-creation: Frankenstein had succeeded in the brilliant task of animating a living being from bits of dead people, yet is unable to save his friend from the depredations of that being. (In fact, by his earlier insistence that they separate, Frankenstein can be seen as contributing to his friend's death. This issue of separation is perhaps, influenced both by the example of

Milton's *Paradise Lost* and by Mary Shelley's experiences with Percy Shelley.) There are even deeper ironies at work, for by the words she uses Mary Shelley seems also to be recalling circumstances around the death of her own first, unnamed baby, several years before. Some days after losing her prematurely-born child in February 1815, she had written in her journal: 'Dream that my little baby came to life again; that it had only been cold, and that we rubbed it before the fire, and it lived' (quoted in the Introduction to the Penguin Classics edition of *Frankenstein*, p. xv).

Frankenstein is convinced he can prove his innocence by calling on 'several persons' he had been conversing with on his Orkney island at the time the body was found. It had been discovered at around ten o'clock at night, yet he had not left the island for a further four or five hours. (In reality it is at least four hundred miles from the Orkneys to the most northerly point of the Irish coast!) Thus he was 'perfectly tranquil as to the consequences of the affair' (170). When he is shown the body, he recognizes it as that of his best friend, and this tranquillity is quickly converted into 'strong convulsions'. After being carried from the room, he lies 'for two months on the point of death', at times raving and screaming 'aloud with agony and terror' (171).

Despite desiring to die and be rid of his torments, he feels 'doomed to live' (another echo of Hamlet). A fatalistic gloom has once again descended upon him concerning the miseries of life and death. The emphasis on this in the text is partly the result of additions made by Mary Shelley in the 1831 revision in which she is conveying her sadness over so many personal losses in her life:

Death snatches away many blooming children, the only hopes of their doating parents: how many brides and youthful lovers have been one day in the bloom of health and hope, and the next a prey for worms and the decay of the tomb! Of what materials was I made, that I could thus resist so many shocks, which, like the turning of the wheel, continually renewed the torture? (171)

It is a good question, of course, and like all profoundly rhetorical questions, unanswerable. There is more to observe in this passage than an uncomplicated biographical borrowing. Does not Frankenstein by his 'creative' actions also merit the title, 'parent'? The irony conveyed here is that by *not* being a 'doating' (or any other kind of) parent to his monstrous 'son', Victor has himself been the major contributory cause of the deaths of his little brother William, and now, Clerval. We are reminded of what makes this possible ('Of what materials', Frankenstein asks himself, 'was I made, that I could thus resist so many shocks?') in an oblique way when he describes his old 'hired nurse' as having a 'hard and rude' face, 'like that of persons accustomed to see without sympathising in sights of misery' (172). In relation to his own son, the same might be said of him. For when the 'benevolent' magistrate Mr Kirwin (whose countenance expresses 'sympathy and compassion' for Victor's plight) offers to make him more comfortable, Victor shows the deadness of his heart by saying that 'on the whole earth there is no comfort which I am capable of receiving'. Kirwin agrees that 'the sympathy of a stranger can be but of little relief to one borne down as you are by so strange a misfortune' (173).

But when he is able to reassure Victor that his family in Geneva are well and that a 'friend' has come to visit him – he assumes Victor will be pleased at this – Frankenstein's obsessive mind gets to work again. He imagines it is the Creature come to 'mock' at his misery and makes the same childish response he did when he first saw him, putting his hand before his eyes and saying, 'I cannot see him; for God's sake, do not let him enter!' (174). The 'friend' is not the Creature, of course, but his own father, who has come to take him home to Geneva. The interesting point to be observed about this is that 'friend' to Frankenstein now means 'Creature'. This confirms what we already know; that, in grotesque parody of the biblical creation myth, Creature and creator are of the same 'kind'.

As we come towards the end of the chapter, we learn he is to be spared the agony of a courtroom trial as the grand jury has rejected the case against him. He is now free to return to Geneva with Alphonse. But there is no 'freedom' for Victor. So plagued is he by fear, guilt and paranoia that the threat of a criminal trial is as nothing compared with the trial his conscience is capable of inflicting upon him. And of course, this is no ordinary conscience, but a 'living' one, embodied in and by the active form of his own Creature. The only outcome he can now gloomily envisage is his own obliteration and that of his family, his own Creature 'executing the award of justice' (175). 'The cup of life was poisoned for ever', he says,

and although the sun shone upon me, as upon the happy and gay of heart, I saw around me nothing but a dense and frightful darkness, penetrated by no light but the glimmer of two eyes that glared upon me. Sometimes they were the expressive eyes of Henry . . . sometimes it was the watery, clouded eyes of the monster, as I first saw them in my chamber at Ingolstadt. (176)

Alphonse finds it impossible to awaken 'feelings of affection' in Victor; we know of course that he lost the essential capacity for these long ago.

When he reminds Victor that Elizabeth and Ernest, his loved ones, eagerly await his return, this only produces 'deep groans' from his son.

On his journey back to Geneva with Alphonse, Victor continues to think obsessively about his Creature, and cannot avoid reflecting on the whole train of events leading up to the present sorry pass, in particular 'shuddering' when he recalls 'the mad enthusiasm that hurried me on to the creation of my hideous enemy, and I called to mind the night in which he first lived. I was unable to pursue the train of thought; a thousand feelings pressed upon me, and I wept bitterly' (177). This maddening inability to think through the events of that night is caused by an unwillingness to recognize two things: (1) that it was his creation and then rejection of the Creature which set off the whole chain of causes resulting in the multiple murders; (2) that the essential identity of him and his Creature are almost completely the same. This last is shown when he is spurred on by the thought of doing his 'duty' to his family, and resolves to confront and destroy what he calls the 'monstrous Image' of his Creature if he should threaten them in Geneva. Almost in the same breath he goes on to describe himself (repeating the 'vampire' characterization) as 'the shadow of a human being' (177); 'shadow' being another term for 'spectral form' or 'phantom', signifying much the same as 'monstrous Image'.

Then, Victor attempts to dispel his sleep-preventing nightmarish state on the boat by taking double his usual dose of laudanum, but this only makes his nightmares more horrible (177). (Just as it did for Percy Shelley, who also had frequent recourse to tincture of opium for his bouts of nervousness. Percy Shelley again seems to provide the model for Victor's behaviour here.) It will be remembered that in trying to dispel the memory of what amounts to an 'original sin', he had attempted to sleep, had been assailed by nightmare and then been awakened by the 'wrinkled' smile of his Creature at the curtain. This time his Creature invades his sleep:

I felt the fiend's grasp in my neck; and could not free myself from it; groans and cries rang in my ears. (177)

Frankenstein is trapped by his own dreams, his own conscience, his own 'monstrous Image', a Gothic spectacle indeed, which once again calls to mind Mario Praz's definition of the Gothic tale as one which embodies an 'anxiety without any possible means of escape'. Alphonse may awake and calm his son, but any assurance of peace Victor may get from the absence of the Creature can only be temporary: the Creature is closing in on him.

Geneva and Marriage (Chapter V)

This chapter is a pivotal one for Victor's destiny, which will henceforth be governed by neurotic defensiveness. Weighed down by remorse and guilt for his 'crime', he is now less than ever able to consider himself worthy of the regard of his fellow humans, and in particular of the love of Elizabeth, whom he nevertheless marries in a kind of daze ('the ceremony was performed', he says, passively). All he can think about is the 'sentence' that the Creature has imposed upon him: 'I shall be with you on your wedding-night.'

The chapter opens with Victor deciding to rest his debilitated frame in Paris. Alphonse encourages him to seek social amusements, but the son feels he has denied himself the 'right to share' the society of people, having 'unchained an enemy among them, whose joy it was to shed their blood, and to revel in their groans' (179). He believes his 'brethren', his 'fellow-beings', would abhor him if they knew what he had done. But 'what he has done' is of course difficult to evaluate. No doubt most people would have been appalled that he had succeeded in creating such a bizarre creature as he has thoughtlessly put together, and would have destroyed it the moment they realized both the impossibility of its being able to survive in a hostile world, and the potential threat it posed.

Yet it is also possible some of them would be even more appalled to learn of Victor's neglect of his Creature, and would feel that, having allowed him to survive, he should at least have given him the chance of a life with one of his own 'kind', a chance which Victor has now denied him. The value put on education in the period in which the novel was set (the late 1790s) is apparent, as shown by the following letter, printed in *The Public Advertiser* in 1792. It appeared under the heading 'Children':

SIR,

It was a maxim which I adopted at thirty, that *the faults of the children* are (generally at least, if not universally speaking) owing to their parents.

If we look round the world, we shall see parents, even the best of them, too negligent of their children, particularly in early infancy; the season in which they receive impressions, which very often a whole life of precept and example cannot entirely eradicate. It is to this neglect, and to the false notion that few vices are contracted by children, and those few easily remedied as they grow up, that I attribute the guilt and misery of more than one-half of the bad children now living. It is too much *trouble* for the mother to suckle it – Here then is the first and most rooted mischief. The brats squall and make a noise, and disturb the business or the pleasures of the parents – they are therefore either put out to hired nurses, or kept up in a distant room of the house, among servants and dependants.

In the higher ranks of life, if the father would spare time from his pleasure and dissipation, and in the middling and lower ranks, from the coffee house, the tavern, or the ale house, to attend diligently to the EARLY, VERY EARLY (let me repeat and repeat it) formation of their children's mind, they would find their labour well re-paid as they advanced in years and discretion.

Yours, &c.

AN OLD BACHELOR (60)

Despite learning that his Creature is a being of refinement, taste and intelligence, Victor has perversely yielded to a structure of fear in himself, convinced that his Creature is 'intrinsically' bad.[2] As with the self-regarding figure of Squire Falkland in Godwin's *Caleb Williams* (see Chapter 9), he has more regard for his own reputation than the needs of others. This determination to make the Creature fearfully and unapproachably 'other' is a product of his own failure to guide and educate the desires and impulses of his 'son'. *That* is what makes the Creature into a real 'monster', the figure of which is a metaphor for human potential gone 'bad', through cultural and educational neglect.

The more he fears his alienated Creature, the more Victor becomes like him. His 'desire to avoid society' (179) is of course not a new impulse – whether in his experiments or in his frequent recourse to revivifying nature, he has been someone who *always* avoided society. We have already discovered the reason for this – it was his mad impulse to Romantic Prometheanism. The word 'mad' is not out of place here. Victor says he has 'a persuasion' he should be 'supposed mad' if he tried to explain his 'fatal secret' to the world, and it is for this reason he checks his 'impatient thirst for sympathy' (180). But Victor is an ill judge of his own character, as he is of most things. When he tells his uncomprehending father 'I am not mad', and that he was unable to save the lives of William, Justine and Henry because 'I could not sacrifice the whole human race', Alphonse is perhaps right to think his son's 'ideas were deranged' (180). To repeat, what deranges him and prevents him from enjoying the sympathy of others is his 'self'-preoccupied Romantic Prometheanism. A tortured Romantic egotism is at the bottom of his grandiose ideas, very much of the sort espoused by Percy Shelley. Frankenstein's radical egotism is characterized by an inability to escape what is essentially a psychotic, isolated self, a 'divinely gifted' self which he himself seems to believe he *alone* has created and 'possesses'. It is this grandiose sense of self-election, of dubious divinity, which also compels him to see the Creature as a 'monster' and not as a being of human feelings.

99

If it is the psychotic nature of the 'double act' of Frankenstein and his conscience, Frankenstein and his troublesome Creature, which keeps Victor from proceeding pragmatically with his existence, then the letter long-suffering Elizabeth sends to him at this time is also and perhaps inevitably fraught with 'double' feelings and responses. Although she has a great fondness for Victor, she is barely able to conceal a certain exasperation with the man who, during the eight years of their betrothal since he left for Ingolstadt, has spent only six months of it in her company. She means to convey sympathy for his losses and sunken condition when she writes. But we who have followed the fortunes of the neglectful Victor will tend to read her remark that 'I expect to see you looking even more ill than when you quitted Geneva' as a reproach. A sense of her annoyance at a further absence in which he has merely succeeded in making himself more miserable than before is augmented when she wonders, as did Alphonse before, whether his seeming reluctance to marry her is actually the result of Victor's heart belonging to 'another':

You have travelled: you have spent several years of your life at Ingolstadt; and I confess to you, my friend, that when I saw you last autumn so unhappy, flying to solitude, from the society of every creature, I could not help supposing that you might regret our connection, and believe yourself bound in honour to fulfil the wishes of your parents, although they opposed themselves to your inclinations. But this is false reasoning. I confess to you, my friend, that I love you, and that in my airy dreams of futurity you have been my constant friend and companion. (182)

Now here are two extracts from a letter Mary Godwin wrote to Percy Shelley in November 1814, early on in their relationship, when they were separated by the latter's need to avoid creditors in London:

I received your letter tonight I wanted one for I had [not] received one for almost two days but do not think I mean any thing by this my love – I know you took a long walk yesterday so you could not write . . .

. . . You dont say a word of Lambert of Harriet of Mrs Stuart of money or anythink – but all the reasonings you used to persuade Mr Peacock love was a good thing. Now you know I did not want converting – but my love do not be displeased at my chattering in this way for you know the expectation of a letter from you when absent always makes my heart jump . . .[3]

Read against the background of this response to Percy Shelley's absence – and his absences were to become a significant part of their future relations together – Elizabeth's letter does seem to convey an essential feature of Mary Shelley's 'double' regard for the poet, a feature produced by love for and resentment of him. William Veeder has character-ized this as an 'express–repress penchant'. As Veeder correctly observes, this method of handling violently difficult emotions is now called the 'approach–avoid' syndrome by psychologists.[4] Describing it as a 'pen-chant' thus hardly seems adequate to the case here. To be fair, Veeder does correct this sense of attributing Mary's differences with Shelley to a kind of impulsive whim. As he goes on to say, the general reader often has little idea of 'two essential biographical facts' lying behind their discord: 'just how incompatible the supposedly blissful Shelleys were', and the fact that Mary Shelley, though sympathetic to liberal political reforms, was 'never essentially a radical'.[5]

Victor's first response to Elizabeth's letter is characteristically oblique, arousing in him not loving thoughts towards her but a reminder of 'the threat of the fiend – "*I will be with you on your wedding-night*"' (182). His commentary on this 'threat', however, embodies an important reminder to *us* of the self-preoccupied way he reads the reality of things:

Such was my sentence, and on that night would the daemon employ every art to destroy me, and tear me from the glimpse of happiness which promised partly to console my sufferings. On that night he had determined to consummate his crimes by my death. (182)

Mary Shelley here effects a number of clever textual ironies. She has Victor indicating how he has created his own impasse – 'Such was *my sentence*' – partly by indulging in his self-obsessed and thus psychotic language. Victor's evaluation of the Creature's threat merely reinforces his radical solipsism – instead of considering Elizabeth's safety, he can only think in terms of a death threat to himself. The reality of that night will prove to be quite different.

The value he attaches to Elizabeth in all this seems minimal. If he should live up to his name in the contest with his Creature that he believes is approaching, the best outcome imaginable for him is the reward of Elizabeth as a kind of inadequate consolation prize for those 'horrors of remorse and guilt' he is now doomed to endure until his death. In his letter of reply he tries to reassure her by saying: 'all that I may one day enjoy is centred in you'. Yet this must be as unconvincing to Elizabeth as it is to us, who, upon reading his remark to Walton that 'in my Elizabeth I possessed a treasure', realize that Victor only ever really perceived her as a possible possession, and never as an erotic and sexually attractive being.

Upon their return to Geneva Alphonse raises the question of an 'immediate marriage' with Elizabeth, but the reluctant Victor says he 'remained silent', implying a continuing desire to delay. When Alphonse asks again whether he has 'some other attachment', we know – though Victor doesn't acknowledge it – that he has. His real 'partner' is the fearful Creature, or, as the Romantic biographical roots driving much of this tale make more and more plain, what this Creature stands for, his 'daemon', the troublesome, God-forsaken atheistic Romantic imagination of Percy Shelley.

Victor now agrees that the marriage day should be fixed. Alphonse attempts to lift his son's spirits by saying how through this marriage 'new and dear objects of care will be born to replace those of whom we have been so cruelly deprived' (184). Significantly (and ironically), Victor makes no comment on this 'pregnant' remark, for he is preoccupied with the threat uttered by the Creature whose very lack of care has made this 'first-born' of his into such a threatening Creature. In telling Walton this part of his story, Frankenstein is reminded of his own stupidity in having misread the real intentions of his Creature:

Great God! if for one instant I had thought what might be the hellish intention of my fiendish adversary, I would rather have banished myself for ever from my native country, and wandered a friendless outcast over the earth, than have consented to this miserable marriage. But, as if possessed of magic powers, the monster had blinded me to his real intentions; and when I thought that I had prepared only my own death, I hastened that of a far dearer victim. (185)

The ironies multiply, of course. Frankenstein, like his Creature, *has* become a friendless outcast wandering the earth. The Creature had not blinded him with magic; rather, Victor has, through his own moral blindness – an incapacity to foresee the consequences of abandoning his offspring – seriously underrated the extent to which the Creature would exact *sexual* revenge upon his creator. Had Frankenstein been attuned to this key dimension of the Creature's desire, he could have read the Creature's threat of 'I shall be *with you* on your wedding-night' more productively. He himself has unconsciously hinted at the Creature's dark sexual intentions by telling Walton of his determination to '*consummate* his crimes' on that night. Read with sexual intentions in mind he should have been able to see that the Creature aimed to become his sexual rival for Elizabeth – to be 'with' him on the wedding-night, rather than to murder him – raping and then murdering his new wife. (Thus cuckolding him *and* depriving him both of sexual pleasure with her and the possibility of reproducing the family line.)

Following their marriage, Victor and Elizabeth travel by boat towards the lakeside town of Evian, where they plan to spend the night before continuing to Lake Como. They will never reach their final destination, however, and Victor recalls how 'a presentiment of evil pervaded' Elizabeth, speculating that she 'perhaps ... thought of the dreadful secret which I had promised to reveal to her on the following day' (186). Underneath her attempts to remain cheerful, Elizabeth is indeed troubled, but the source of her anxiety, though unspecified, would from her point of view seem to concern the honeymoon encounter she is about to have with her new husband, rather than the 'dreadful secret' to be imparted to her from a person whose melodramatic character she knows only too well: 'Something whispers to me not to depend too much on the prospect that is opened before us, but I will not listen to such a sinister voice' (186–7). She seems to be entertaining doubts about Victor's consummatory capacities, and, indeed, we are given evidence that the cause of Victor's sexual debilitation is near at hand with the description that: 'The sun sank lower in the heavens,' until finally 'The sun sunk beneath the horizon as we landed ...' (187). The scene is set once again for the appearance of the Creature.

Honeymoon, Death, and Desperation (Chapter VI)

The language deployed by Mary Shelley at the opening of this chapter is truly 'Gothic':

> The moon had reached her summit in the heavens and was beginning to descend; the clouds swept across it swifter than the flight of the vulture and dimmed her rays ... (188)

The Creature, symbolically announced by the arrival of the moon, is about to 'descend'. Meanwhile, a 'heavy storm' of rain is building up, the 'restless waves' signalling Victor's increasing emotional agitation at the forthcoming 'combat' – though he little suspects it is to be a (somewhat one-sided) contest for the sexual favours of Elizabeth. Blind to the danger facing her, he thinks only of how 'fearful' it would be for her to witness his life-or-death struggle with the Creature. Thus he makes the 'fatal' error of sending her to their bedroom while he hunts through the ('Gothic') 'passages of the house' for his 'adversary' (188). When he hears the 'shrill and dreadful scream' of Elizabeth from the bedroom, he reports how 'the whole truth' now rushed into his mind. In a novel where the truth is constantly under question, one wonders what he could really mean by this. Part of the answer is provided by the ambiguous language used to describe the scene confronting Victor when he arrives in the bedroom:

She was there, lifeless and inanimate, thrown across the bed, her head hanging down, and her pale and distorted features half covered by her hair. Every where I turn I see the same figure – her bloodless arms and relaxed form flung by the murderer on its bridal bier . . . For a moment only did I lose recollection: I fell senseless on the ground. (189)

Elizabeth is dead. But the circumstances of her death are made ambiguous by the use of the word 'its' here. Does 'its' refer to Elizabeth's dead body, or to Frankenstein's Creature? Superficially read, the ambiguity seems even-handed. But we know how the Creature is convinced of being doomed to the deprivation of human – especially female human – contact. The only way he is going to attain his sexual end with a woman is by brute force, by rape, a crime in which the female is regarded by the attacking male as an object, an 'it'. The asocial Creature, deprived of the possibility of society by Frankenstein, has sought and gained sexual revenge for his denial of a Creature-wife, and thus feels justified – as Frankenstein perhaps recognizes by his use of the phrase – in regarding the wedding-bed of his creator as 'its bridal bier' by rights. This interpretation gains more credence when we realize that the posture of Elizabeth's dead body on the bed is much the same as that depicted in Fuseli's famous (male) erotic image of night-time rape, *The Nightmare* (1781).

That the creator has been cuckolded by his Creature seems confirmed when Victor returns to the bedroom after recovering from his faint. The shutters of the window had been closed before, but now they are 'thrown back', suggesting the Creature had been secretly watching him when first he discovered the body. Victor now 'felt a kind of panic on seeing the pale yellow light of the moon illuminate the chamber' (189). He realizes what we have known for some time: that the appearance of the moon signals the presence of the Creature. He perceives 'a figure the most hideous and abhorred' at the window:

A grin was on the face of the monster; he seemed to jeer, as with his fiendish finger he pointed towards the corpse of my wife. (189–90)

This time it does seem Frankenstein is entitled to regard the Creature as expressing ill-will: for with his gesture he is telling his creator in no uncertain terms that his latest act of revenge has two aspects: he has murdered his new wife, but he has also cheated him of the sexual favours he was to have enjoyed on his wedding-night. Victor fires his pistol in a predictable attempt to destroy the Creature, but equally predictably the Creature eludes him as he runs off into the lake 'with the swiftness of lightning' – appropriate enough for one animated by galvanic electricity.

Aware that the lives of Alphonse and Ernest could be in danger, Victor gives chase in a boat. But whereas before he had 'always experienced relief from mental torment in bodily exercise', his excessive mental agitation now renders him 'incapable of any exertion', and he falls to brooding on his miserable lot. The Creature's acts of revenge have finally made the scientist as miserable as he is, a fact unconsciously acknowledged by Victor when he says:

A fiend had snatched from me every hope of future happiness: no creature had ever been so miserable as I was; so frightful an event is single in the history of man. (191)

Of course, there has indeed been a 'creature' as miserable as he is – his own. Aware that the telling of yet another after-tale of misery will prove 'tedious' to his auditor Walton, Victor seems set to spare him and us from another account of his neurotic guilt. Instead the tale of misery is continued in another direction. With the news of Elizabeth's death, Alphonse collapses, dying after a few days in Victor's arms, unable to live under 'the horrors that were accumulated around him'. The death toll has now reached five: William, Justine, Clerval, Elizabeth and Alphonse. It is no wonder that Victor once again succumbs to madness, and is incarcerated in 'a solitary cell' for 'many months' (192).

Upon his recovery, Victor is determined to have recourse to the law in securing the capture and destruction of the Creature. But the criminal magistrate to whom he makes his deposition is doubtful of catching him, expressing his doubt in the text's frequent recourse to Milton:

'Who can follow an animal which can traverse the sea of ice, and inhabit caves and dens where no man would venture to intrude?' (193)

Indeed. In *Paradise Lost*, while Satan seeks a way out of Hell, his devils are condemned to wander through

> . . . many a region dolorous,
> O'er many a frozen, many a fiery alp,
> Rocks, caves, lakes, fens, bogs, dens, and shades of death,
> A universe of death. (II. 619–22)

The criminal law cannot deal with Frankenstein's problem, because it is a problem of the human soul, of the spirit, and of human psychology. Put briefly, it is the problem of how to survive in a universe where man has displaced God – and found himself wanting. Frankenstein has broken through the 'ideal bounds' of life and death by creating life, and death has been the result of his inadequacy in dealing with the consequences. That is why Victor's 'rage is unspeakable' at the thought that 'the murderer, whom I have turned loose upon society, still exists' (193). The Creature he brought to life was no murderer before universal rejection gave him cause for revenge. The murderer whom Frankenstein is talking about is himself; he it is whose thoughtless actions have brought about the death of God, a modern 'existential' dislocation of the spirit from which many of us suffer still. He it is whom he addresses when – as representative of the new godless order of 'Man' – he reproaches the reluctant magistrate like 'the martyrs of old' with: 'Man, how ignorant art thou in thy pride of wisdom! Cease; you know not what it is you say' (194). Victor is really talking about his own ignorance and the 'pride of wisdom' which had set the whole train of events in motion. Without God, and now without any friends or relations who might offer him a reason to live with any happiness (faulty plotting at this point means that Ernest his brother has been forgotten), Frankenstein now compulsively turns to the only mode of action seemingly left open to him. The problem he alone has created, he must alone resolve.

To the Arctic (Chapter VII) (1)

In its last chapter, Mary Shelley's *Frankenstein* ends as all revenge tragedies must, with death. (However, we shall see that the novel's resolution is by no means straightforward.) The Creature had told his creator that they were bound together 'by ties only dissoluble by the annihilation of one of us' (96). Frankenstein's refusal to create a living mate for his Creature has ensured that that annihilation must now take place – on one side or the other. The Creature's avenging actions for his untenable isolated existence have brought Frankenstein to the same pitch of motivation as himself, for, as he says,' revenge kept me alive; I dared not die, and leave my adversary in being' (195).

Frankenstein is now forced, in effect, to re-confront the moment following the Creature's animation, the moment when he had literally run away from the problem in the hope that it would disappear of its own accord. Such problems, 'of one's own creation', never do disappear, of course, but must at some point be dealt with. Once again, then, Victor finds himself wandering 'many hours round the confines of the town, uncertain what path I should pursue' (195). By dusk he has ended up at the gravesides of William, Elizabeth and his father. Here he makes a resolution, calling on the 'spirits of the dead' and the 'wandering ministers of vengeance' to witness the pledge he makes to avenge their deaths. But he finds his fervid oath answered 'by a loud and fiendish laugh', and his Creature, pleased to see his master reduced to his own 'wretched' condition, says in an 'audible whisper': 'I am satisfied: miserable wretch! you have determined to live, and I am satisfied' (196). We have come to expect the Creature's night-time appearances to be accompanied by the moon, and this occasion is no exception, with its entrance being even more melodramatic than usual:

Suddenly the broad disk of the moon arose, and shone full upon his ghastly and distorted shape, as he fled with more than mortal speed. (196)

With the Creature's flight Frankenstein's relentless pursuit of him begins. This takes him from the river Rhône to the 'blue Mediterranean', thence via the Black Sea through the inhospitable 'wilds of Tartary and Russia' and finally into the snows and ice of the Arctic, where he is eventually picked up, exhausted, by Captain Walton's ship. The journey is not merely physically draining for Victor; it is also a massive test of his psychological and spiritual capacities, which are now shown to be virtually indistinguishable from those of his 'devilish' Creature. 'I was cursed by some devil,' he says, 'and carried about with me my eternal hell' (197), an echo of the Creature's earlier invocation of Milton's Satan when he complained that 'I, like the arch-fiend, bore a hell within me' (132). The hellishly unrelieved resentment at the root of this resemblance, which some commentators describe as a double or *doppel-gänger* effect,[6] at times grossly distorts Frankenstein's perceptions. His derangement is revealed, for instance, when he believes a 'repast' he finds in the desert has been left by 'the spirits' he invoked to aid him in his pursuit of the Creature. But it is clear to the reader that the food left to 'restore and inspirit' him in the wilderness (again an ironical allusion to the topic of 'bringing back to life') has been provided by the Creature in order to prolong his creator's agonies. Again, when Victor believes it is his 'guiding spirit' that conducts him in safety to the place where he will finally 'meet and grapple' with the Creature, he does not seem to realize that it is the Creature himself enabling this process to take place.

When Frankenstein reaches the edge of the northern land-mass, he is told by 'horror-struck' villagers how a heavily armed 'gigantic monster' had put to flight 'the inhabitants of a solitary cottage, through fear of his terrific appearance' (199). So even at this stage, it is made clear that the Creature has no evil intentions towards society in general, as Frankenstein had feared he would. The Creature's animosity is directed solely at his creator; any fear generated in others is caused, as ever, by his 'terrific appearance', and not by any innate murderous aggression. This is a far cry from the plays and films supposedly retelling Mary Shelley's story over the following two centuries, where the Creature is more often than not portrayed as a grunting, criminal imbecile. In James Whale's famous Universal film of the story (*Frankenstein*, 1931), for instance, despite Boris Karloff's occasional success in portraying the pathetic dilemma of the Creature, he is nevertheless up against the script's demand that he be endowed (by mistake) with a 'criminal' brain. This was an idea clearly feeding off the then current notions of genetically determined 'criminal types', as developed in the fringe-scientific theories of the Italian criminologist Cesare Lombroso in his *Criminal Man* (1875).

In what are now the concluding scenes of Frankenstein's narrative, when he exchanges his 'land-sledge for one fashioned for the inequalities of the Frozen Ocean' (200), we are offered perhaps the most striking allusions yet to the punishing voyage of atonement which the Mariner undertakes in Coleridge's poem:

Immense and rugged mountains of ice often barred up my passage, and I often heard the thunder of the ground sea, which threatened my destruction. But again the frost came, and made the paths of the sea secure. (200)

The wind arose; the sea roared; and, as with the mighty shock of an earthquake, it split, and cracked with a tremendous and overwhelming sound. (201)

Here is the Coleridge:

> And thro' the drifts the snowy clifts
> Did send a dismal sheen;
> Ne shapes of men ne beasts we ken –
> The Ice was all between.
>
> The Ice was here, the Ice was there,
> The Ice was all around:
> It crack'd and growl'd, and roar'd and howl'd –
> Like noises of a swound! (ll. 53–60)

Three weeks of pursuit bring Frankenstein in sight of his Creature, but just as every other satisfaction in life has been denied him, so is he now denied the chance of a life-and-death duel when the ground sea splits the ice, marooning him on a 'scattered piece'. The Creature is now out of reach, but after some hours Victor sees Captain Walton's ship riding at anchor, and he is induced to hope, not that he might be rescued, but that a boat might be given him in order that he can pursue his obsessive mission. At which point he is noticed and picked up by Walton's crew.

To the last, he maintains the fiction that the Creature is out to pursue 'dark crimes', possessing a soul 'as hellish as his form, full of treachery and fiendlike malice' (202). And with these attempts to persuade Walton of such intrinsic evil, and a plea that, should he die, the explorer will instead 'thrust your sword into his heart' if he appears, we hear the last words of the narrative recording Frankenstein's story as kept by Walton.

7 Robert Walton's Narrative (2)

'Lost in darkness and distance' (Chapter VII) (2)

It has taken from the 19th to the 26th of August for Frankenstein to relate his story – and that of his Creature – to Walton; that is to say, eight days. Another twelve days will pass before the remaining action of the novel is complete. This will involve a near-mutiny by Walton's crew, the death of Frankenstein, and the final appearance of his Creature before he is carried off into 'darkness and distance' on the 'ice-raft which lay close to the vessel' (215).

In resuming his own narration to Margaret, Walton is initially much preoccupied with the manner in which Frankenstein has told 'the strangest tale that ever imagination formed' (203). His 'eloquence is forcible and touching', he says, and he cannot 'hear him, when he relates a pathetic incident, or endeavours to move the passions of pity or love, without tears' (203). Yet it is these very histrionic skills which make Victor's tale seem incredible and 'imagination formed':

His tale is connected, and told with an appearance of the simplest truth; yet I own to you that the letters of Felix and Safie, which he showed me, and the apparition of the monster seen from our ship, brought to me a greater conviction of the truth of his narrative than his asseverations, however earnest and connected. (202)

For Walton, Victor's word is untrustworthy, however compelling, just as, for Frankenstein, the story-telling of his Creature is suspect: 'He is eloquent and persuasive; and once his words had even power over my heart: but trust him not' (202). On the other hand, Walton is content to allow Victor to 'correct and augment' his notes of Frankenstein's narrative 'in many places', presumably agreeing with the scientist that a 'mutilated' form of this should not 'go down to posterity'. He may allow this concession because the corrections he makes are 'principally in giving the life and spirit to the conversations he held with his enemy' (203). However sceptical he may be about Frankenstein's story, we have to remember that Walton himself is deeply imbued with the spirit of over-reaching Romantic Prometheanism, and as such has been desperately curious to 'gain from Frankenstein the particulars of his creature s formation'. Like Frankenstein, Walton wants, adapting a phrase from Sylvia Plath, to 'masturbate a glitter',[1] to 'create life' in an existence where the life of the imagination is all. Frankenstein, the epitome of the Romantic 'creative' genius, will not yield, and 'on this point he was impenetrable' (202). Why? Creative gods do not give up the secret of their proud powers easily. This is shown by the fact that even when he compares himself with 'the archangel who aspired to omnipotence' and was punished by being 'chained in an eternal hell' – presumably meant as a dire warning to Walton – Frankenstein is still obsessed enough with reflections on his own creative powers to go on blindly celebrating them. For he now reveals how he has for many years seen himself as a Romantic genius, in his youth much beyond 'the herd of common projectors':

'My imagination was vivid, yet my powers of analysis and application were intense; by the union of these qualities I conceived the idea, and executed the creation of a man . . . I trod heaven in my thoughts, now exulting in my powers, now burning with the idea of their effects. From my infancy I was imbued with high hopes and a lofty ambition; but how am I sunk! Oh! my friend, if you had known me as I once was, you would not recognize me in this state of degradation. Despondency rarely visited my heart; a high destiny seemed to bear me on, until I fell, never, never again to rise.' (204)

Powerful irony is at work in Mary Shelley's language here. She questions the nature of Romantic 'creativity' by deploying metaphors concerning the act of procreation. Instead of male and female producing a baby, we have the 'union' of imagination with 'intense' powers of 'analysis and application'. These 'conceive' first the 'idea', and then the 'creation' of a man'. But we need to note the unmistakably chilling rider Mary Shelley adds to this process by the ambiguous use of the word 'executed'. Because this 'creation of a man' was 'executed', his possibilities seem doomed from the outset. This is obviously confirmed by the 'non-life' produced by rejection which the Creature has been forced to endure.

In the more 'practical' terms experienced by the characters of the novel, as we have seen, such a death is felt more as an irretrievable loss in the capacity for generating or experiencing human sympathy. This is Walton's enormous regret in relation to Frankenstein. He has 'longed for a friend', has 'sought one who would sympathise with and love me', but having found that person, has 'gained him only to know his value, and lose him'. He would 'reconcile [Frankenstein] to life, but he repulses the idea'. To repeat, that is because, in the process of creating life, Frankenstein has also 'executed' his capacity for sustaining it in human, sympathetic terms. Frankenstein thanks Walton for his 'kind intentions' towards him (we should note the ambiguous use of 'kind' again), but regrets he is unable to make 'new ties, and fresh affections', linking this incapacity to his loss of Elizabeth and Clerval. There are companions of our childhood, he says, who 'always possess a certain power over our minds, which hardly any later friend can obtain' (204).[2] Only one thing would persuade him to 'preserve' his life: to be 'engaged in any high undertaking or design, fraught with extensive utility to my fellow-creatures' (205). But of course, this is heavily ironic, revealing once again the moral blindness of Frankenstein, for these motives of 'extensive utility' were of the very sort which had originally driven him to make the Creature!

With his offer of friendship effectively repulsed, Walton again writes to Margaret, twice addressing her as his 'beloved sister', as if marking a shift in his affections. He is losing all confidence in himself, and in Frankenstein too, of whom he reports as talking only '*as if* life were a possession which he valued' (205, emphasis added). At what will be his most testing time, Walton's anxieties have returned. The ship is 'surrounded by mountains of ice, which admit of no escape', bringing about an anxiety without any possible means of escape. He worries about the distressed state of his sister's mind, should he die under these entrapped circumstances. But it is really his own mind that concerns him most. The 'brave fellows' of his ship are looking to him for aid in their predicament, but he has 'none to bestow'. After the fascination of listening to Frankenstein's story for a week, his own characteristically oscillating state of mind is now asserting itself. At one moment he feels his 'courage and hopes' have not deserted him, but then is concerned that it is his 'mad schemes' which have endangered his men's lives (205). And not simply endangered them. Listening to Frankenstein, the sailors may 'feel the power of his eloquence', and have their energies 'roused' in such a despairing situation. But Walton observes that 'these feelings are transitory'. Why so? It is because the crew are acutely aware that many of Frankenstein's 'unfortunate comrades have already found a grave amidst this scene of desolation' (206). Each sailor knows he may be the next to die, and so does Walton. The captain thus dreads that their increasing despair in such a situation will provoke a mutiny.

This fear seems about to be realized when Walton receives a deputation of sailors whose leader insists he should direct his course 'southwards', if the ice should dissipate, making a free passage possible. In what to us appears as an unmistakable echo of the Creature's demand for a mate, Walton feels that 'in justice' he cannot refuse such a 'requisition' (206). But before he is able to respond to their demand, Frankenstein, whose 'eyes sparkled' and whose cheeks are 'flushed with momentary vigour', addresses the men with a rousing speech designed to persuade them to continue with their 'glorious expedition'; to imagine their return 'as heroes who have fought and conquered', rather than as 'cowards' who have turned their backs on the 'foe' (207). This is very similar to the attempt Dante's Ulysses makes to rouse his sailors to heroic action: 'Do not deny yourselves the experience, following the sun, of the unpeopled world. Consider your origin: you were not formed to live like beasts, but to pursue power and knowledge' (*Inferno*, XXV.118–20). Ulysses' reward for persuading his men to join him in his over-reaching project is to be consigned to the domain of the flaming ditch, reserved for evil counsellors. Walton is more cautious than either Frankenstein or Ulysses. He says he will not 'lead them farther north' if they 'strenuously desire' the contrary, even though he hopes they will be courageous enough to continue. He tells the men to 'retire' to consider all that has been said. Prudence is almost certainly the deciding factor here, for Walton would have known, from his reading, about the celebrated case of the explorer Henry Hudson, whose ship had been stuck in Arctic ice for several months in 1610. When warmer weather liberated the vessel, the starving crew mutinied, setting Hudson and eight sick men adrift to perish on the ocean. Walton's men, in his eyes 'unsupported by ideas of glory and honour', persist in their demands to turn south at the first chance, and so their captain 'consented to return'. He states that his hopes have thus been 'blasted by cowardice and indecision' and that it requires more philosophy than he possesses 'to bear this injustice with patience' (208).

In his last letter, which brings the novel to a close, Walton's attitude hints at the values which Mary Shelley espouses, concerned as they are with human sympathy. With Frankenstein dead and his 'hopes of utility and glory' lost (208), Walton now looks towards England and his sister for 'consolation', saying he 'will not despond' (210, 208). Yet in a novel which has consistently troubled itself with the theme of loss, this preoccupation continues, with Walton determined to chronicle to the end the 'bitter circumstances' surrounding the death of his friend. These involve the final speech and death of Frankenstein, and the last appearance, and then disappearance, of his Creature, whose own parting speech is one of the most moving of the whole novel.

Even as the tragic denouement unfolds, Mary Shelley persists in conveying the difficult issues of life and death, (re)animation and bodily extinction, that have been at the heart of her text. This is shown when the ice recedes and Walton tells Frankenstein he cannot lead his men unwillingly into danger, indeed, that he 'must return' (208). In contrast, Frankenstein responds with the classically defining gesture of the tragic hero who says he 'dare not' give up his 'purpose' since this 'is assigned to me by Heaven'. But his effort to follow up this resolve with an attempt to 'spring from the bed' ends in collapse. A kind of parody of the scene where the Creature was brought to life (56) follows, where Walton tells us that:

It was long before he was restored; and I often thought that life was entirely extinct. At length he opened his eyes; he breathed with difficulty, and was unable to speak. (209)

Whereas 'the sentence' which Frankenstein had earlier imagined the Creature to have imposed upon him – death – had not materialized, this time 'his sentence was pronounced', ironically enough, by a fellow-doctor, the ship's surgeon, who says that he 'had certainly not many hours to live' (209).

Then in his dying speech to Walton, he offers a review of his 'past conduct', which he does not consider 'blameable':

In a fit of enthusiastic madness I created a rational creature, and I was bound towards him, to assure, as far as was in my power, his happiness and well-being. (209)

This 'power' had been decidedly limited, as his abandonment of the Creature, the event from which all the subsequent drama flows, proves. He admits that it was his 'duty' to ensure his Creature's happiness and well-being, but then, in a sleight of hand which overlooks the nil effort he made in this direction and also totally discounts the long and moving story the Creature had had to tell, he pragmatically weighs this neglected duty against the 'duties towards the beings of my own species'. These he feels had 'greater claims' upon his attention, 'because they included a greater proportion of happiness or misery' (209). But this appeal to 'utilitarian' values is deeply ironic. The compulsive Promethean missions of both Frankenstein and Walton had been undertaken in response – quoting Walton – to 'hopes of utility and glory'. But instead of benefiting their fellow-creatures, both men have occasioned misery and death through their literally care-less actions.

Frankenstein's limited moral vision and over-reaching Promethean logic are sustained to the last. He feels he 'did right in refusing to create a companion' for his Creature, whom he insists showed unparalleled malignity and selfishness, in evil; he destroyed my friends; he devoted to destruction beings who possessed exquisite sensations, happiness, and wisdom; nor do I know where this thirst for vengeance may end. (209)

Faulty logic, enormous ironies, and some truth are all to be found in this statement. Firstly, he fails to recognize that the vengeful murders of Clerval and Elizabeth were actually occasioned by his own refusal to create a mate for the Creature, the 'unparalleled malignity and selfishness' of which he talks being produced *after* this refusal, not before. Secondly, the 'exquisite sensations, happiness, and wisdom' of his friends were precisely those fully human qualities which his own Creature had given evidence of possessing or aspiring to in his long narrative, qualities which got roughened into their opposites as he repeatedly encountered social rejection. Finally, Frankenstein's perception that the Creature's thirst for vengeance has triggered a similar motivation in him is an accurate one, and this deadly revenge mechanism does indeed promise to become an endless prospect. As René Girard has said, 'Everyone wants to strike the last blow, and reprisal can thus follow reprisal without any true conclusion ever being reached.'³ If this is so in the case of human beings, then it is so much more the case when the death which is really being confusedly mourned and avenged in this novel is what Nietzsche later called the 'death of God'. This is far from apparent as Victor Frankenstein, the man the Creature has been compelled to regard as his creator, makes his last, dying statements. Confusion overcomes this technical divinity, and is shown in several ways.

Worn out by remorse and his failure to destroy that which he had once in jubilation created, he half-heartedly urges Walton to 'undertake my unfinished work'. Yet he quickly realizes that this request is a dubious one, and is right to say that in making it he 'may still be misled by passion' (210). For whether this avenging 'task of destruction is motivated by 'Selfish and vicious motives' or 'induced by reason and virtue', the violent outcome will be the same – death. This is a troubling conclusion for him, and for us. If one cannot be sure whether the motives for one's actions are guided by vicious or virtuous impulses, where is one to get one's sense of moral purpose from? This issue is left unresolved. Victor, eager to join the 'forms of the beloved dead' who 'flit before' him, shows himself little concerned with the affairs of this world, his parting advice to Walton being both cautious *and* spirited on the subject of scientific pursuits:

'Farewell, Walton! Seek happiness in tranquillity, and avoid ambition, even if it be only the apparently innocent one of distinguishing yourself in science and discoveries. Yet why do I say this? I have myself been blasted in these hopes, yet another may succeed.' (210)

That he now views his attempts to distinguish himself in science as only *apparently* innocent seems to indicate a certain degree of insight about the dangers of his Promethean motivations. Yet his comment about 'success' reveals the character trait which predominates in him – self-deception. He cannot grasp the essential point that his real failure is intimately linked to the price paid for his success: the sacrifice of his capacity for social sympathy, the sacrifice of his conscience. Frankenstein cannot, or will not, see this. It is not simply a question of correcting what nowadays would be called a 'design fault' in his product. Creating a human being involves taking responsibility for it, whether beautiful or ugly. Frankenstein's tragedy is that, like Percy Shelley, his major preoccupation is not merely beauty, but 'intellectual' beauty, a valued process which they admiringly abstract and isolate out of daily existence at their moral peril.

Mary Shelley's values are much nearer 'home'. (Indeed, one of the best critics of *Frankenstein*, Anne K. Mellor, has maintained that Mary Shelley's fiction as a whole shows her to be 'in search of a family'.[4]) That is to say, she is much concerned with exploring the concrete situation of someone like the Creature, whose intellectual capacity forces him to question and cope with an existence in which no one accords him recognition or value. In Charles Dickens's novel *Little Dorrit*, a good deal of the rage felt by the Meagles' maid Tattycoram is caused by her name being a permanent reminder to her of her lowly birth and orphan status. How much more enraged and alienated must Frankenstein's Creature then be? For not only has he been given no name: neither has he found, nor been offered, any role whatever in social existence. Rather the opposite; his only truly social experiences have been those teaching him to regard himself as a threat, as an ugly outcast. He is a being defined by total rejection.

And it is with the touchingly human distresses of this rejected and reviled Creature, whose narrative was strategically placed at the 'heart' of this brilliant text by Mary Shelley, that the story comes to its emotionally painful conclusion, and what Walton calls a 'final and wonderful catastrophe'.[5] No one is going to be spared the full force of the Creature's dreadful predicament, the account of which begins when Walton, continuing to write to his sister, suddenly hears 'a sound as of a human voice' coming from the cabin where 'the remains of Frankenstein still lie'. He decides he 'must arise, and examine' (210).

In the cabin he finds the 'gigantic form' of the Creature hanging over his dead creator, uttering 'exclamations of grief and horror'. He has 'one vast hand extended' towards him, just as he had on the night of his 'birth', when he approached Frankenstein at his bedside, benignly seeking 'to detain' him (57). In the way that everyone else has before him, Walton 'involuntarily' shuts his eyes when he sees the Creature's face. It strikes him with 'such loathsome, yet appalling hideousness' that for a moment he finds it hard to 'recollect what were my duties with regard to this destroyer' (211). While he endeavours to 'recollect' his shattered self, the Creature, angry and distraught, rages distractedly over his creator in a 'suffocated' voice, calling him *both* a 'generous' *and* a 'self-devoted being'. The Creature's useless begging for forgiveness in front of the body which created his own checks Walton's impulse to attack him, and the explorer feels overcome by 'a mixture of curiosity and compassion'. Yet he soon gathers sufficient resolution, even in the presence of a being whose 'scaring and unearthly' ugliness prevents him from gazing at him directly, to say that his self-reproaches are too late – that he should have heeded the 'stings of remorse' earlier, and Frankenstein might 'yet have lived'. But the Creature argues that Frankenstein's suffering had been nothing compared with his own, even though, when killing Clerval and Elizabeth in revenge for Victor's failure to make him happy, he had momentarily cast off his misery and 'rioted' in the excess of his despair:

'My heart was fashioned to be susceptible of love and sympathy; and when wrenched by misery to vice and hatred, it did not endure the violence of the change, without torture such as you cannot even imagine.' (212)

As with the rebellious Satan in *Paradise Lost*, he says, 'Evil thenceforth became my good.' He felt he had had no choice but to act as he did.

Walton's response to this defence is interesting. One must assume he has listened with his gaze still averted from the Creature, for he says he was 'at first touched by the expressions of his misery'. But the evidence of his ears is insufficient. Like Frankenstein before, he must convince himself that the essential impulses of the Creature are as ugly as his countenance. Thus he encourages himself to call to mind 'what Frankenstein had said of his powers of eloquence and persuasion', and turning to the scientist's lifeless body, he experiences the anger he has been looking for. 'Indignation was rekindled within me', he says, and proceeds to accuse the Creature of hypocrisy: '. . . you lament only because the victim of your malignity is withdrawn from your power' (212).

117

Six of the last seven paragraphs of the novel are then devoted to what amounts to one of the most moving accounts of thwarted human existence ever written. The Creature agrees that it must 'appear' (his word) to Walton that he grieves only because Frankenstein is now beyond his control. But he asks now for nothing, no 'fellow-feeling' in his misery, having learned from bitter experience that he is unable to evince sympathy from anyone. (Significantly, it was only the old De Lacey, forced through blindness to see 'beyond appearance', who had offered him anything like the beginnings of sympathy.) He had once delighted in the prospects of existence, he says. His fancy had been 'soothed with dreams of virtue, of fame, and of enjoyment' and he was 'nourished with high thoughts of honour and devotion' (213). Just as Victor had been! we might observe. But whereas Victor had been a member of society and chose to isolate himself in the hope that scientific discovery would bring him these things, the Creature had been forced to suffer an isolation without any hope whatsoever of social redemption, and this had corrupted his spirit. Using his reading as a paradigm for good and evil human possibilities and psychology, the Creature once more compares himself to Satan: 'the fallen angel becomes a malignant devil'. However, he notes poignantly that 'even that enemy of God and man had friends and associates in his desolation; I am alone' (213).

Importantly, he challenges Walton as to whether he can really understand his appalling situation. He may have listened to Frankenstein's version of his story, he says, but it is impossible that the 'hours and months of misery' he had to endure, 'wasting in impotent passions', could be adequately communicated:

'For while I destroyed his hopes, I did not satisfy my own desires. They were forever ardent and craving; still I desired love and fellowship, and I was still spurned.' (213)

Spurned for his ugliness, he was even attacked when he tried to do good. 'Why do you not execrate the rustic who sought to destroy the saviour of his child?' he asks Walton. More naively, he wonders why Walton should not hate Felix, 'who drove his friend from the door with contumely'. But this naivety not only makes our sympathy for his friendless plight even more poignant, it confirms once more that this is a novel both of psychological realism and of telling ethical value, in the deepest human sense. Those who railed against him merely because of his ugly visage, making the mistake of reading his intentions by his appearance only, 'these are virtuous and immaculate beings!' he observes, with touching irony.

He sees no irony in what now lies before him. Ultimately he makes no excuses for himself. Admitting to the base impulses of a wretched murderer, he echoes Frankenstein's own sentiment that no one can hate him more than he hates himself, and looks forward to a self-destruction using the hands which destroyed others (214). Yet there is irony aplenty and enormous power in the statements he makes concerning the self-extinction he now anticipates. For he tells Walton that upon leaving his ship on an ice-raft he will 'seek the most northern extremity of the globe'. Though the Creature does not know it, such an action will of course cheat Walton of the glory of being first to the North Pole. Not only this, but once in that domain of 'eternal light' (13), of which the explorer had only dreamed, this victim of Prometheanism will 'consume to ashes this miserable frame', and ensure by so doing that

its remains may afford no light to any curious and unhallowed wretch, who would create such another as I have been. (214)

This provides a powerfully ironic comment upon Frankenstein's un-hallowed (i.e. unholy) desire to 'pour a torrent of light into our dark world' (52) by creating human life. He continues the ironic play upon the language of 'light' and 'sense' right up to the end, describing how in his death all 'light, feeling, and sense will pass away'; how the 'burning miseries' of his existence will disappear, when he 'triumphantly' endures the 'agony of the torturing flames' of his funeral pile; and how 'the light of that conflagration will fade away', just as his form now does, when leaping from the ship on to his ice-raft, he is soon 'lost in darkness and distance' (214, 215).

Walton tells us that the Creature is 'lost in darkness and distance', but in a deeply ironic text where nothing is quite what it seems, perhaps this is only how things 'appear'? The Creature is still alive when he departs the ship. And even if tragic death should end this novel – for it is an open question whether it finally does – it is a death we should perhaps learn to understand as contributing to the force of a potentially 'great' life and an existence of hope for us, the readers.

Part Two: Interpretation

At the beginning of Part One I suggested that the primary theme of *Frankenstein* was what happens to human sympathies and relationships when men seek obsessively to satisfy their Promethean longings to 'conquer the unknown' – supposedly in the service of their fellow-humans. Our reading of the novel has demonstrated quite graphically the consequences of Mary Shelley's central argument: that compulsive enterprise destroys such sympathies and relationships. Walton's voyage of exploration to the North Pole ends in defeat and many deaths; Frankenstein creates a living Creature whose neglect ultimately produces misery and an incitement to destructive acts. The male protagonists all *mean* well, but their curiosity-driven, misguided efforts are rewarded with negative outcomes. In the next chapter I discuss how this theme was one Mary Shelley had found in the novels of her father William Godwin, particularly in *Caleb Williams* (1794) and in *St Leon* (1799). Here I am first of all concerned to explore how Mary Shelley achieves the various literary effects and meanings she does so powerfully, concentrating on some of the uses she makes of metaphor and irony. (The central political metaphor of the book is discussed in Chapter 11, as is the use of sexual metaphors for Frankenstein's 'penetration' of nature.) This leads into a discussion of what I have called Romantic Prometheanism, which in turn gives rise to a consideration of the book's preoccupation with the vexed theme of fathers, mothers and parenting. This subject allows us to approach the theme of the 'absent father', both in the language of the book and in society.

Ice and Fire

In the set of opposing binary terms I listed on page 11 are the contrasts heat/cold. Of all the metaphors employed by Mary Shelley, those linked to heat and cold are the most pervasive and operative for conveying her meanings, the various underlying 'messages' of her book. We should notice that all three narratives making up the novel – those of Walton, Frankenstein, and the Creature – are told amidst remote icy surroundings. Walton's account begins as he journeys towards the North Pole and ends in its icy wastes. Frankenstein tells his tale to

Walton while they are trapped aboard ship in the solid Arctic ice. And the Creature relates his story to his maker in the 'hut upon the mountain' overlooking the sea of ice above Chamonix. Having these stories told in such icy surroundings symbolically draws our attention to the conditions of social isolation under which the whole effort of Promethean creative over-reaching takes place. As a Romantic Promethean one *necessarily* becomes self-preoccupied with one's heroic mission, and must therefore stand aloof from exercising the social sympathies – the active and real caring practice of making everyday 'warm' contact with one's fellow human beings – those affective ties which make social life worth living.

Mary Shelley again and again throughout her text uses images of cold and heat, ice and fire, dark and light, to symbolize ironically the destructive effects which attempts by the protagonists to 'unite' these contrasts bring about, the ultimate and central irony of the book being Frankenstein's experiment to bring together the worlds of life and death. These metaphors are brought to bear right from the beginning. In Walton's first letter home to his sister Margaret we have already noticed how the icy wind blowing from the North Pole was for him a 'wind of promise'. As he physically moves further and further away from his sister, the sustaining warmth of a family relation gives way to the warmth of his Romantic image of the North Pole as 'a country of eternal light', a place to which he is also 'attracted' by its supposedly being the location of the 'wondrous power of the needle'. The warmth then of his Romantic dream enables him to put a distance between himself, his bodily senses, and the real world. We know that there is 'eternal light' at the North Pole, but we also know that it is a light which shines on freezing, uninhabited white wastes, where little or no sentient life exists. What then is the lure of it? The only answer can be that this is really a light representing the 'living' power of the imagination. This is graphically represented in the novel by Frankenstein's use of language when describing the experience of discovering the method of 'bestowing life upon lifeless matter'. 'A sudden light broke in upon me', he says, a light 'so brilliant and wondrous' that he became 'dizzy with the immensity of the prospect which it illustrated' (51). This is something like the Romantic artist's alternative conception of heavenly eternity, akin to the quality or element P.B. Shelley had in mind when he coined a favourite expression for his poetry, the 'white radiance of eternity'. Indeed, it is not surprising to find that it was Percy Shelley who actually wrote these words of Frankenstein, just one of the many additions he made to the manuscript when Mary had finished the novel in 1817.

Where Walton's imagination gets fired by the 'immensity of the prospect' of the North Pole as a kind of icy Paradise, Frankenstein's eagerly youthful mind is stunned when he confronts the awesome power of nature at work in the form of an electrical storm at Belrive. This is the raw energy of 'life' which, harnessed in and deployed from (one presumes) an electrical battery, he is able to impart to the giant Creature of disparate human parts which he assembles at Ingolstadt. Using electricity, he animates death into life. But in doing so, he finds he has 'thoughtlessly' (though 'imaginatively') and forcibly penetrated the domain of Mother Nature. Not only does this metaphor of mother-rape trigger thoughts in us about other domains of presumptuous violation – like Wordsworth, Mary Shelley shows us that she is an environmental 'green' long before it is fashionable to be so. But it also produces yet another metaphor, perhaps the most powerful of the whole book, because it is potentially the most uncontrollable. This is the metaphor of the 'monstrous' Creature itself. Without the energy of the Creature to drive the story along, there would be no Frankenstein story or Frankenstein myth.

It will be remembered that on his return to Geneva in I. VII, Victor witnesses a stupendous electrical storm in which he sees 'the lightnings playing on the summit of Mont Blanc in the most beautiful figures', and that shortly afterwards he perceives 'in the gloom a figure which stole from behind a clump of trees' (73). The use of 'figure' here can be no accident. In what is a kind of bizarre parody of the 'God-Man' character of Jesus Christ, Mary Shelley is offering us a figurative vision of the Creature both as pure natural energy and as worldly earth-bound being. We have already observed how the Creature is a figure (metaphor) for human potential 'gone bad' through cultural and educational neglect. Now we must also recall once more that what drives the Creature along is the 'daemon' – the demonic energy – of Frankenstein himself, which I earlier characterized as the 'troublesome, God-forsaken atheistic Romantic Imagination of Percy Shelley'. The reason this energy is so frightening is that it has 'no home' to call its own, nothing to 'register' itself upon, or attach itself to. It is a concept of power Mary found in Shelley's poem *Mont Blanc* (1816), and which he had evoked as 'untameable wildness'. But to be endowed with the spark of existence by a man of overheated imagination – and yet whose heart is cold towards his vital creation – where does this idea of a creative 'spark' come from?

Romantic Prometheanism

In my critical reading of Mary Shelley's novel I have frequently used the term 'Promethean' to describe the over-reaching motivations of its male protagonists. This was not an arbitrary use but derives from the author's description of Frankenstein in the sub-title as *The Modern Prometheus*. Who was Prometheus? He is a figure who appears both in Greek and Roman mythologies. In Greek mythology Prometheus (meaning 'forethinker') was a Titan, one of the dynasty of gods who ruled heaven before the younger Olympian gods, led by Zeus (Jupiter, in Roman mythology), took over. When Zeus confiscated fire from human-kind, Prometheus stole it and gave it back to man, of whom he had been the original creator. Zeus punished his presumption by chaining him to a rock on Mount Caucasus, where an eagle devoured his liver, which was daily renewed, until eventually he was set free by Herakles (Hercules). In the later Roman account, the focus is on Prometheus as *plasticator*, fashioner of human creatures from the earth. Ovid's *Metamorphoses* records this version (translated by John Dryden):

> Whether with particles of heavenly fire,
> The God of Nature did his soul inspire;
> Or earth, but new divided from the sky,
> And, pliant, still retain'd th'ethereal energy:
> Which wise Prometheus temper'd into paste,
> And, mix't with living streams, the godlike image caste ...
> From such rude principles our form began;
> And earth was metamorphosed into man.

Mary Shelley was very familiar with the figure of Prometheus both through this account and Aeschylus's drama *Prometheus Unbound*, as were the other Romantic writers of the 1816 Genevan summer, Lord Byron and P.B. Shelley. In fact, the Romantic poets were so drawn to the rebellious and suffering saviour of humanity that both wrote works drawing on the myth. Like Mary's father Godwin, Byron and Shelley were fierce opponents of arbitrary power and sympathetic to the idea of serving humankind beneficently – even at the cost, perhaps *because* of the personally heroic cost, of eternal torment. Byron published his three-stanza *Prometheus* in 1816 (with its final defiant line, 'making Death a Victory'), and the poem in some measure captures his parting disgust with an English society that had all but thrown him out of the country, to which he would never return. Percy Shelley's poetic drama *Prometheus Unbound* (1819), which some regard as his finest achievement, is a long, elaborate lyrical drama of four acts in which the uncompromising, idealistic Promethean figure struggles to liberate man from the chains of tyranny.

Mary Shelley's own adaptation of the Promethean myth is clearly not developed along the same lines as those of her male companions. How does it differ? As Romantic writers living in an age of upheaval when established beliefs, values, and political and social structures were under radical challenge, the appeal of Prometheus for Byron and Percy Shelley seems to have been twofold. They admired the figure both as hero, revolutionary and freedom fighter, but also as an artist, a creator. Byron had a less idealistic view of the human possibilities suggested by the rebellious benefactor Prometheus than did Shelley. Though Shelley may have agreed that Prometheus –

> . . . art a symbol and a sign
> To Mortals of their fate and force

and that this figure could inspire us to develop

> . . . a firm will, and a deep sense,
> Which even in torture can descry
> Its own concentr'd recompense,
> Triumphant where it dares defy,
> And making Death a Victory
> (Byron, *Prometheus*)

Byron could never have been so idealistic as to believe that evil can be eradicated from the world by willpower and mental determination. But Shelley, with what Mary called his 'more abstract and etherialised inspiration',[1] was just such an idealist. As Mary observed in her note on *Prometheus Unbound*:

The prominent feature of Shelley's theory of the destiny of the human species was, that evil is not inherent in the system of the creation, but an accident that might be expelled . . . That man could be so perfectionized as to be able to expel evil from his own nature, and from the greater part of the creation, was the cardinal point of his system. And the subject he loved best to dwell on, was the image of One warring with the Evil Principle, oppressed not only by it, but by all, even the good, who were deluded into considering evil a necessary portion of humanity.

As she goes on to say, attracted by the Prometheus myth, 'Shelley adapted the catastrophe of this story to his peculiar views' and wrote *Prometheus Unbound*.[2]

Mary Shelley wrote these notes twenty years after the composition of *Frankenstein*, so it may be argued that we are not entitled to read these critical points back into the concerns of the novel. Yet it is plain from our reading that P.B. Shelley's 'abstruse and imaginative theories with regard to the Creation' – as she calls them[3] – are of fundamental importance for its genesis. Frankenstein may be the 'modern' Prometheus – a Romantic scientist of the sort I discuss in Chapter 11. But in her 1831 Introduction he is described as an 'artist' (9) – a creator – and the text (for instance) has him desiring to 'banish disease from the human frame and render man invulnerable to any but a violent death' (40). That is to say, he wants to use science to banish those 'weaknesses' of human mortality which (to quote Hamlet) 'flesh is heir to' – death and decay. He wants men to become gods and live for ever. But they cannot become gods fired by Romantic Promethean imaginations if they are conceived and born in the normal way. 'Man that is born of a woman is of few days, and full of trouble,' says the Bible (Job 14:1). The answer, then, is for men to conceive men without the aid of women. Mary Shelley has the deepest scepticism about what we may now call without hesitation this mad, masculinist goal. 'What would happen if' one could sidestep the normal constraints of mortality by discovering the power of 'bestowing animation' (52)? What would happen is conveyed by the novel *Frankenstein*. In making his choice against what Mary Louise Pratt has called 'heterosexual conjugal life and women',[4] Victor Frankenstein sees himself as father of a new species which he believes will bless him as 'its creator and source'. But in realizing a conception that should have remained a masturbatory fantasy, all (as we well know) goes horribly wrong and his 'son' comes to curse rather than to bless him. This mis-conceived plan of Frankenstein's brings us to a key theme of the novel: the 'monstrous' problem of men who want to conceive and have children, but for some reason are no good at being fathers.

Inadequate Fathers

Throughout the text of *Frankenstein* the position of 'father' is severely under question, mainly at two levels: religious and familial. The absence in the novel of a God – 'God the Father', a universal Creator – has been noted already, and this is discussed further in Chapters 9 and 12. The social functioning, or rather malfunctioning, of fathers in the story may seem less easy to pin down, yet once noticed, the absence, narrow-mindedness or ineffectuality of its fathers is striking. In making a contrast between Victor Frankenstein's 'total failure at parenting' and the 'loving fathers' Alphonse Frankenstein and De Lacey, Anne K.

Mellor seems to be drawing out one of the text's important themes, one that has been much discussed by feminist critics, as she says.[5] But her argument that it is 'Frankenstein's failure to mother his child' which puts him at fault, whereas Victor's and Felix's fathers 'assiduously care for their motherless children',[6] is one with which I must take issue. The implication is that these fathers in contrast have successfully taken on the 'mothering' role. But however hard a father may try to take on the role of mother, he can never be a mother. This is because the kind of intimate tie a mother or mother-figure has with its child cannot be replaced by a man, regardless of the intensity of love and social attention which a father might be able to give. It therefore seems pointless to blame Victor Frankenstein for not being something he can never be – even if he (thoughtlessly, unconsciously) imagined he could be both father and mother to a 'new species'. As Victor himself says, 'No *father* could claim the gratitude of his child so completely as I should deserve theirs' (52–3, emphasis added). It is on his shortcomings as a father, and the shortcomings of many of the other males of the text as fathers, that Mary Shelley wants us to focus. It is well worth considering the presentation of some of the men of the text in order to demonstrate this.

Let us begin with the two 'loving fathers', Alphonse Frankenstein and the old De Lacey. Early on in Part One of our close reading I made the point that Alphonse seems to have been a somewhat distant figure for Victor, and a man whose hasty dismissal of Victor's enthusiasm for the old alchemists marks him out as a thoughtless father, rather than one who cares responsibly for his son's proper understanding of things. Furthermore, when he sends him away to Ingolstadt, he is sending him to the very place where Victor's unfortunate 'creative bent' will be put to its best/worst use. In Milton's *Paradise Lost*, God upbraids Adam for allowing Eve to separate from him in the garden of Eden, since this gives Satan in the shape of a serpent the opportunity to seduce her into sin. Something of the same kind of point is being made by Mary Shelley's having Alphonse send Victor away to Ingolstadt, where the knowledge which brings his 'downfall', is imbibed. 'Learn from me', Victor earnestly tells Walton,

if not by my precepts, at least by my example, how dangerous is the acquirement of knowledge and how much happier that man is who believes his native town to be the world, than he who aspires to become greater than his nature will allow. (52)

East West, home's best? To people of traditional cultures and to those enamoured of the bourgeois family (as Mellor – correctly, I believe – argues that Mary Shelley was), this statement represents an outlook on life that is not to be underestimated. A final point on Frankenstein's father is that, even when he comes to take Victor home from his Scottish and Irish ordeals, his greatest concern in the end is to persuade him to marry Elizabeth in order that the Frankenstein family line can be continued, not for any obvious reasons concerning Victor's happiness.

The case of the old De Lacey is perhaps easier to deal with, in that he is almost completely incapable of carrying out his fatherly functions because of his incapacitating blindness. Mary Shelley may have deliberately made him blind so that he will be the only character who can offer sympathy to the hideous-looking Creature. But the portrayal of him as completely dependent upon Felix and Agatha makes him into a figure of impotence, however much he may love his son. He undoubtedly comes across to us as a benign old man putting forward the Godwinian ideal of universal benevolence. But even as a putative paternal agent of such benevolence, he is a figure of passivity.

In terms of passivity there is of course no more inert father in the whole book than Robert Walton's dead parent. And although I pointed out early on in Part One that an important component in the motivation of the explorer's Promethean quest was a wilful determination to challenge his father's 'dying injunction' that he be denied a seafaring life, nevertheless this was, finally, the injunction of a father soon to be dead. In turn, Robert's uncle Thomas seems not to have been too strict in ensuring that the father's wishes were enforced. But then his avuncular role had not been a fatherly one. And since it is his own collection of voyages which excites Robert to thoughts of marine exploration, we may expect that the uncle is anyway somewhat reluctant to discourage the youth from thoughts of seafaring, when he is clearly enamoured of the life himself. It is perhaps significant that no wife of his is mentioned. Uncle Thomas as a frustrated Promethean, perhaps?

Another father in the text who is not merely unsatisfactory but an exploiter to boot is Alphonse's friend, Beaufort. Perhaps embodying in him something of Godwin's incompetency in handling money and his exploitation of Fanny, her half-sister, as a domestic drudge, Mary Shelley here seems to be mounting a critique of fathers once again. This time it is a father who stubbornly seeks to defend his threadbare reputation by escaping from the society he knows and which could actually help him (in the shape of Alphonse), were he to allow it to. Instead, isolated, inactive and self-preoccupied, 'his grief only became more deep and rankling' (32). He turns away from any trust in feelings of sociability, and ends as a hopeless father relying on the miserable efforts of his daughter 'to earn a pittance scarcely sufficient to support life' (32). In giving him a 'proud and unbending disposition' (31), Mary may also have been injecting into Beaufort's character an element of the fiercely independent personality of Godwin's playwright friend, Thomas Holcroft. Holcroft was a fervent unbeliever whom Coleridge once described as 'Fierce, hot, petulant, the very High priest of Atheism', a man who '*hates* God with all his heart, with all his mind, with all his soul & with all his strength'.[7]

On the subject of 'unbending dispositions', there is one other father in Frankenstein whose 'shortcomings' should be mentioned. This is Safie's father, whom it is perhaps enough to characterize as a scheming figure of 'oriental despotism'. As has already been pointed out, for many writers of Mary Shelley's period, the deployment of this kind of stereotyped figure from 'tyrannical' Islamic culture was a commonplace way of mounting a critical gesture against what was conceived of as some rigid aspect of one's own culture, in this case, its patriarchal character. Here the father conforms so much to the 'unbending' demands of patriarchal fatherhood that he is an abuser of it.

It has been mentioned before how the behaviour of Victor Frankenstein sometimes echoes the way Rousseau describes himself in *Reveries of a Solitary Walker*, which Mary Shelley had been reading in 1816. Although she also seems to have drawn on Rousseau's educational theories in his *Émile* (1762), where he had argued that 'a man left to himself from birth would be more of a monster than the rest',[8] in her later biographical essay on the Romantic philosopher she is extremely critical of his own real-life performance as a father. Rousseau admitted in his ninth Promenade that the action of putting his own children in a foundling home had been 'enough to get me misrepresented as an unnatural father'. Mary Shelley was clearly out of sympathy with his complaint, saying in her essay: 'Our first duty is to render those to whom we gave birth, wise, virtuous and happy – Rousseau failed in this.'[9] She is extremely sympathetic to his philosophical vision in most other ways, but believes that his example proves that 'a father is not to be trusted for natural instincts towards his offspring'. And the same might be said of Frankenstein's failure, when she comments on Rousseau as a father: '. . . can we wonder that his after course was replete with sorrow?'[10]

Language without the father in *Frankenstein*

When discussing the Creature's enthusiastic encounter with what he calls the 'godlike science' of human speech in Part One, I quoted Locke's observation that language was 'the great instrument and common tie of society'. I went on to say that the very impossibility of the Creature's being able to learn human speech by passively 'listening in' and mimicking words that describe things he has no way of linking to his own experience – this not only illustrates Locke's central idea, but serves to point up the crucial fact that 'being human' requires *active* participation in a shared language community. The Creature tells us that it was by 'great application' that he 'discovered the names that were given to some of the most familiar objects of discourse' by the De Lacey family (109). But no amount of 'application' will enable the Creature to gain real access to meaning, to make 'the word' his own, unless he is actively involved, through experience, in linking together what one twentieth-century linguist sees as the two dimensions of a word necessary for the real signifying/affective experience of meaning to be apprehended.

Intuitively, Mary Shelley was exploring territory that was not to be developed in linguistic studies for at least another hundred years, until, in fact, the work of the Russian Mikhail Bakhtin appeared. As David Lodge has pointed out, for Bakhtin the word is a

> two sided *act* . . . It is determined equally by whose word it is and for whom it is meant . . . A word is territory *shared* by both addresser and addressee, by the speaker and his interlocutor.[11]

Essentially, then, the Creature *over*hears others involved in this kind of activity, but he himself only really hears and experiences words in the abstract, within his own private world. He desperately *wants* to join in the shared life of the De Laceys, whose 'articulate sounds' he notices produce 'pleasure or pain, smiles or sadness, in the minds and countenances of the hearers' (108). Though conveyed as a rural idyll, in linguistic terms it is a (public) language community from which his (private) desires are excluded. All that he learns about the public world of human values, social systems and governments are conveyed to him through his books and Safie's lessons. These he cannot be reconciled to while he is denied social recognition and esteem as a human. And he never achieves these things. In many ways this kind of enclosed privacy is also experienced by his creator Frankenstein, who admits early on in the novel that neither the structure of languages, nor the code of governments, nor the politics of various states possessed attractions for me. It was the secrets of heaven and earth that I desired to learn ... (37)

In his essay on *Frankenstein* utilizing the psychoanalytic theory of Jacques Lacan, David Collings has taken this evident division between the public realm and the private in the book to be reproducing what Lacan calls the Symbolic and Imaginary orders. 'Lacan's theory of the Imaginary and Symbolic orders,' he says, 'makes apparent a pattern within the novel that pre-Lacanian psychoanalytic readings missed: its persistent contrast between the world of the mirror-image, or double (the Imaginary), and that of kinship, language, and social life (the Symbolic). Yet the novel', he goes on,

demonstrates that the Symbolic order's insistence on denying the Imaginary comes at the enormous cost of excluding the maternal body. As Mary Shelley's novel suggests that the situation Lacan describes is neither inevitable nor necessary, it opens up new directions for psychoanalytic theory.[12]

Whether *Frankenstein* opens up new directions for psychoanalytic theory or not is not my concern here. What does concern me is to emphasize my sense of a text in which the figure of the father – what Lacan calls the 'paternal metaphor' – is seen to be failing. What Mary Shelley is achieving in her novel is not so much an exclusion of 'the maternal body' as a discovery that the paternal body – masculinity if you like – is losing its power, its potency. Man – both 'God the Father' in the transcendent symbolic sense, and man in the familial/social setting – is losing his potency. In deciding to destroy his Creature's would-be wife, Frankenstein is clearly displaying a fear of where 'monstrous' sexual reproduction might lead; but this is merely an extension of his originally 'monstrous' reluctance to indulge his sexual feelings towards Elizabeth, and instead to produce a 'son' of his own, avoiding the use of a real female womb. Frankenstein and Walton cannot be 'men' in the conventional sense, because they deny the reality of women.

Collings says there is a 'private, almost delusional relation between Victor and the monster'.[13] But it is more than that. The adolescent-minded Victor cannot cope with females – just as Walton cannot – and so, turning his back on the Symbolic order of society, social sympathies, and so on, succeeds in translating his masturbatory dream of creating 'beautiful' life into monstrous reality. The denial of the female is repeated when he refuses to allow his Creature's 'Eve' to live. But the consequence of such a fundamental denial of free sexual functioning – or perhaps one should even say a disavowal, or renunciation of this, more precisely – is to leave Frankenstein and the Creature as 'clingers to the outside of words' (to paraphrase Virginia Woolf). Through Frankenstein's self-denial of normal sexuality and then the denial of the same for his Creature, their only resource is words without a potent language, a speech and a language where the 'other' – the 'third' which makes society (as opposed to a duo, a double) possible – is put out of reach. This is the meaning of the text's cleverly ironic play on words given at Frankenstein's expense in his response to the Creature's state- ment that 'I shall be with you on your wedding-night'. Victor says of this statement, 'such was my sentence'. Yes, it *was* his sentence! He has ensured his own entrapment in words by denying the demands of the desiring body.

But the 'private' relation between Frankenstein and the Creature, trapped as they are within the same 'sentence', is more than delusional – it is psychotic. As Anthony Wilden has said (following Lacan), psychotic language is language where

a 'regression' to treating words like things leaves the speaker in the grip of an uncontrollable shifting between opposites . . .

. . . there is no dialectic, no 'dia-logos', because [the discourse of the psychotic], in Lacan's view, is composed of nothing but words, rather than the Word.[14]

Frankenstein has trouble in distinguishing words from things, a diffi- culty he ensures his Creature inherits through his monstrous isolation. But the Word which really carries weight involves language and speech which, to return to the sanity of Bakhtin, functions rather in the following way:

The word in living conversation is directly, blatantly, oriented towards a future answer word: it provokes an answer, anticipates it and structures itself in the answer's direction.[15]

Literary texts are always influenced to some degree or another by literary texts that have gone before. In giving shape, meaning and significance to their writing, authors will make allusions and references to other works, consciously or unconsciously echoing a predecessor or precursor. In the case of Mary Shelley's *Frankenstein* these influences are numerous. This is no doubt partly explained by the fact that this was her first book, written while still in her teens, when the 'materials' which she described in her 1831 Introduction as being necessary before 'invention' could take place were to a great extent provided by her reading. As we have already seen in Part One, even the ideas and aspirations of Frankenstein's Creature are in large part shaped by his reading (Plutarch, Goethe, Milton, Volney). With a stimulating and rigorous education firstly provided by her father, the voluminously well-read radical philosopher and novelist William Godwin, and the extensive programme of reading she undertook in the company of Percy Shelley from 1814, there is little doubt that for her age Mary had one of the most compendiously informed and intellectually capable minds of her generation. Smarting after an argument with the precocious seventeen-year-old in the year of her elopement with Percy, the latter's friend and trainee lawyer Thomas Jefferson Hogg realized, in the words of Richard Holmes, he would do better in the future 'by omitting to run the Wollstonecraft gauntlet'.[1]

Knowing that Mary was an intelligent and compendious reader means it is valuable to identify and explore some of the texts which had a major influence upon *Frankenstein*. What were these? I have already mentioned how the poetry of Milton, Coleridge, Byron and Shelley, and the writings of Rousseau and John Locke, found their way into her novel, and to some of these I shall want to return below. In the sketch of the 1816 Geneva summer she gave in her 1831 Introduction to the novel, she cited conversations she believed had occurred then between Percy Shelley and Lord Byron concerning 'the nature of the principle of life'. These she claimed formed the primary 'material' that set her mind to work on her story, eventually inspiring her to imagine how 'the component parts of a creature might be manufactured, brought together, and endued with vital warmth' (8). In terms of 'new historicist' literary theory, this form of stimulus could be accommodated into a wider notion of intertextuality by seeing it as part of a 'significant interconnectedness between a literary text and nonliterary discussions of or discourses about contemporary culture'.[2] But I leave that level of contextualizing to Chapters 10 and 11. Here I shall concentrate on literary texts *per se*.

By Mary Shelley's own account the source which initially prompted Lord Byron to suggest the 'ghost-story contest' was a group of German ghost stories, translated into French, which the Byron–Shelley parties read to each other during that 1816 'wet, ungenial summer' at Geneva. She describes two of the ghost stories in her 1831 Introduction. The first tells of 'the *History of the Inconstant Lover*, who, when he thought to clasp the bride to whom he had pledged his vows, found himself in the arms of the pale ghost of her whom he had deserted' (7). Since she tells us in the same Introduction that the Frankenstein story was begun with a transcription of those 'grim terrors of my waking dream' (9) constituting the beginning of Volume One, Chapter V ('It was on a dreary night of November . . .', etc.) it is not so surprising to find an echo of this story in the account Frankenstein gives of the nightmare he had when trying, through sleep, to escape the Creature he brought to life. Victor has been an 'inconstant lover' by neglecting Elizabeth in favour of the Creature of his 'beautiful dream'. And instead of his lover turning into a 'pale ghost', Victor's intended bride becomes transformed into an image of his dead mother's corpse. His conscience, deeply guilty for neglecting his family, is clearly punishing him by brandishing what to him is a primary image of nurturance and generosity – his mother – now dead and gone, and out of comforting reach.

The other story Mary Shelley recounts is also closely connected with *Frankenstein*, for it is about 'the sinful founder of his race whose miserable doom it was to bestow the kiss of death on all the younger sons of his fated house' (7). In the novel, Frankenstein also brings about the death of his young brother William, albeit indirectly. It will be remembered that Victor's 'sinful' goal had been to break through the 'ideal bounds' of life and death so as to create a 'new species' which 'would bless me as its creator and source; many happy and excellent natures would owe their being to me' (52). Of course, forgetting what *he* owes to the first of his new species finally brings reprisal on his own family and friends, extinguishing the lives of all but one of the 'fated house' of Frankenstein.

In Part One we have already encountered Mary's use of several of Percy Shelley's poems. For instance, she deployed *Alastor* to characterize the obsessive psychology that lay behind his erection of the Creature. In the previous chapter the concept of awful Power which she drew on from *Mont Blanc* to symbolize the life-force of the Creature was also discussed. And Frankenstein focusses his bitter regret over where the tragic unruliness of his imaginative impulses have led him by quoting from *Mutability*. But in the first stanza of this poem that he repeats to Walton we find the following line: 'We rest; a dream has the power to poison sleep' (94). This is very reminiscent of an important passage in Milton's *Paradise Lost*, a source for *Frankenstein* we have bumped into frequently in Part One, and one we must now consider in more depth. For of the two major literary sources for Mary Shelley's novel – the other is William Godwin, to be considered next – Milton is the one to whom Mary Shelley is most indebted.

Paradise Lost

Intent on corrupting the innocence of God's 'new race called Man' in revenge for his expulsion from Heaven (II.348), Satan determines that the unconscious desires of Eve's dream-life offer the best point of entry for success in this and proceeds to 'poison' her sleep in the guise of a 'squat toad':

> . . . close at the ear of Eve;
> Assaying by his devilish art to reach
> The organs of her fancy, and with them forge
> Illusions as he list, phantasms and dreams . . .
> (IV.800–803)

These efforts to arouse Eve's carnal desires are of course successful. So that Milton is then able – more or less – to 'blame' her (gendered) emotional weakness for the Fall of Man. His famous intention in the poem was to 'justify the ways of God to men'. But this he succeeds in doing only at the expense of exposing for the careful reader just how vulnerable the Christian belief in God has become to the power of human desire in late seventeenth-century English culture. All such readers come to discover how Milton undermines his intentions, in two main ways. Firstly he has the supposedly omnipotent, immutable and infinite being of God represented in the form of a speaking character who displays human emotions and impulses. This not only subverts the credibility of God as infinite Creator of the universe, but puts him on the same level as his evil opponent Satan, Milton's fallen Lucifer. This is the second undermining point. Milton demoralizes and finally crushes

Satan to make his remoulding of the biblical story 'work', yet to the reader – and in particular to later rebellious Romantic writers like Godwin, P.B. Shelley and Byron – Satan actually comes across as the most impactful character of the poem. As William Blake famously characterizes this effect for us, despite his intentions Milton demonstrated with his epic poem that he 'was of the Devil's party without knowing it'.

For the Enlightenment-influenced and atheistic Percy Shelley this fact made Satan unproblematically into the justified and virtuous rebel, with God seen as an evil tyrant. For Mary Shelley such a simplistic reading was not possible. Her deployment of *Paradise Lost* for *Frankenstein* shows that, as Christopher Small observes, the 'moral ambiguity was restored' of the former text.[3] But this moral ambiguity is achieved in a most radical way. She does not simply wish to reverse the moral roles of God and the Devil as P.B. Shelley and other male Romantic political radicals might be inclined to do. Rather, to accomplish her ironic critique of the power-mongering patriarchy around her she excludes God from the text altogether. George Levine sums up this exclusion well by noting that *Frankenstein* echoes 'with the language and the narrative of *Paradise Lost*, but it is *Paradise Lost* without angels, or devils, or God'.[4] This absence of God in *Frankenstein* has been mentioned several times already and is a crucial topic to which I return in Chapter 12. So how does Mary Shelley get Milton's poem to work for her, given her radical use of it?

The first reference to *Paradise Lost* in the novel comes with the epigraph to the 1818 edition:

> Did I request thee, Maker, from my clay
> To mould me man? Did I solicit thee
> From darkness to promote me? –

This is part of a long lament spoken by Adam in Book X.743–5, in which he bemoans his fall from the innocence of Paradise and what he sees as his hopeless, unredeemable state. In *Frankenstein* the lines are clearly meant to apply to the miserable condition of Mary Shelley's 'Adam', the Creature that Victor Frankenstein has manufactured. In turn Frankenstein functions as the god-figure of the novel, as is made explicit in the Creature's appeal to him:

Remember, that I am thy creature; I ought to be thy Adam, but I am rather the fallen angel, whom thou drivest from joy for no misdeed. (96–7)

So here there is a complication. Frankenstein has acted like a god, but he is not like the God of *Paradise Lost*. When Milton's God creates a female partner for Adam, then offers him and Eve redemption for the sin of eating lustfully of the Tree of Knowledge, he does this by having the Archangel Michael tell Adam that though he must leave Paradise, he is to discover and possess 'A paradise within thee, happier far' (XII.587). There is here a sense in which a spiritual value is still available to be shared by God and man. But Victor Frankenstein can offer no form of redemption because, as Paul A. Cantor has perceptively put it, in Mary Shelley's version of the creation myth, 'the creation becomes identified with the fall,' a 'gnostic twist'[5] ensuring that the self-regarding motivations of the creator produce a spiritual vacuum where no life worthy of the name can flourish. Victor has relinquished all claim to spiritual value by the creation and rejection of a being for whom he feels (ultimately) no responsibility and with whom he feels no identity or sympathy. As he tells the Creature so significantly, 'There can be no *community* between you and me; we are enemies' (97, emphasis added). But if there can be no community between them, there is nevertheless the paradox that in their isolated conditions they share very similar – though negative – experiences. Hence the so-called *doppelgänger* effect already mentioned. Instead of the 'paradise within' of Milton's poem, they both partake of Satanic attributes: 'I, like the arch-fiend, bore a hell within me,' says the Creature (132), while his creator states how he was 'cursed by some devil, and carried about with me my eternal hell' (197). Cantor sums up with admirable brevity how this double effect has been achieved:

Frankenstein retells *Paradise Lost* as if the being who fell from heaven and the being who created the world of man were one and the same. In *Frankenstein* one can no longer speak of an original divine plan of creation which is perverted by a demonic being; the plans of Mary Shelley's creator-figure are both divine and demonic from the beginning.[6]

So it does seem the case that Frankenstein and his Creature are in many ways doubles of each other, tarred as they are with the same Satanic brush. Yet of course they are in no way *completely* alike. As we have already discussed, Mary Shelley was at pains to show that her monster was a noble savage whose capacity for goodness and eagerness for society and knowledge potentially made him a being of great transcendent spiritual quality. And this is shown to be the case in the episode on the mountain when the Creature insists that Frankenstein hear his story before rashly condemning him. He says to Frankenstein:

'The sun is yet high in the heavens; before it descends to hide itself beyond yon snowy precipices, and illuminate another world, you will have heard my story and can decide.' (98)

This is a further clever allusion to *Paradise Lost* – and more. In Book V of the poem God sends the angel Raphael down to Paradise to inform an ignorant Adam of his history and place in the order of things, 'and whatever else may avail Adam to know'. Halfway through the Book Raphael halts his discourse, but a curious Adam insists he continue with the story, saying that he has:

> . . . more desire to hear, if thou consent,
> The full relation, which must needs be strange,
> Worthy of sacred silence to be heard;
> And we have yet large day, for scarce the sun
> Hath finished half his journey, and scarce begins
> His other half in the great zone of heav'n.
>
> (V. 555–60)

Mary Shelley has inverted the Miltonic roles of divine messenger and ignorant mortal. In doing so she not only strengthens our sense that Frankenstein is an incompetent and weak creator-figure, but also suggests that the Creature perhaps has something of the angelic in him, something of the divine substance to impart to his wanting creator.

Using Milton in this way is a brilliantly inspired method of taking the story forward, and it will finally have the desired effect of delivering the Creature to us as a being of heroic potential, rather than as simply a victim of circumstance. In a book which otherwise reveals the novels of her father Godwin as the most powerful narrative influence, it is this quality of transcendent potential in the Creature which sets her text apart from those of her father. As I shall argue, Mary could, as a relatively 'emancipated' female of the early nineteenth century, deal with emotions and desire in a way that her Calvinistically trained father found impossible. And yet, to get to the point where I can argue this properly, we must first of all acknowledge the deep literary debt that Mary did in fact owe to her father's work.

William Godwin

When Mary Shelley dedicated her novel to William Godwin, she did not do this because she was a dutiful daughter, for as Chris Baldick has observed, she forfeited that title when she eloped with P.B. Shelley in 1814. It was because, as Baldick correctly states, 'Godwin was in so many ways the novel's intellectual begetter.'[7] One of the first critics to notice this literary kinship was Sir Walter Scott.

Although Scott dominated the scene as best-selling prose author in the first decades of the nineteenth century, it is not generally known that (according to his friend **James Ballantyne's** personal report) Sir Walter

greatly preferred Mrs Shelley's *Frankenstein* to any of his own romances. I remember one day, when Mr Erskine and I were dining with him, either immediately before or immediately after the publication of one of the best of the latter, and were giving it the high praise we thought it deserved, he asked us abruptly whether we had read *Frankenstein*. We answered that we had not. 'Ah', he said, 'have patience, read *Frankenstein*, and you will be better able to judge of —.'

This may have been false modesty on Scott's part, but I think not. My sense is that he felt *Frankenstein* represented a publishing achievement quite beyond his own capability. This comes across in the lengthy review he wrote of the novel, published in Blackwood's *Edinburgh Magazine* of March 1818. From the outset Scott states his difficulty in being able to categorize the 'species' – his word – to which *Frankenstein* belongs. It conforms to a class of fiction, he says, that has sometimes been applied to

the purposes of political satire, and sometimes to the general illustration of the powers and workings of the human mind. Swift, Bergerac, and others, have employed it for the former purpose, and a good illustration of the latter is the well-known *St Leon* of William Godwin . . .
. . . *Frankenstein* is a novel upon the same plan with *St Leon*.

One may wonder what the features of Godwin's *St Leon* (1799) were that led Scott to believe Mary Shelley was 'modelling' her own novel on it. Especially as his intriguing phrase, the 'general illustration of the powers . . . of the human mind' might almost have been lifted from one of Godwin's chapter headings in *Political Justice*. Perhaps the most obvious similarity is the device employed in both novels, whereby their heroes, possessed of 'superhuman' powers which each believes will benefit mankind, proceed to exploit them – only to find their ideas have seriously backfired. Frankenstein discovers how to bestow 'animation on lifeless matter', and creates a man he is completely ill-equipped to care for, with the result that an alienated and resentful Creature brings ruin down on the head of his creator, family and friends. In the case of St Leon, when he acquires the secrets of the 'philosopher's stone' and the 'elixir of life' and attempts to use these gifts for the good of mankind, all his efforts produce misunderstanding, danger and unhappiness. Both men become intoxicated by the prospects which the use of their superhuman powers hold out, and believe that by utilizing them they can benefit mankind: but both men fail. Why do they fail?

Two key features of the situations of both characters from the time they become possessed of their respective powers is that they are compelled (1) to abandon their capacity for human sympathy, and (2) to operate in secret. In order to gain his powers, St Leon is sworn to an oath of the utmost secrecy. His consequent mysterious behaviour alien- ates him from his family, causes his only son's departure, brings about the illness and death of his wife, and is the occasion for a relentless series of persecutions which harass him across Europe. As we have seen, Victor Frankenstein's inability to tell Clerval, Elizabeth or indeed anyone about his predicament, following the murder of his little brother by the Creature he has created, means that the latter is never brought into any productive relation with society. He is neither nurtured, nor, when things have gone too far, stopped in his tracks from creating further mayhem. He is like Samuel Beckett's man of action – absurdly unable to act.

Where – we might ask – does this compulsion to 'not tell' really come from? And why is it such a powerfully arresting factor in both texts? Indeed, if the ground plots of each are designed, as Scott suggests, to effect an 'illustration of the powers . . . of the human mind', just what kind of psychological 'powers' are we here looking at? Of what 'species' is the psychology driving along these novels, at a time when the 'psychological novel' seems hardly to have been born? One obvious place to begin tracing the source of this psychology is in the work of Godwin. But not in *St Leon*. Rather we must look at the novel which established his literary fame, *Caleb Williams* (1794). For if any novel of the Romantic period can lay claim to being the first 'psychological novel', it is that one. Let us see why.

The plot of *Caleb Williams* revolves around high-minded Squire Falkland's anxious attempts to keep secret the fact that he is a murderer. His insatiably curious servant Caleb – who, we should note, *vis-à-vis* Victor Frankenstein, describes himself as 'a sort of a natural philoso- pher' desiring to trace 'the variety of effects which might be produced from given causes' – eventually and mischievously wheedles the secret out of his master. But then he lives to regret it, since Falkland, desperate to defend his reputation, will go to any lengths to enforce Caleb's silence. For Godwin in the early 1790s, such concern with 'silencing' had specific historical roots. As a close follower and supporter of the French Revolution, he was horrified when a fearful British government began sponsoring a 'media campaign' against the political radical Thomas Paine when Part Two of his *Rights of Man* was published in 1792. To escape prosecution for treason, Paine had fled to France. Early in 1793, a week before Godwin finished *Political Justice*, his own radical though more philosophical onslaught on a deeply unequal society, he wrote a series of letters to the press, all relating to the defence of his favourite Enlightenment weapons in the rational struggle for the reign of 'independent man': the freedoms of 'opinion' and 'speech'. As he advanced with the writing of *Caleb Williams* during 1793, the process of silencing the radicals deepened, eventually culminating in the so-called 'Gagging Acts' of 1795. Such silencing comes to operate at the very heart of Godwin's novel, written between February 1793 and May 1794, at the height of the Terror. But it operates in a way that requires careful analysis.

Falkland catches the obsessively curious Caleb in the act of opening his mysterious trunk – to which Caleb says he has been drawn 'by some secret fatality' – in the very same way Frankenstein characterizes his being drawn to his life-creating experiments. This act of Caleb's, *vis-à-vis* Frankenstein's experiments, is something that he not only in retrospect calls 'monstrous', but which he evokes with as numerous an array of metaphors to describe his inner state at the time as there are names given to the unnamed Creature in Mary Shelley's book. It was, he says, the 'moment of an instantaneous impulse', a 'passing alienation of mind', 'in some sort an act of insanity' – and so on. Falkland has finally confessed himself a murderer to the probing secretary, but the price to be paid for this knowledge is grim, as Caleb gloomily reports:

I had made myself a prisoner, in the most intolerable sense of that term, for years – perhaps for the rest of my life. Though my prudence and discretion should be invariable, I must remember that I should have an overseer, vigilant from conscious guilt, full of resentment at the unjustifiable means by which I had extorted from him a confession, and whose lightest caprice might at any time decide upon every thing that was dear to me. The vigilance even of a public and systematical despotism is poor, compared with a vigilance which is thus goaded by the most anxious passions of the soul. Against this species of persecution I knew not how to invent a refuge.[8]

At a time when, as Godwin says in the Preface he restored to his novel for the second edition, 'Terror was the order of the day', what we find him doing, instead of sinking into despair at the way radical hopes for political change are being dashed, is rather to become *fascinated* by the sense of empty resentful impotence that this situation has engendered in him. To simplify very drastically, a French Revolution to which he and many others had looked with enormous expectation had now turned 'bad'.

The consequences of such a shift into terror for the British political reform movement was disastrous. Government coercion and control did not merely have the effect of discrediting the arguments of the political radicals. For the novel-writing Godwin, who, in his *Political Justice*, had delivered a whole treatise confidently predicated on the claims of Reason for a better society, it forced him into a mode of textual investment that actually reproduced the force of this political coercion. In this sense, Marilyn Butler is correct to describe *Caleb Williams* as a novel which 'enacts coercion'. But that coercion we must explore, elaborate, and attempt to name. 'Word divinities' like Truth and Virtue had functioned in *Political Justice* as privileged signifiers that the Enlightenment philosopher Godwin uttered with a simple and unproblematic confidence. He had proclaimed, as if quoting a mathematical axiom:

Sound reasoning and truth, when adequately communicated, must always be victorious over error: Sound reasoning and truth are capable of being so communicated. Truth is omnipotent: The vices and moral weakness of man are not invincible: Man is perfectible, or in other words susceptible of perpetual improvement.

But the coercion 'working' *Caleb Williams*, written immediately after *Political Justice*, shows there to be a crisis now occurring in Godwin's system of signification. This is what is at the heart of the novel's repetitive 'can't tell' strategy, a pattern repeated in *St Leon* and in *Frankenstein*. Caleb 'can't tell' anyone the 'secret' that Falkland is a murderer. He cannot tell Falkland's brother of his dilemma, or anyone else, including Laura, the Mary Wollstonecraft figure added for the third edition of the novel in 1797.

However, Laura *is* able to get to the heart of the problem, when Caleb, having escaped to Romantic and rural Wales to forget his past and start anew, cannot. Fumbling for words to explain himself after Laura, shocked, has read about his being wanted in a government pamphlet, he is desperate to establish his 'virtue', yet is compelled to repeat the old 'can't tell' formula. At this point the text offers a major clue about the key feature of what has become the novel's maddeningly compelling neurotic mechanism to make 'bad' repetitions. The 'difference' that starts loosening the text up at this point is captured in Laura's simple and direct statement to the fumbling Caleb: 'Virtue, sir, consists in actions, and not in words.' One can almost hear the shrewdly perceptive Mary Wollstonecraft playfully delivering these lines to a Godwin who in serious discussion – if we are to believe an anecdote of his friend Charles Lamb – invariably prefaced his responses with the dismaying phrase, 'Of course it depends how one *defines* the problem of . . .'

This brings us back to considering Godwin the author, a man whose character typology was deeply invested by Enlightenment values and signification. It is this investment which links Mary Shelley to Godwin and which allows us to call *Frankenstein* a Godwinian novel. Yet it is an investment which also lies at the root of the crucial *difference* between the two major novels of father and daughter, too. It is the loss of the Enlightenment signifier, carrier of sympathy and optimism, which creates the pain and anxiety afflicting Caleb, Squire Falkland – and Frankenstein too. But the desires animating the Creature in *Franken- stein* are always – potentially at least – of a different order from those propelling along these driven characters. Godwin, whose fiction ex- plores the emotionally crippling effect that deep investment in the soul- chilling doctrines of ultra-Calvinist Sandemanianism had had on him, was compelled to write novels repeating a story of loss and exclusion. *Frankenstein* shows us that Mary Shelley, though in many ways her 'father's daughter', was a personality animated by different concerns – in particular ones which stemmed from her being the daughter of Mary Wollstonecraft.

And so we move on to an examination of the biographical context for *Frankenstein*.

Part Three: Contexts

It is not my concern in this chapter to provide an exhaustive account of Mary Shelley's life. This can be read now in many of the proliferating biographical and literary studies which have appeared over the last twenty years (and some of which are listed in 'Suggested Further Reading' at the end of this book). Neither is it my intention to explore how *Frankenstein* and its Creature can be seen as a kind of imaginative compensation for the deficiencies Mary Shelley had suffered in her family life, 'pregnant' with possibility as this suggestive approach might be. Certainly the subject of birth, treated so ably by feminist critics, is important, although my own version of what 'birth' is really registered by *Frankenstein* is reserved for Chapter 12. But what I think the close reading of Part One, the interpretative discussion of Part Two and now the contextual accounts of Part Three will rather come to show is that *Frankenstein* is one of the most protean novel texts to have appeared in English, and is susceptible of many readings, none of which can be considered as absolutely 'correct'. Which is how, for any profound work of art, things of course should be. What is more, since previous chapters have already to a degree introduced some of the important figures in Mary Shelley's life up to the time of first publication of *Frankenstein* – above all, Mary Wollstonecraft, William Godwin and Percy Shelley – I prefer here merely to elaborate a little more on the part these people and some others played in helping to shape Mary Shelley's life and character up to 1818.

Mary Shelley begins her Introduction to the 1831 edition of *Frankenstein* by repeating the question 'so very frequently asked' of her over the years since 1818: 'How I, then a young girl, came to think of and to dilate upon so very hideous an idea?' Her answer begins: 'It is not singular that, as the daughter of two persons of distinguished literary celebrity, I should very early in life have thought of writing' (5). She thus states a very obvious yet profound fact. That as the daughter of what Anne Mellor has called 'the most famous radical literary marriage of eighteenth-century England',[1] and which Richard Holmes dubs 'a significant new marriage between Imagination and Reason',[2] she was the product of a physical and cultural match of which extraordinary expectations could and would be entertained, not least by herself.

Mary Shelley was born on 30 August 1797 in Chalton Street, off Euston Road, near today's new British Library at St Pancras in London. Her mother Mary Wollstonecraft had achieved fame as the author of *A Vindication of the Rights of Woman* (1792), a text 'now recognized as the progenitor of the women's rights movement',[3] but which at the time made her a notorious figure for drawing attention to women's second-class status in society. She was a woman of extraordinary accomplishment in other ways too. She had gained her intellectual and political education from Dr Richard Price and other Radical Dissenters in the London suburb of Newington Green, where she kept a small school with her sister in the 1780s. She then became an author, publishing as an educationalist (*Thoughts on the Education of Daughters*, 1787), a novelist (*Mary, a Fiction*, 1788), a writer for children (*Original Stories from Real Life*, 1788), and as a reviewer for Joseph Johnson's *Analytic Review*. And then, at a time when common men had failed as yet to secure the vote in any measure, she published the first radical response to Edmund Burke's *Reflections on the Revolution in France*, the 1790 blueprint of British conservatism for some generations to come. This was *A Vindication of the Rights of Men* (1790), which appeared some months before the first part of Thomas Paine's *The Rights of Man* came out. It was written with a characteristic 'glow of indignation' (as she put it) at Burke's 'unprincipled filial affection [for] the venerable vestiges of ancient days'. Attacking the principle of hereditary property and honours, she insisted that

there are rights which men inherit at their birth, as rational creatures, who were raised above the brute creation by their improveable faculties; and that, in receiving these, not from their forefathers but, from God, prescription can never undermine natural rights.[4]

After receiving his own rather unconventional education Frankenstein's Creature would no doubt have agreed.

Her argument in the book that 'true happiness' can only arise 'from the friendship and intimacy ... enjoyed by equals' was one she took further in *A Vindication of the Rights of Woman*, yet it was to be another four years before she achieved such happiness – all too short-lived – in her own life. First she took the daring step of going alone to Paris to witness at first-hand the progress of a French Revolution she and so many of her radical friends believed was heralding a new dawn in the history of humanity. She met and mixed with leading Girondin revolutionaries and became for a period prominent in a group of mainly British and American exiles and expatriates. One of these, an

American merchant adventurer and radical writer called Gilbert Imlay, she fell in love with. When the fall of the Girondins came and the Terror deepened in 1794, they made the Romantic decision to emigrate to the United States with their illegitimate baby Fanny, much like the characters in Imlay's novel, *The Emigrants*. But before this could happen, Imlay seems to have used his long business trips in France and beyond as an excuse to extricate himself from the relationship. Mary Wollstonecraft took their daughter with her to Scandinavia in a brave attempt to help with his business, but when she returned to meet him in London he had betrayed their relationship by initiating another affair. When the relationship seemed finally to have collapsed she grew desperate and made what was a second suicide attempt, throwing herself off Putney Bridge, having first walked up and down in the rain to weigh down her clothes. It was the lowest point in her existence. As Richard Holmes says, 'Everything she believed in, and above all her vision of woman's independence and equality, had been tested to breaking point.'[5] Yet having survived her suicide attempt when boatmen rescued and revived her, she opted once again for life, and this time found love as well.

William Godwin had first met Mary Wollstonecraft at a dinner given by publisher Joseph Johnson in 1791, when she monopolized the conversation with her eager feminist talk. Godwin was more than irritated, since he wanted to listen to the star guest of the occasion, Thomas Paine. In January 1795, soon after the suicide attempt, they met again, this time at the home of Mary's friend and Godwin's disciple, the novelist Mary Hays. She was clearly drawn to the philosopher-novelist, for after a period of some weeks' recovery in the country, she boldly and characteristically paid him a lone visit at his Chalton Street home. In the meantime, Godwin had obtained an advance copy of her *Letters Written during a Short Residence in Sweden, Norway, and Denmark*, which Richard Holmes describes as 'the most imaginative English travel book since Sterne's *A Sentimental Journey* (1768)'.[6] At a time when Pitt's 'Gagging Acts' were all but throttling British political radicalism, Godwin now found the more Romantic side of his otherwise militantly rationalistic character yielding to a new influence in his life. 'If ever there was a book calculated to make a man fall in love with its author,' he wrote later, 'this appears to me to be the book. She speaks of her sorrows in a way that fills us with melancholy and dissolves us in tenderness, at the same time that she displays a genius which commands our admiration.'[7] Following her visit, Godwin called on her for tea the next day. They now visited each other regularly, though it was not until August 1796 that they finally became lovers, the climax of an attachment which grew, in Godwin's words,

with equal advances in the mind of each. It would have been impossible for the most minute observer to have said who was before, and who was after. One sex did not take the priority which long-established custom has awarded it, nor the other overstep that delicacy which is so severely imposed.[8]

And then, in a most un-Godwinian passage, the man his friend Charles Lamb dubbed 'the Professor' tells in the most sensuous terms how they secretly became lovers:

It was friendship melting into love. Previously to our mutual declaration, each felt half-assured, yet each felt a certain trembling anxiety to have assurance complete ... Mary rested her head upon the shoulder of her lover, hoping to find a heart with which she might safely treasure her world of affection – fearing to commit a mistake, yet, in spite of her melancholy experience, fraught with that generous confidence, which, in a great soul, is never extinguished. I had never loved till now; or, at least, had never nourished a passion to the same growth, or met with an object so consummately worthy.[9]

Wollstonecraft felt the same about him, had finally found someone who could give her the 'true happiness' she had been seeking 'from the friendship and intimacy . . . enjoyed by equals'.

Only five months before the birth of the future Mary Shelley, Godwin and Wollstonecraft decided to marry, much to the disappointment of their friends and the amusement of Society people. It was felt by the radical intelligentsia to be somehow regrettable that the leaders of the rationalistic New Philosophy should, as William St Clair says, 'be so human as to fall in love'.[10] More importantly, they were both seen to be flying in the face of Godwin's famous view of marriage in *Political Justice* as 'a system of fraud' and 'the most odious of monopolies'. But in urging Godwin to marry her, Wollstonecraft was merely being practical. Books are one thing, but survival is another. She had already been 'left with the baby' once in a society that more and more poured scorn on unmarried mothers, and which was largely geared (who should know it better?) to the economic dominance of men. Godwin put it all more eloquently when he said that 'nothing could have induced me to submit to an institution which I wish to see abolished', but Mary was pregnant, and he wished to protect her happiness, 'which I have no right to injure'.[11] So they married and for five months enjoyed their new-found happiness. Then the severest blow of Godwin's life occurred when Mary died ten days after giving birth to little Mary. The placenta had been retained, and attempts by the doctor to extract it poisoned her blood, which led to a fatal puerperal fever.

This terrible loss not only haunted Godwin for the rest of his life, but was something Mary Shelley also grew up with, was forced to take on. She no doubt embraced the memory of her mother both as an irreplaceable loss, and as a guilty burden – at a time when septicaemia had yet to be discovered she must have subconsciously blamed herself for the death. But she was also encouraged to reverence her mother by Godwin, and through this and reading her writings she embraced Wollstonecraft into her character in ways we can perhaps partly understand, yet hardly hope to feel ourselves. An indication of the mother-reverence that was bred in her by the father is shown in Godwin's last novel, *Deloraine* (1833). Even at seventy-three, Godwin reveals in the portrayal of 'the beautiful Emilia Fitzcharles' both the extraordinary impact his short liaison with Mary Wollstonecraft had had on him, and also a suggestive intimation of how the little Mary would have been encouraged to regard her mother. In Godwin's study at Chalton Street and in all the later houses he lived in, John Opie's now famous portrait of Mary Wollstonecraft occupied a prominent position on the wall. In Godwin's novel, when Deloraine and Emilia leave their little daughter Catherine in the charge of a close friend while they are abroad, the girl is taught to view a picture of her mother, placed in a special alcove, with deep reverence:

Emilia's friend told the child that that was its mother; and, when the child was able to speak, the first articulate sound she uttered, as she saw the picture, or thought of the picture, was, Mamma! ... A curtain was spread before the recess in which the portrait was placed; and this curtain was drawn back with a certain degree of ceremony ... each exhibition concluded with a kind of epilogue, judiciously adapted to the capacity of the spectator, of which Love and a sort of worship formed, if I may express myself, the concluding notes. In quitting the scene, the child was taught to kneel, and join its little hands as in the attitude of supplication ... All this made a deep impression upon the little Catherine.[12]

And, no doubt, if the same routine was initiated in the Godwin household after Mary Wollstonecraft's decease, upon the infant mind of little Mary Godwin too. In another incident of the novel there is little reason to think that Deloraine's memory of Emilia's 'last injunctions' to him before she tragically dies are anything other than a thinly disguised account of the words Mary Wollstonecraft spoke to Godwin just before she died about the future care of baby Mary:

I remembered the last injunctions of the adored partner of my life. She had adjured me to watch anxiously for the welfare of our only child. She had said to me, 'Now that our Catherine is about to be deprived of her mother, it is your office to take care that you discharge to her the duties of both, and be to her a father and a mother.'[13]

Godwin did his best to be a mother and a father both to little Mary and to Fanny when Wollstonecraft died, but soon found himself wilting under the strain. The 'poor children' were suffering for the lack of a mother, and he felt 'totally unfitted to educate them'. He was openly frank about the 'scepticism which perhaps sometimes leads me right in matters of speculation [but] is torment to me when I would attempt to direct the infant mind'. Painfully aware of the uniquely advantaged mother who had been lost, the ex-Dissenting preacher laments the fact that he 'is the most unfit person for this office; she was the best qualified in the world'. As a result, after several refusals from various quarters, in 1801 at the age of forty-five his proposal to a neighbour, Mrs Mary Jane Clairmont, was accepted. The apocryphal words, 'Is it possible that I behold the immortal Godwin?' were supposedly uttered from a neighbouring balcony, and the vain philosophical advocate of universal benevolence could not resist. Mary Jane and the daughter Jane she brought with her were to be the bane of Mary Shelley's life for many years to come. Mary had never known a real mother and she would not find a caring one in the new Mrs Godwin. Yet to her father she became exceptionally devoted, and despite his often cold, insensitive and 'philosophical' manner, she maintained a filial loyalty that lasted for the whole of his long life. In letters to friends she talked of 'my excessive and romantic attachment to my father' and said that: 'Until I met Shelley I could justly say that he [Godwin] was my God ... I remember many childish instances of the excess of attachment I bore him.' Again, if *Deloraine* is to be trusted as biographical guide, this is not surprising, since the widower of Emilia 'gradually came to regard her child as her living representative. I desired to heap all sorts of benefits upon its head. I sought its society, not always, but often ...'[14] In the novella *Mathilda* she wrote after *Frankenstein*, Mary Shelley explored the theme of a father's incestual feelings for his daughter; when she sent the manuscript to Godwin, he was so disgusted he refused to allow publication, and the story only finally appeared in 1959.

These powerful feelings between father and daughter were neutralized throughout Mary Shelley's childhood, for two main reasons: Godwin's essentially undemonstrative, severely Calvinist-trained manner made for a peculiarly detached relationship; and the resentment felt towards her by the stepmother Mrs Godwin meant that hardly a day went by without Mary Wollstonecraft's daughter being admonished for some misdemeanour, real or imaginary. Nevertheless there were compensations in growing up in Godwin's household. She had the run of his enormous library, and the personal tuition of one of the most compendious, orderly and teacherly minds in Britain. In 1805, when the family moved to Skinner Street near Holborn, Godwin and his wife opened a bookshop and began publishing children's books, the most famous of which would be Charles and Mary Lamb's *Tales from Shakespeare* (1807). Encouraged to write by Godwin, the youngest author to appear in print was Mary Godwin herself, whose thirty-nine-quatrain satirical expansion of a Charles Dibdin five-stanza song, 'Mounseer Nongtongpaw', was published by M.J. Godwin's Juvenile Library early in 1808 when she was only eleven. In addition, although political reaction had by the early 1800s plunged Godwin's name into near obscurity, his house was yet visited by some of the most famous writers, artists and scientists of the day. As well as hearing Coleridge recite the whole of the *Ancient Mariner* from behind a sofa – Mrs Godwin threatened to pack the two girls off to bed, but the poet persuaded her to allow Mary and Jane to listen – Mary Godwin would have listened keenly to her father's conversations with such people as William Hazlitt, Charles Lamb, Humphry Davy and many others.

At seventeen Mary wrote: 'I detest Mrs G. She plagues my father out of his life.' But long before this, the time came when the antipathy between Mary and her stepmother was so strong that Godwin was forced to intervene. For him it must have been a regrettable action to take, but for Mary the opportunity for true companionship and freedom – which she never attained in a household where Mrs Godwin's own children were always given preference – came when Godwin asked one of his Scottish admirers if she could stay with his family in Dundee for an extended period. The wealthy merchant William Baxter agreed. Thus it was that Mary found her first great friend in the person of Isabel Baxter, and on the banks of the Tay (as she tells us in her 1831 *Frankenstein* Introduction) discovered 'an eyry of freedom ... where ... I could commune with the creatures of my fancy' (6). In a letter to Baxter, Godwin gives us a good idea of Mary's character as she approached the age of fifteen: 'I am anxious that she should be brought up ... like a philosopher, even like a cynic. It will add greatly to the strength and worth of her character. I shall also observe that she has no love of dissipation, and will be perfectly satisfied with your woods and your mountains.' But he should be warned of her tendency to 'formation of castles in the air: I wish, too, that she should be *excited* to industry. She has occasionally greater perseverance, but occasionally, too, she shows a great need to be aroused . . .' In another letter, Godwin contrasted Mary with her 'indolent' stepsister Fanny by describing the former as 'singularly bold, somewhat imperious, and active of mind. Her desire of knowledge is great, and her perseverance in everything she undertakes almost invincible. My own daughter is, I believe, very pretty . . .'[15] He might almost have added, 'In fact she's inherited all the qualities her mother possessed.'

Upon her return to Skinner Street in 1814 she encountered a young man who very quickly came to believe just this, and as a result drew her into an existence that was to be wild, creative and exhilarating – but also full of disappointment and death. Percy Bysshe Shelley was a hot-headed but eloquent Romantic of nineteen who had attached himself to Godwin as a disciple, often visiting Skinner Street with his young wife Harriet. His ardent hatred of tyranny and his idealistic political notions had caused him, as it had many other young men before him, to be drawn as though by a magnet to Godwin's *Political Justice*, and thence to the ageing philosopher's own house. The now almost forgotten philosophical radical must have more than welcomed the attentions of the young man who considered him 'a luminary too dazzling for the darkness which surrounds him'. He was used to this kind of praise from idealistic youths, but when it came from a young man who had announced in his initial letter that he was 'the heir by entail to an estate of £6,000 per an', the ever-needy Godwin was more than ready to accept this new disciple. And when Percy·dined at Skinner Street in May 1814 to discuss money matters with Godwin, he could not take his eyes off Mary Godwin. The blooming but poised intellectual young woman of sixteen that she had become attracted him from the first – and the feeling quickly became mutual. Here is a brief extract from Hogg's account of a visit they paid to Skinner Street at this time. As he and Shelley waited in Godwin's library, wondering whether the venerable author was at home,

the door was partially and softly opened: a thrilling voice called 'Shelley!' A thrilling voice answered, 'Mary!' And he darted out of the room, like an arrow from the bow of the far-shooting king. A very young female, fair and fair-headed, pale indeed, and with a piercing look, wearing a frock of tartan, an unusual dress in London at that time, had called him out of the room. He was absent a very short time – a minute or two; and then returned. 'Godwin is out; there is no use in waiting.' So we continued our walk along Holborn.

'Who was that, pray?' I asked; 'a daughter?'

'Yes.'
'A daughter of William Godwin?'
'*The daughter of William and Mary.*'[16]

By the end of June, Percy, completely disenchanted with his marriage to Harriet, had become a daily visitor to the house, and was in effect courting young Mary upon their now frequent walks to Mary Wollstonecraft's grave at St Pancras cemetery. Often they were accompanied at a discreet distance by Mary's stepsister Jane Clairmont. Soon they declared their love for each other, and were making love too (though the idea that this was done on top of Wollstonecraft's tombstone, as some claim, will seem a little far-fetched to those who have seen its limited dimensions).

On 28 July 1814 Percy and Mary eloped to the Continent, taking with them Jane, now romantically styling herself 'Claire' Clairmont. Godwin had been outraged when he discovered the amorous entanglement, and even more stunned when he had to deal with the elopement. 'Jane has been guilty of an indiscretion only, Mary has been guilty of a crime' was his grave judgement, a censure that Mary Poovey thinks was to 'haunt Mary Shelley for much of the rest of her life.'[17] Whether this is so or not (it seems doubtful) the Continental 'adventure' which the three undertook turned out to be a pretty miserable affair, although Mary described it later as 'acting a novel, being an incarnate romance' and turned it to useful literary account by publishing *History of a Six Weeks' Tour Through a Part of France, Switzerland, Germany and Holland* in 1817. As her first adult publication, it can in some ways be seen as an attempt to emulate the travel-writing of her mother. But the young threesome had found little enjoyment wandering from European town to town, friendless and with little money. Moreover, Mary found the presence of Claire virtually intolerable. Towards her middle age she wrote: 'Now, I would not go to Paradise with her for a companion – she poisoned my life when young . . . she still has the faculty of making me more uncomfortable than any human being.' At the end of the summer, when they returned to England, Mary and Percy took lodgings which Shelley hardly lived in, pursued as he was by creditors (his father, as outraged as Godwin, had withheld his allowance). Claire had gone home, but Mary refused to do so, and was now estranged from her own family. In February 1815 her first child was born prematurely, and died a few days later, still unnamed. It was the first of many deaths to cast a shadow over her existence. Some days after the death, she wrote in her journal: 'Dream that my little baby came to life again;

that it had only been cold, and that we rubbed it before the fire, and it lived.' For those who wish to look for a preoccupation with 'death coming to life' in Mary Shelley's biography, perhaps they have little further to look than this.

In August 1815 Mary and Percy set up house in Bishops Gate, near Windsor. Then in the first two weeks of September, only nine months before Mary began writing *Frankenstein*, Percy, his friend Thomas Love Peacock, Mary, and Charles Clairmont (brother of Claire) all embarked from Old Windsor on a boating expedition. Mary may be alluding to this trip in Walton's first letter to his sister. The 'enticements' of discovery, which Walton says are sufficient to enable him to overcome all fear of danger and death, have also induced him, he says, to commence the voyage

with the joy a child feels when he embarks in a little boat, with his holiday mates, on an expedition of discovery up his native river. (14)

Organized by Peacock, the Bishops Gate party had set out in a small wherry to try and reach the source of Percy's own 'native river', the Thames. Narrowly prevented from attaining their goal by thick weeds above Lechlade, a delighted Percy wanted to prolong the expedition by taking diverse canals and rivers up into Scotland, in what eventually would have become a 2,000-mile round trip. But they had insufficient money for the Severn canal sailing fee, and were forced to turn back, with Shelley continuing to talk elatedly long afterwards about his 'endless river expedition'.[18] It was also on this trip that a key stimulant for the Frankenstein story may have been fed to Mary's brain when they stopped off at Oxford. 'We saw the Bodleian Library, the Clarendon Press, and walked through the quadrangles of the different colleges,' Charles reported, adding, 'We visited the very rooms where the two noted infidels, Shelley and Hogg (now, happily, excluded from the society of the present residents), pored, with the incessant and unwearied application of the alchymist, over the certified and natural boundaries of human knowledge.'[19]

In January 1816 Mary gave birth to her first surviving child, William, an event roughly coinciding with the publication of Percy's poem *Alastor*. But by May they were preparing for another Continental trip. The motive for the adventure this time was different. Claire, romantically desiring a poet to call her own, had in April managed to effect a liaison with Lord Byron, and had soon become pregnant by him (Allegra, her daughter, was born the following January). Without telling Mary, Claire had persuaded Percy to head for Geneva, where she knew Byron was planning to settle for the summer, he having decided once and for all to leave England. It may be, as Richard Holmes suggests, that the as yet unknown poet Shelley saw the possibility of using Claire to engineer a meeting with Byron, the most famous poet in Europe. Everything finally went according to plan. The Shelley party waited ten days at Geneva until Byron arrived in his Napoleonic coach. Although initially reluctant to take up once again with the insistent Claire, he finally relented, writing to his half-sister Augusta that 'I could not exactly play the stoic with a woman who had scrambled eight hundred miles to unphilosophize me.'[20] When he wrote to a friend six months later about the summer he spent with the Shelley party at Geneva, this erotic element figured prominently in his recollections: 'I was half mad . . . between metaphysics, mountains, lakes, love unextinguishable, thoughts unalterable and the nightmare of my own delinquencies,' he said (xix).

And in the midst of this extreme mood of fecundity was Mary Godwin. Her sensations had been awakened to the full when she encountered and fell in love with Shelley. The endless play of the body that Caleb Williams could only experience voyeuristically, and which Godwin ecstatically encountered in reality with his all too brief relationship with Mary Wollstonecraft, had for a time satisfied her exorbitant adolescent cravings. By now Mary had matured a great deal, yet her sensations were as eager for 'creative' outlets as ever. In her first letter home to Fanny we glimpse in her excited descriptions of her surroundings just how joyously overtaken by the effects of nature she was. These are responses that will be paralleled by the Creature's 'new born' encounters with the world in a story she as yet had not an inkling of writing:

To what a different scene are we now arrived! To the warm sunshine and to the humming of sun-loving insects. From the windows of our hotel we see the lovely lake, blue as the heavens which it reflects, and sparkling with golden beams . . . We have hired a boat, and every evening at about six o'clock we sail on the lake, which is delightful, whether we glide over a glassy surface or are speeded along by a strong wind . . . the tossing of our boat raises my spirits and inspires me with unusual hilarity.

. . . coming to this delightful spot during this divine weather, I feel as happy as a new-fledged bird, and hardly care what twig I fly to, so that I may try my new-found wings. A more experienced bird may be more difficult in its choice of a bower; but in my present temper of mind, the budding flowers, the fresh grass of spring, and the happy creatures about me that live and enjoy these pleasures, are quite enough to afford me exquisite delight, even though clouds should shut out Mont Blanc from my sight. Adieu![21]

Of course, the weather did not hold, and the Byron and Shelley parties, as is famously known, were forced to remain indoors by inclement weather, telling each other ghost stories and talking (as Polidori reported) 'till the ladies' brains whizzed with giddiness, about idealism' (xix). But the anarchic 'hilarity' which the rushing winds and fragrant scents of nature had awakened in Mary's mind at this time, *did* hold, when the imaginations of the other participants in the 'ghost-story contest' failed to produce much. And thus did the '*The daughter of William and Mary*', progeny of a 'significant new marriage between Imagination and Reason', come to invent one of the most startling stories of modern times.

Perhaps the most telling observation to be made about what Mary calls her 'waking dream' (9) is that it offers 'living' evidence that an intellectually sophisticated but modest young woman living in the shadow of her male companions could wrench the initiative from them, and by 'experiment' (i.e. testing from experience) discover both the power source of her own literary talent and in the same movement devise a plot for the story she was so desperate to invent. The account she gives of her dream supports this (8–9). And the creature of her imagination having been brought to life with its 'speculative eyes' – as with all living organisms – is determined to live, and to prosper.

11 Politics, Science, and the 'Frankenstein Idea'

Politics

In August 1823 Mary Shelley returned to London from Florence after her five-year stay in Italy and – as she wrote in a letter to Leigh Hunt – 'I found myself famous! Frankenstein had prodigious success as a drama & was about to be repeated for the 23rd night at the English opera house.' She went on to describe in detail her reaction to Richard Brinsley Peake's *Presumption; or The Fate of Frankenstein*, beginning:

The playbill amused me extremely, for in the list of dramatis personae came, — by Mr T. Cooke: this nameless mode of naming the unnameable is rather good.[1]

That the Creature is nameless and denied any status or recognition by the Creator to whom he owes his miserable existence has indicated to one Marxist critic of *Frankenstein* that he is a symbol of the emerging industrial proletariat of early nineteenth-century England. Interpreting Mary Shelley's story as one born of 'the fear of bourgeois civilization', Franco Moretti argues that: 'Between Frankenstein and the monster there is an ambivalent, dialectical relationship, the same as that which, according to Marx, connects capital with wage-labour.'[2] Such a view is certainly suggestive in beginning a consideration of the political context of the novel. This is partly because a struggle for political reform involving a growing but as yet hardly recognized working-class movement was indeed taking place in the second decade of the century. Equally important, it was a struggle which Mary Shelley followed with interest, as I shall presently discuss.

The years following the end of the war with France in 1815 were ones of acute political discontent in England, brought about by a number of factors. Most important in this period of post-war economic depression was the underlying situation of an almost permanent surplus of labour in many areas, due to the high rate of population growth. Returning military forces formed an army of unemployed and as machines increasingly displaced manual labour, particularly in textile production, the collapse of traditional industries added further to this number. It is not surprising to find the consequent agitation for political reform, which many workers now saw as the means to protect their interests, being perceived by the government as threatening the very fabric of the social order. But interestingly, although such agitation did often involve large gatherings and sometimes spilled over into riot during the critical phase of 1816–20, for the most part political demonstrations and meetings were peaceful affairs. This was extremely disturbing to some of the authorities. For instance, during the great strike of Manchester cotton-spinners of 1818, General Byng's comment on their mass march was that: 'The peaceable demeanour of so many thousand unemployed Men is not natural.'[3] This kind of disquiet and difficulty on the part of the political establishment in knowing how to respond to such orderly protest lends support to David Musselwhite's notion that 'the problem of "naming" was perhaps the most critical *political* problem of the period'.[4] More importantly, knowing that Mary Shelley took a good deal of interest in these political struggles as they were happening – her letters reveal this – shows that politics could well be an important factor in the formation of the *Frankenstein* text.

Her appreciation of the political situation is shown in her letter of 2 March 1817 when, still deeply engrossed in writing the first draft of *Frankenstein*, she wrote to Leigh Hunt from Peacock's house in Marlow:

Shelley & Peacock have started a question which I do not esteem myself wise enough to decide upon – and yet as they seem determined to act on it I wish them to have the *best advise*. As a prelude to this you must be reminded that Hamden was of Bucks and our two worthies want to be his successors for which reason they intend to refuse to pay the taxes as illegally imposed – What effect will this have & ought they to do it is the question? Pray let me know your opinion.

Our house is very political as well as poetical and I hope you will acquire a fresh spirit for both when you come here . . .

. . . I have not yet seen the Examiner but when I do I shall judge if you have been disturbed since we left you – The present state of affairs is sufficient to rouse any one I should suppose except (as I wish to be contemptuous) a weekly politician – This however as I have not seen your paper is rather cat's play – . . .[5]

In this mixture of playful bantering and incisive hectoring we see some of the most distinctive of the young Mary Shelley's capacities and energies at work. Surrounded by idealistic (male) political enthusiasts, as an intelligent, informed female – yet thereby somewhat socially displaced and undervalued – she feels goaded into displaying her knowledge and being confidently provocative to the 'weekly politician' Hunt, editor of the *Examiner*. As we have seen, Godwin had taught her well in giving her a 'masculine' understanding. The 'illustrious Hampden', as she describes the leading Parliamentary opposer to Charles I in *Frankenstein* (155), was a heroic figure for many other political radicals, as well as Shelley and Peacock. By 1816–17, a large number of Hampden Clubs had sprung up in England, particularly in Lancashire and the east Midlands.[6] These were dedicated to political reform, which by now meant petitioning for universal (male) suffrage and annual parliaments, activities that had resurfaced after being curbed from the mid-1790s by Pitt's war with revolutionary France. 'The present state of affairs' in Mary's letter refers to the government's latest repressive response to the various acts of political agitation that had been taking place. These had begun with the Spa Fields riots of December 1816 and culminated in the Prince Regent's carriage being mobbed and its window broken as he returned from the opening of Parliament on 28 January. As a result, 'In the last days of February and in March a succession of measures were passed against the reformers, re-enacting in their full severity the repressive legislation of the 1790s. Habeus Corpus was suspended until 1 July 1817', and the Seditious Meetings Act suppressed and prohibited all reforming 'Societies and Clubs . . . as unlawful combinations and confederacies'.[7]

Why, we might ask, were such repressive measures necessary? The answer can be summed up in one word: fear. To talk of 'the fear of bourgeois civilization' being provoked by the demands of a discontented and threatening 'working class' is probably too simplistic. As E.P. Thompson has said:

We have spoken of the *artisan* culture of the Twenties. It is the most accurate term to hand, and yet it is not more than approximate. We have seen that '*petit-bourgeois*' (with its usual pejorative associations) will not do; while to speak of a 'working-class' culture would be premature. But by artisan we should understand a milieu which touched the London shipwrights and Manchester factory operatives at one side, and the degraded artisans, the outworkers, at the other. To Cobbett these comprised the 'journeymen and labourers', or, more briefly, 'the people'.[8]

'The people' did not define a uniform class but a heterogeneous collection of working and unemployed groupings. This provoked William Hazlitt in 1818 to pose the question, 'What is the people?', a question which, as David Musselwhite has said, 'to a very large extent remained, and remains, unanswered'.[9] Nevertheless the perceived *threat* posed by 'the people' was real enough for the political establishment and the property-owning orders. And this is where 'gothic' fiction and political reality can and do overlap.

Since the eighteenth century, 'the mob' had been a convenient shorthand for describing the social order's image of a hostile crowd composed of the lower echelons of society. Now the threat had come of age, had reached the gates of Westminster, and it was demanding a piece of the political action. For many this was no longer merely the mob, but a Monster whose provocative demands were not to be endured. Mary Shelley herself, though brought up a republican by Godwin, found violent revolution in England a hateful prospect. As she said in a letter to Percy about the incitement to violence she found in Cobbett's *Political Register*:

Have you seen Cobbett's 23 No. to the Borough mongers – Why he appears to be making out a list for proscription – I actually shudder to read it – a revolution in this country would not be *bloodless* if that man has any power in it. He is I fear somewhat of a Marius perhaps of a Marat – I like him not – I fear he is a bad man – He encourages in the multitude the worst possible human passion *revenge* . . .[10]

As we have seen in Part One, the Creature's 'disappointed sympathies' finally provoke him into a downward spiral of revenge upon his maker Frankenstein, offering us a graphic demonstration of what the 'worst possible human passion' can produce. Mary Shelley's reference to Marat in this regard is instructive. Marat was a journalist who championed the cause of the lower orders in the French Revolution, advocating the massacre of those formerly in power as a form of revenge for the injustices of the *ancien régime*. Then he was famously assassinated himself during Robespierre's Reign of Terror in 1793. As well as being *au fait* with the political struggle of her own time, then, Mary shows familiarity with the politics of the pre-war 1790s. Indeed, as one commentator has said, both 'Mary et Shelley étaient enfants de la Révolution'.[11]

This may be somewhat overstating things in the case of Mary, yet the influence of the French Revolution on them both is crucial to consider if we are to pursue the notion that (as William St Clair has said) 'Frankenstein's discovery of life was an obvious political metaphor'.[12] It may be true that this is obvious, and it has been noted many times before that 'it is possible to see *Frankenstein* as a kind of anti-jacobinical tract with the Monster representing all that the social order most deeply feared and resented'.[13] Yet it is no less powerful a metaphor for all that. Particularly when applied to the situation of the French Revolution, this becomes even more important to notice, because what we see alerts us to the central *ethical* considerations being projected in Mary Shelley's text. Anne K. Mellor's description of how the making of the Creature can be read as a metaphor for the French Revolution is admirably succinct. But first she mentions that all-important inspirer of the revolutionaries, Rousseau, noting how one can see Frankenstein's creation 'as an attempt to achieve the final perfecting of Rousseau's natural man, to produce an immortal being of great physical strength and powerful passions who transcends the chains of social oppression and death'. She goes on:

Mary Shelley conceived of Victor Frankenstein's creature as an embodiment of the revolutionary French nation, a gigantic body politic originating in a desire to benefit all mankind but abandoned by its rightful guardians and so abused by its King, Church, and the corrupt leaders of the ancien régime that it is driven into an uncontrollable rage – manifested in the blood-thirsty leadership of the Montagnards [Jacobins – M.H.] – Marat, St Just, Robespierre – and the Terror. Frankenstein's creature invokes the already existing identification of the French Revolution with a gigantic monster troped in the writings of both Abbé Barruel and Edmund Burke.[14]

During their systematic efforts to understand the Revolution and its outcome in Napoleonic imperialism, Mary and Percy Shelley read not only the works of radicals like Thomas Paine, Mary Wollstonecraft and Godwin, but also conservative writers and anti-Jacobins like Burke and Barruel. In 1793 a deposed Danton, one of the Revolution's original leading activists, despairingly told his successor Garat how the Girondins 'had forced us to throw ourselves into sans-culottery – which devoured them, which will devour everyone, which will devour itself'. And Danton was indeed 'devoured' himself, guillotined along with other revolutionary scapegoats during Robespierre's Reign of Terror. Such 'devouring' imagery was also to be found in a highly developed state in the books of Burke and Barruel. As early as 1790 in his *Reflections on the Revolution in France*, Burke had warned that a military democracy (such as he predicted would be the outcome of the French Revolution) is a 'species of political monster, which has always ended by devouring those who have produced it'.[15]

In the case of Barruel, whose four weighty tomes, *Memoirs Illustrating the History of Jacobinism*, Mary and Percy took with them on their 1814 Continental trip, he explicitly makes use of the parent–child metaphor in describing how the 'Illuminizing Code' had 'engendered that disastrous monster called Jacobin'. The French Revolution, he says, 'has been a true child of its parent Sect; its crimes have been its filial duty; those black deeds and atrocious acts the natural consequences of the principles and systems that gave it birth'.[16] As we already noted in Part One, Barruel's argument was that the French Revolution and its associated disasters had originated at Ingolstadt, famous as the home of the Illuminati, a secret revolutionary society founded by the university's Professor of Law, Adam Weishaupt, in 1776, year of the American Revolution. When Percy Shelley began his novel *The Assassins* in 1814, he used Barruel's negative account of the Illuminati, but perversely and enthusiastically 'reading white where Barruel wrote black' in order to portray his own utopian political society.[17]

There seems every reason to suppose that Mary Shelley had both Shelley and his zeal for the Illuminati's conspiratorial cause in mind when she located Frankenstein's creative 'experiment' at Ingolstadt. Although the plot being hatched was not now recognizably political, but scientific, that Mary Shelley wanted to show significant links between the two spheres is evident from the unpublished (and incomplete) biography of her father she began writing after Godwin's death in 1836. Writing of Godwin's radical politics in 1789, she describes the moment of the French Revolution in the following terms:

The giant now awoke. The mind, never torpid, but never rouzed to its full energies, received the spark which lit it into an unextinguishable flame.[18]

Science

It is now important to explore just what the scientific context for this 'spark' of life really was in the first decades of the nineteenth century. Why so? Some people have dealt with the 'science' of *Frankenstein* by simply dismissing it in the way James Rieger does, by saying that 'Frankenstein's chemistry is switched-on magic, souped-up alchemy, the electrification of Agrippa and Paracelsus'. Indeed, because (as he puts it) Mary Shelley 'skips the science' in her account of the Creature's animation by Frankenstein, he goes on to assert that the novel cannot therefore even be considered as science *fiction*.[19] But when *Frankenstein* is read (particularly in its 1818 edition) against the background of ideas, concerns and disputes being thrown up by scientific endeavour in the early decades of the nineteenth century, we gain quite a different perspective on the novel's scientific context. Without doubt this was an exciting period when a mushroom growth of scientific experimentation and discovery was taking place. In fact, the mood of excitement attending these discoveries – above all in chemistry – can be witnessed in the pages of *Frankenstein* itself. Telling Walton how deeply absorbed he had become at Ingolstadt University 'in the pursuit of some discoveries which I had hoped to make', Victor perorates on the attractions of science:

None but those who have experienced them can conceive of the enticements of science. In other studies you go as far as others have gone before you, and there is nothing more to know; but in a scientific pursuit there is continual food for discovery and wonder. (49)

We have noticed a number of times that the phenomenon of Victor Frankenstein embodies in many ways what Christopher Small calls the 'Shelleyan Idea'. In terms of politics he was imbued with what Mary Shelley described as a 'passion for reforming the world'. But from his earliest years Percy had been as obsessed with science as he was with politics. It therefore comes as no surprise to discover it was Shelley who added to Mary's manuscript Victor's paean to science. Thomas Jefferson Hogg, his friend at Oxford, remembered Percy's avid reading of 'treatises on magic and witchcraft, as well as those more modern ones detailing the miracles of electricity and galvanism'. Recalling the 'experiments' with chemical apparatus that Percy conducted there, he tells how at Oxford Shelley

proceeded, with much eagerness and enthusiasm, to show me the various instruments, especially the electrical apparatus; turning round the handle very rapidly, so that the fierce, crackling sparks flew forth; and presently standing on the stool with glass feet, he begged me to work the machine until he was filled with the fluid [i.e. electricity – M.H.], so that his long, wild locks bristled and stood on end. Afterwards he charged a powerful battery of several large jars; labouring with vast energy and discoursing with increasing vehemence of the marvellous powers of electricity, of thunder and lightning; describing an electrical kite that he had made at home, and projecting another and an enormous one, or rather a combination of many kites, that would draw down from the sky an immense volume of electricity, the whole ammunition of a mighty thunderstorm; and this being directed to some point would there produce the most stupendous results.[20]

James Whale's 1931 *Frankenstein* film was undoubtedly indebted to spectacular images of this sort for its portrayal of the Creature's creation, depicting these very methods of 'drawing down' electricity from a violent storm in order to assist his 'galvanic' animation.

Yet the essential attraction of this sensational 'thunder and sparks' image of electrical animation for a twentieth-century cinema audience was not so different from that which excited the curiosity of people about *real* scientific developments in Mary Shelley's period. We must remember that she was writing at a time of phenomenal transformation in the productive and social structures of English society – in short, the transformation we call the 'Industrial Revolution' – and as in all times

167

of perplexingly rapid change, people wanted answers. In the early decades of the nineteenth century the increasingly powerful and commercially-minded middling orders had a desire to hear what the new science, especially chemistry, had to say about this new world. Science historian David Knight has evoked well the heightened sense of expectation excited by the work of chemists in these years:

> Lecturers in London, Glasgow, and Paris attracted enormous audiences to their orations and demonstration experiments. The chemical philosopher was expected to develop and discuss a world-view; his science seemed the key to the nature of matter, and he was in a position to throw light upon such questions as the truth of materialism or the role of mechanistic explanations in psychology and biology. It seemed possible that chemists, using novel methods of analysis such as the electric battery of Alessandro Volta, might pin down the Proteus of matter and discover the one basic stuff which, in different arrangements or electrical states composed all the manifold substances which we find in the world. Coleridge compared the chemist to the poet as one searching through a multiplicity of forms for unity of substance.[21]

The chemist who attracted the biggest audiences for his demonstrations was Humphry Davy. Davy is now best known as the inventor of the miner's safety lamp, but in the early years of the century he was regarded as 'perhaps the greatest of Romantic scientists'.[22] It was through his friendship with Davy, who believed that 'chemical affinity and electricity were manifestations of one power', that Coleridge became absorbed in the possibilities of chemistry. But Davy can also be linked directly to Mary Shelley, for during her girlhood he was one of the many distinguished people to visit Godwin's household. Did she therefore go to any of Davy's spectacular demonstrations as part of her Godwinian education? The 1818 edition of *Frankenstein* contains a passage (subsequently cancelled) strongly suggesting she did:

> My father expressed a wish that I should attend a course of lectures upon natural philosophy, to which I cheerfully consented . . . The professor discoursed with the greatest fluency of potassium and boron, of sulphates and oxyds, terms to which I could affix no idea; and I became disgusted with the science of natural philosophy, although I still read Pliny and Buffon with delight . . .[23]

This is no proof of course, yet one can quite imagine Mary wanting to exchange the tetchiness of her stepmother the former Mrs Clairmont for the dazzling displays put on by Davy. Certainly, at a time when she was writing the 'animation' scene of *Frankenstein* at Bath in 1816, she records having studied 'Davy's Chemistry' for two months, with the result that both the tone and content of Davy's enthusiastic views find their way into her novel. In the 'panegyric on chemistry' delivered by Professor Waldman, for instance, Victor's new scientific mentor claims that modern 'philosophers' (i.e. scientists, a word not coined until 1834),

'have indeed performed miracles. They penetrate into the recesses of nature, and show how she works in her hiding-places. They ascend into the heavens: they have discovered how the blood circulates, and the nature of the air we breathe. They have acquired new and almost unlimited powers; they can even command the thunders of heaven, mimic the earthquake, and even mock the invisible world with its own shadows.' (47)

Compare this with the Davy:

Science has ... bestowed upon [man] powers which may be called almost creative; which have enabled him to change and modify the beings surrounding him, and by his experiments to interrogate nature with power, not simply as a scholar, passive and seeking only to understand her operations, but rather as a master, active with his own instruments ...
   ... who would not be ambitious of becoming acquainted with the most profound secrets of nature; of ascertaining her hidden operations; and of exhibiting to man that system of knowledge which relates so intimately to their own physical and moral constitution?[24]

We can be fairly sure Mary Shelley was not imbued with these ambitions. But many men of science, whether amateurs like Percy, or gifted professionals like Davy, were. And although the techniques for harnessing electricity (commanding the thunders of heaven), making explosives (mimicking the earthquake) and making moving pictures (mocking the invisible world with its own shadows) had been of more recent development, the *ambitions* to 'penetrate' the secrets of nature so as to take command of it for the supposed good of mankind had existed for a long time. One of Percy Shelley's heroes, the famous and influential statesman, essayist and scientist Francis Bacon, had committed himself to this scientific creed as long ago as 1620 in the Preface to his *De Interpretatione Naturae*:

Believing that I was born for the service of mankind, I set myself to consider what service I was myself best fitted to perform. Now if a man should succeed, not in striking out some new invention, but in kindling a light in nature – a light that should eventually disclose and bring into sight all that is most hidden and secret in the universe – that man (I thought) would be benefactor indeed of the human race...[25]

Brian Easlea has highlighted how this early modern blueprint for

European scientific endeavour was essentially a 'masculinist' affair, with 'Patriarck of Experimental Philosophy' Bacon (as he was called by one of his admirers) explicitly calling on his fellow-men to inaugurate with him a 'truly masculine birth of time' designed to accomplish 'the domination of man over the universe'.[26] Easlea is careful to note that throughout Bacon's writings a strong motivation of compassion for human suffering is often evident. But as he says, this humane purpose is deeply incompatible with Bacon's other overriding concern, 'not merely to *know* nature (which is the goal of insufficiently masculine philosophers) but to *gain power* over "her"'. He records how Bacon ceaselessly derides Aristotle for having adopted a passive attitude towards nature. 'I had not supposed, sons,' Bacon writes sarcastically, 'that we were on such familiar terms with nature that, in response to a casual and perfunctory salutation, she would condescend to unveil for us her mysteries and bestow on us her blessings.' Instead, aggressive experimental action must be taken to achieve the following end:

The end of our Foundation is the knowledge of Causes and secret motions of things, and the enlarging of the bounds of Human Empire, to the effecting of all things possible.

As a result of this kind of desire to subdue the earth, 'official' attitudes towards nature became transformed from Bacon's time onward, as Carolyn Merchant explains:

The new image of nature as a female to be controlled and dissected through experiment legitimated the exploitation of natural resources. Although the image of the nurturing earth popular in the Renaissance did not vanish, it was superseded by new controlling imagery. The constraints against penetration associated with the earth-mother image were transformed into sanctions for denudation. After the Scientific Revolution *Natura* no longer complains that her garments of modesty are being torn by the wrongful thrusts of man.[27]

While science remained in the hands of masculinist men it was hardly likely to, of course, and by Humphry Davy's time the Romantic Baconian scientist was using the 'new controlling imagery' with all the poetry at his disposal. Writing of the chemistry involved in living systems, he seems hardly able to contain his excitement, for 'The skirt only of the veil which conceals these mysterious and sublime processes has been lifted up, and the grand view is as yet unknown.'[28]

But by the mid-twentieth century, as Easlea argues, this 'grand view' had been achieved, with scientific conquest reaching a kind of paroxysm of success when the American scientists at Los Alamos in California finally 'penetrated' the mysteries of the atom, using the knowledge to create an atomic bomb. To describe this creation the Baconian 'controlling imagery' of female penetration now gave way to metaphors of birth. Marie Mulvey Roberts explains how, when the nuclear scientists went to the Nevada desert to witness the first nuclear blast, they were described by their wives as about 'to midwife the birth of the monster'. As she says, this was in effect to be the chief scientist 'Oppenheimer's Baby', and the bomb he was responsible for developing was called 'Little Fat Boy'.[29] On 6 August 1945 a 'Little Fat Boy' bomb was dropped on Hiroshima, its single blast virtually destroying the city and killing 100,000 of its citizens.[30]

Electricity and the Vitalist Debate

But now let us return to the important topic of electricity and that of 'life' itself, the nature and essence of which had been of intense interest to writers and scientists long before Victor Frankenstein came on the scene. Recalling that Percy Shelley and Byron had discussed experiments by Erasmus Darwin, who 'preserved a piece of vermicelli in a glass case, till by some extraordinary means it began to move with voluntary motion', Mary Shelley in her 1831 Introduction was sure that 'Not thus, after all, would life be given.' Instead, perhaps 'a corpse would be re-animated; galvanism had given token of such things. . .' (8). For many in the early years of the century it had indeed. Davy had been most impressed by the 'penetrating genius of Volta', whose means of creating a continuous electric current promised for him to 'lay open some of the most mysterious recesses of nature'.[31] Maybe even Mary Shelley herself had been wondrously jolted by the experience of electricity. In 1816 Percy had taken her to see experiments performed by the French scientist Garnerin in which an electric current was made to flow from person to person as they held hands.[32] But even more sensational were the 'life-restoring' experiments using electricity performed in London in 1802 and 1803 by Giovanni Aldini; these had entered into the folklore of scientific achievement by 1818, when another popular lecturer, Andrew Ure, conducted similar experiments.

Aldini, nephew of the famous Italian physiologist and experimenter Luigi Galvani, had given himself the task of demonstrating to the world the truth of his uncle's claim that animal tissues were the source of the 'galvanic fluid', i.e. the 'electrical fluid' some early Victorians believed ran through the nerves of the body and which kept it alive.[33] Whereas Galvani had confined himself to experiments with frogs' legs,

171

Aldini's performing repertoire was more extensive, including electrical experiments on the bodies of dead criminals when the opportunity arose. On 17 January 1803, it did. In the presence of Thomas Keate, President of the Royal College of Surgeons, the poles of a large galvanic battery were attached to various parts of Forster, a murderer whose dead body had been made available for experimentation after his execution at Newgate. The resulting contractions and convulsions provided a startling exhibition when the current was turned on, as *Tilloch's Philosophical Magazine* reported:

On the first application of the process to the face, the jaw of the deceased criminal began to quiver, the adjoining muscles were horribly contorted, and one eye was actually opened. In the subsequent part of the process, the right hand was raised and clenched, and the legs and thighs were set in motion. It appeared to the uninformed part of the by-standers as if the wretched man was on the eve of being restored to life.[34]

Reported in the press and patronized by the fashionable, including the Prince of Wales, Aldini's experiments created a sensation. Many were convinced he had indeed demonstrated the existence of animal electricity. *Nicholson's Journal* asserted that 'whilst it had been indistinctly apprehended or conjectured in the way of theory, that the galvanic or electric matter was excited, collected or generated in the bodies of animals, where it was considered as the great cause or instrument of muscular motion, sensation, and other effects highly interesting,' Aldini's experiments had been successful in 'having placed this proposition in the rank of established truths'.[35] William Nicholson, founder of the *Journal*, had been a close a friend of William Godwin since the days of *Political Justice*, and was another of the distinguished scientific visitors who regularly visited his house and met his family, and no doubt came into contact with the precocious young Mary. Aldini's experiments were by no means regarded as cranky by contemporary orthodox opinion. In fact, believing them to have established the possibility of restoring life in cases of drowning and suffocation, the Royal Humane Society applauded his work and the experiments also found favour with the Royal College of Surgeons.

Yet at this very same College by the year 1816 a controversy sprang up between 'vitalists' and 'materialists' that not only challenged the 'electrical fluid' theory of life-energy, but set in motion a 'science versus religion' debate destined to re-surface explosively later in the century with the publication of Darwin's *Origin of Species* (1859) and the notorious *Essays and Reviews* (1860), a collection of writings by Anglican divines that challenged the historical veracity of the Christian Bible. William Lawrence, a newly-appointed Professor of Anatomy and Surgery at the College, delivered in March two public lectures, one an introduction to the comparative anatomy and physiology then being undertaken in France, and the other entitled 'On Life'. In these lectures he saw fit to attack the 'vitalist' ideas of his former teacher at the College, the 'established' Professor of Anatomy, John Abernethy. The moderately-minded Abernethy had given a series of anatomical lectures in 1814 in which he claimed that life had its own principle, distinct from the 'organization' of the body. Criticizing modern materialists for using such concepts as 'organization', 'function', and 'matter' to explain the workings of living bodies, in his own 'Theory of Life' he asserted that mere words could never reveal the distinctive quality of the life-principle. He argued instead that this depended on a subtle substance, similar to, though not necessarily identical with, electricity. He supported this avowal by referring to his own teacher the famous eighteenth-century anatomist John Hunter, and to the work of Humphry Davy, who was also convinced that the 'vital fluid' of electricity animated all living things. In his lectures Lawrence contended that there was no separate 'principle of life' independent of the body, and ridiculed the notion of a subtle, invisible, animating substance by comparing it to the personifications found in ancient and medieval mythology, and by quoting from Pope:

Thus we find at least that the philosopher with his archeus, his anima, or his subtle and mobile fluid is about on a level, in respect to the mental process, by which he has arrived at it, with the

> Poor Indian, whose untutor'd mind,
> Sees God in clouds, and hears him in the wind.[36]

If these were the beliefs of untutored poverty, then they were also beliefs shared by Rousseau, Wordsworth, Coleridge, (the later) Godwin and, arguably, by Mary Shelley herself, for they all could be said to be Romantic deists of one sort or another. That is to say, they all believed, not in a conventional Christian God, but in a deity, a beneficent universal principle governing the universe, something like the 'theism' that Godwin, weaned off his atheism by Coleridge in 1800, described as consisting in 'a reverent and soothing contemplation of all that is beautiful, grand, or mysterious in the system of the universe'.[37]

The debate raged on. In 1817 Lawrence defended his materialistic position in an outright attack on Abernethy where he again ridiculed the idea that electricity, or 'something analogous' to it, could do duty for the soul – 'For subtle matter is still matter; and if this fine stuff can possess vital properties, surely they may reside in a fabric which differs only in being a little coarser.' Abernethy replied in a series of lectures delivered the same year, and alleged that the sceptics were afraid of a substance superadded to structure, since to believe in such a thing could imply belief in a soul. This, he said, would thereby endanger 'the privileges of scepticism', that is, the assurance that 'gratifying their senses, and acting as their reason dictates, for their own advantage, independently of all other considerations' (we should now say, perhaps, being 'selfish'), was true philosophy.[38]

How is all this fascinating controversy linked to Mary Shelley and *Frankenstein*? There is good evidence to show that, just as Mary Shelley took a close interest in the radical politics of her period, so was she intimately aware of the vitalist debate going on in science. First of all, in the late summer of 1815, when Percy and Mary were living in Bishops Gate, near Windsor, we know that Shelley, suffering a bout of abdominal illness as well as consumptive symptoms, put himself under the care of William Lawrence, and the treatment was a success. According to Marilyn Butler, Lawrence's involvement with Mary and Percy at a time when his radical publications in the vitalist and evolutionary field coincided with the 'years of the conceiving and writing of *Frankenstein*', suggests a dialogue between them that 'continues, embraces the novel, becomes its essential context and at times the text'.[39] This is certainly tantalising, as is Butler's more detailed speculation:

Mary and Percy Shelley, Lawrence's friends, were living near London in that March of 1816, when Lawrence's materialist case against spiritualized vitalism was first sketched out. It would not be surprising, then, if Mary's contribution to the ghost-story competition to some degree acts out the debate between Abernethy and Lawrence, in a form close enough for those who knew the debate to recognize. Frankenstein the blundering experimenter, still working with superseded notions, shadows the intellectual position of Abernethy, who proposes the superadded life-element is analogous to electricity.[40]

When Shelley and Byron went off on their famous eight-day trip around Lake Geneva in June 1816, Mary was left behind in the company of Polidori and Claire. Polidori's diary shows that he either dined or spent each of these days at her house during this time. Because of this, there is as much reason to suppose that Polidori 'revived' and reinforced the topic of the vitalist debate for Mary as there is to believe that Lawrence himself planted the idea during 1815. In fact, it may even be that the brilliantly accomplished – if insufferably vain – Polidori is himself a model for Frankenstein. Writing a dissertation on 'The

Psychosomatic Effects of Sleepwalking and/or Nightmares', he had left Edinburgh University in 1815 with a doctoral degree in medicine at the unprecedentedly early age of nineteen – the age at which Victor begins his 'creative' experiments. He was in London in the spring of 1816, and since there is every reason to suppose he would be keen to keep up with contemporary medical controversy concerning the human body, he is likely to have attended Lawrence's provocative lectures. Certainly in his diary entry for 15 June he states that 'Shelley and I had a conversation about principles, – whether man was to be thought merely an instrument'. Butler says that Polidori frames this question 'in a theologically sensitive way like Abernethy's, by using a word associated pejoratively with materialism – is man to be thought merely an instrument?'[41] She adds that in her initial summary of the conversation in 1831 Mary Shelley 'inclines to the materialist perspective of Lawrence', but that within a page 'her tone changes markedly', partly affected by the 'reasonable fear that *Frankenstein* would be contaminated by its thinly covered associations with Lawrence's brand of materialism'. As Butler argues, in the 1831 edition of her novel Mary did indeed make additions offsetting the originally more materialist base of the book with religious attitudes and judgements attuned to the prevailing conservative religious climate; we should add that these additions were also stimulated by her own desperate feelings of Romantic loss after losing Shelley some years before.

And yet, even if one relies wholly on the 1818 version of the novel, one cannot get away from the fact of a text in which something much *more* than a controversy about whether man has a soul or not is conveyed. I have said that Mary Shelley could arguably be considered a Romantic deist, someone believing in an active principle governing the workings of the universe, including the 'working' of human beings. At the very heart of her novel the Creature tells his story, and it is a story which is pervaded by a delight in benign nature, and an active joy at feeling alive in the world:

'The pleasant showers and genial warmth of spring greatly altered the aspect of the earth . . . The birds sang in more cheerful notes, and the leaves began to bud forth on the trees. Happy, happy earth! fit habitation for gods, which, so short a time before, was bleak, damp, and unwholesome. My spirits were elevated by the enchanting appearance of nature; the past was blotted from my memory, the present was tranquil, and the future gilded by bright rays of hope, and anticipations of joy.' (112)

These observations are not the product of 'rationality', but reveal a deeply felt experience of joy at being alive, and a soulful *desire* to remain alive: a celebration of 'aliveness'. Such a feeling is unmistakably conveyed in the Creature's long, moving speech at the end of the novel, too. In the last chapter I shall argue that although in a conventional sense 'God is dead' in *Frankenstein*, nevertheless the powerfully 'positive' desires which find expression in the Creature's narrative demonstrate that a new force has arisen in the world of literature by 1818. This is an awareness that it is *desire itself* and the language used to express it which is what now really counts in telling what it means to be human.

12 *Frankenstein*: the End of Enlightenment and the Birth of Desire

At the head of the Preface of his influential classic of Enlightenment thought, *The Spirit of the Laws* (1748), Montesquieu wrote the following phrase from Ovid: 'an offspring made without a mother'. Judith Shklar says he did not mean to imply by this that all the ideas of his book were new, but that he had 'put together a distinctive political theory that was unlike any of its predecessors'.[1] Given what must be for us provoking descriptions of an important Enlightenment work, we are in a position to pose an interesting question, and one which I hope allows us to conclude this study in a challenging way. What kind of relationship might exist between Montesquieu's 'motherless' work and Mary Shelley's novel, bearing in mind that the subject-matter of the latter is 'an offspring made without a mother', unlike anything to have gone before? Noting when each book appeared offers a first clue. Montesquieu's text was published with instant success in Geneva at the height of mid-eighteenth-century Enlightenment confidence in rational methods of inquiry. *Frankenstein*, begun at Geneva, was also published with great success (to an entirely different kind of audience), but seventy years later. Much cultural change had occurred in this period between the two motherless literary births, such that one recent comment on Mary Shelley's text has claimed that by 1818 *Frankenstein* could reveal the 'bankruptcy' of the 'Enlightenment project'.[2] This might be overstating the case a little. In a world where 'market forces' were making life very unpleasant for many people (see Chapter 11) there was still certainly a need for late Enlightenment notions of democratic political 'progress' to be put into practice. Nevertheless, the more extravagant speculations concerning the 'perfectibility' of man entertained by some Enlightenment thinkers (for example Godwin in England, Condorcet in France[3]) had now to be taken with a most generous pinch of salt. If we compare and contrast the text of Montesquieu with that of Mary Shelley (taking the former as broadly representative of Enlightenment thinking), we can also begin to trace in broad outline how over the period between them there was a shift in European cultural concerns from rationality and 'ideas' towards desire and 'the body'. These latter preoccupations are emblematized finally in imaginative terms by *Frankenstein*, whose author, importantly, 'was a child of the Enlightenment'.[4] And it will come as no surprise to find that it was a woman's piece of imaginative writing rather than a man's which achieved this, the most radical literary critique of the 'Enlightenment project' available in modern literature.

Let us start tracing the outline of this shift in cultural preoccupation from ideas to desire by once again considering science. Roy Porter tells us how by the eighteenth century the 'new sciences' of astronomy, cosmology and physics had 'destroyed the old harmonies of an anthropocentric (man-centred) universe, that small closed world focussed upon man himself, which both Greek science and the Bible had endorsed'.[5] As early as the beginning of the seventeenth century, metaphysical poet John Donne had declared 'And new philosophie calls all in doubt'. By its end the moral authority of the Church had been sapped by religious squabbles between Protestant and Catholic biblical theologians arguing over the fundamentals of faith.[6] Then during the first half of the eighteenth century rationally-minded Enlightenment thinkers came to believe that the 'crisis' of the late seventeenth-century 'European mind' (as the French historian Paul Hazard characterized it) could be overcome by the 'execution of a programme for the scientific understanding of man'.[7] Knowledge of the natural world, thought to be governed by 'natural laws', could reinforce (and for some perhaps even replace) an uncertain faith. So that, as Porter says, it was now that the idea of a true 'science of man' became 'central to the aspirations of enlightened minds'.[8] (We should notice how this phrase 'science of man' signifies in a neat fashion those masculinist assumptions concerning gender, knowledge and abstract ideals that we have found *Frankenstein* is so concerned to challenge.)

Montesquieu was one among a small number of philosophically-minded intellectuals (known in France as the *philosophes*) who sought to apply the methods of Isaac Newton in physical science to the study of man in society, in order to establish the 'science of man'. Although in the mid-eighteenth century there was much less specialization in academic subject areas than there is now (Newton for instance wrote more theology than he did science), thinkers did have their distinctive interests. Montesquieu's was politics. In the first comparative analysis of political systems to be undertaken, his goal was to see which type of government was the most satisfactory for the exercise of power. Narrowing it down to republic, monarchy, and what he called 'despotism' – the rule by fear of a monarch or prince manipulating the law – his systematic and supposedly objective study concluded that England's constitutional monarchy offered the best example to date of a system balancing liberty with order. The essential factor for genuine political liberty, as he saw it, was an independent judiciary; by separating the law from that of other agencies of government (the basis for his celebrated 'separation of powers' theory), the old autocratic systems wielding arbitrary power would be undermined.

Taught by science to base their thinking on facts and observation rather than ideas blindly repeated from the past, the concern of Enlightenment thinkers then was to establish 'progressive' analyses and evaluations of the world around them gleaned from rational reflection and the trials of experience. They believed that theories derived from the tests of rationality and experience would also have 'universal' application. John Locke has been described as 'the father of the central philosophical and political tradition of the Western world, especially in America'.[9] This influence was deep upon the *philosophes* and yet there was still a tendency for the French 'science of man' to be rationality-led and theoretical, an inheritance from the powerfully deductive philosophy of René Descartes (Cartesianism). In down-to-earth Britain, the bias was more towards experience and demonstration as the test of truth, hence John Locke, George Berkeley and David Hume have always been known as 'empiricist' rather than 'rationalist' philosophers. Despite its effort to focus on the real conditions of existence that shaped the 'spirit' of the 'body politic' of different nations, Montesquieu's efforts still tended to be speculative, abstract and wish-fulfilling in many ways, especially in the rose-tinted view he seems to have had of British public life (though compared with France it must have seemed a land of liberty). The concerns of Scottish Enlightenment thinkers Adam Smith and David Hume were more closely concerned with the bodies of real (though chiefly male) experience. Thus although Smith's *Wealth of Nations* (1776) has often been cited as both blueprint for and apologia of market capitalism, his discovery that human labour under that system is the real basis for economic wealth, rather than gold or silver, still remains true. Nevertheless he was more concerned to fashion a theory explaining how the productive process of wealth creation works 'universally' than to examine how the capitalist economic system would inevitably require the exploitation of workers. Smith tended to avoid this by arguing that the 'invisible hand' of Providence would 'naturally' assist the laws of the competitive market to promote the overall common good. Whereas he seems to have taken it for granted that God or a providential Deity had the interests of market society at heart, David Hume, famous for his radical scepticism in matters religious, was highly dubious about the evidence for Divinity's hand being behind the work

179

of human creation. And this brings us back to issues we have met before; those of atheism and the 'death of God'.

One of the features of the new science pioneered by Francis Bacon was that belief in God could be dispensed with, and replaced by a creed putting Man in charge of a universe whose discoverable laws would give him control over Nature, 'effecting all things possible'. Indeed, Bacon was himself an atheist. But when the idea that changing the world by gaining knowledge of its workings could be applied to the realm of society, people and political systems, the example of the 'progressive' Enlightenment-inspired French Revolution showed that there was perhaps something severely wanting in this scientific, knowledge-based secular outlook. Clearly 'ideas' were not enough. Edmund Burke recognized this long before the worst excesses of the French Revolution revealed the mistake, and used all his rhetorical powers to mount a crusade against the 'new philosophy' which dispensed with ideas of God, putting a supposedly self-sufficient Man at the centre of things. In England Godwin was viewed as representative of this godless new order of Independent Men, Burke describing his opinions as 'pure defecated atheism . . . the brood of that putrid carcase the French Revolution'.[10] Despite such sensational imagery, it was nevertheless true that the Revolution based on Reason had degenerated into Terror and military dictatorship, and so failed. And it would take more than a Bible-thumping evangelical movement to restore a confident belief in God again. (Victorian culture would do its best.) For the effect of the French Revolution and of the knowledge-based materialist science (like anatomist Lawrence's) which grew out of its typically secular thinking was in the end not a partial one, but absolutely total. Though the Revolution failed, the world it brought with it was a changed one. To his dismay, Burke realized this as early as 1796: 'The French Revolutionists complained of everything; they refused to reform anything; and they left nothing, no nothing at all *unchanged*.' He also indignantly observed that 'Ambition is come upon them suddenly; they are intoxicated with it, and it has rendered them fearless of the danger, which may from thence arise to others or to themselves. These philosophers, consider men in their experiments, with no more regard than they do mice in an air pump, or in a recipient of mephitic gas.'[11]

The fact that a supposedly all-embracing knowledge would try but be unable to replace divinity was not lost upon Mary Shelley either, whose appropriation of these observations of Burke's we can surely see represented in *Frankenstein*. I say 'represented' rather than 'reproduced' because it is no more a matter of thinking that she totally agreed with

Burke's ideas than it is of saying she was a fully paid-up Godwinian. This latter but mistaken view is represented in the 1818 Tory *Quarterly Review*, when John Wilson Croker wrote of *Frankenstein* that the novel was 'a tissue of horrible and disgusting absurdity piously dedicated to Mr Godwin [and] written in the spirit of his school'. What of course Croker and nearly everyone else was unable to understand about *Frankenstein* (including Percy Shelley himself) was that it was no straightforward Godwinian text celebrating the 'spirit' of the 'new philosophy', but an ironic critique *both* of that philosophy *and* of conservative traditions. The novel shows her instinctive grasp that the post-French Revolutionary situation had produced new certainties and uncertainties, in equal measure. And it is here that I want now to focus more carefully still on the significant shift captured and conveyed by *Frankenstein* of man as an Enlightenment being of ideas, to man as a Romantic being of desire.

Having known, one cannot 'unknow' knowledge. By Mary Shelley's time, the 'science of man' had advanced so far in its various studies of the workings of human beings that it was forcing people to perceive 'man' anew. To those imbued with the new secular scientific view, man was now to be seen in many ways as one animal creature among others; yet the human scientist was also careful to point out the superior position his species occupied at the commanding apex of creation. So although it was being recognized that he was shaped by and subject to laws of nature and his own social environments, Enlightenment thought had also informed him of his status as a creature whose perceptive capacities, thoughts, desires, and ability to make and manipulate the world had progressively enabled him to achieve a new 'self-sufficiency'. With such understanding also came the recognition that he was no longer necessarily under the protection of a benevolent God. Such was the bargain struck for true, human 'stand-alone' independence. There had already been various responses to the discovery of man as a creature of reduced significance when viewed in the new 'universal' scale of things. As long ago as the mid-seventeenth century, French philosopher Blaise Pascal, stunned by the discoveries of the new sciences, had written of the human condition as one of terror:

Observing the blindness and mean condition of Man and the extraordinary contradiction visible in his nature, and seeing the universe silent, and Man without light or guidance, thrown back on his own resources, as if lost in a remote corner of the universe, not knowing who has placed him there, or what he is supposed to be doing there, or what will happen to him when he dies, I fall into terror, like a man who has been carried while asleep to some fearful desert isle, and will wake up not knowing where he is or how to get away; indeed, at this point, I wonder how one does not fall into despair at our abject situation.

Pascal had become a pessimistic victim of a science declaring universal nature to be a vast, explicable but 'silent' mechanism in which man and his earth were meaningless because so insignificant and uncared for: he might just as well be dead. At his worst moments, there is more than a hint of Pascal's feelings to be glimpsed in the narrative of Frankenstein's rejected Creature. But Voltaire in the next century breezily upbraided Pascal for being so gloomy:

Why try to give us a horror of ourselves? Our existence is not as unhappy as people would have us believe. To regard the universe as a prison, and all men as like criminals about to be executed, is the notion of a fanatic. To believe that the world is a place of delights, where there is to be nothing but pleasure, is the daydream of a Sybarite. To think that the earth, and men, and the animals are what they should be according to the order of Providence – that, on the other hand, is, to my mind, to be a wise man.

However attractive this typical Voltairian riposte might appear to the sanguine and secure, the luxury of Providence was by 1818 something a rejected Frankenstein Creature could have little confidence in as he struggled for an answer to the meaning of his existence. And according to Michel Foucault, neither could anyone else in western European culture from the end of the eighteenth century onwards be afforded such confidence. This is because:

Before the end of the eighteenth century *man* did not exist – any more than the potency of life, the fecundity of labour, or the historical density of language. He is quite a recent creature, which the demiurge of knowledge fabricated with its own hands less than two hundred years ago: but he has grown old so quickly that it has been only too easy to imagine that he has been waiting for thousands of years in the darkness for that moment of illumination in which he would finally be known.[12]

It is Foucault's contention that when 'natural history becomes biology, when the analysis of wealth becomes economics, when, above all, reflection upon language becomes philology', then 'man appears in his ambiguous position as an object of knowledge and as a subject that knows'.[13] The consequence of this is that instead of being able to represent himself *to* himself as a creature having a coherent, comfortable relationship with the rest of the universe about him, as a being benignly seeing himself as created in the image of, and therefore resembling,

God – despite all his 'philosophy', he is now, finally, forced to regard his human condition as profoundly *finite* and limited. This new self-perception forced upon man as a being both conditioned and unconditioned may not strike him so much as one of terror, as it did the pessimistic Jansenist Pascal, but perhaps more typically as a circumstance over which to puzzle and grieve. Even that supreme philosophical champion of Individual Man William Godwin, when operating in his more insightful mode as psychological novelist, seems to have recognized this irrevocably 'double' status of modern man, when he has the despairing Caleb Williams reflect how

The pride of philosophy has taught us to treat man as an individual. He is no such thing. He holds necessarily, indispensably, to his species. He is like those twin-births, that have two heads indeed, and four hands; but, if you attempt to detach them from each other, they are inevitably subjected to miserable and lingering destruction.[14]

The difficulty of coming to terms with this 'betwixt and between' state, where one is fully aware of 'being' but cannot easily find a definitive place for oneself in the order of things, reminds us of the self-questionings of Frankenstein's Creature:

'My person was hideous and my stature gigantic. What did this mean? Who was I? What was I? Whence did I come? What was my destination? These questions continually recurred, but I was unable to solve them.' (125)

In antiquity some gnostic religious sects had posed similar 'existential' questions, and had invariably come up with explanations couched in psycho-spiritual or mythological terms. Thus for a second-century Valentinian gnostic, 'What liberates is the knowledge of who we were, what we became; where we were, whereinto we have been thrown; whereto we speed, wherefrom we are redeemed; what birth is, and what rebirth.'[15] The modern alienated Creature of Frankenstein on the other hand is never able to solve his self-questionings to any great satisfaction. He knows from reading Frankenstein's journal that he owes his life to the intensive labours of his creator. He has learned from overhearing Safie's lessons, and from observing the lives of the De Laceys, about poverty, scarcity and wealth. And he comes to know only too well from his own reading and from the stirrings of his body about the intensities of desire it is possible for humans to feel. But these knowledges and feelings, while providing him with strong motivations for wanting to be in the world, are also deeply frustrating. He finds himself in the condition of the modern man that Foucault describes as an 'empirico-transcendental doublet'.[16] That is to say, he discovers himself as a creature who is 'the produced effect of a labour, a body and a language not its own' and also that 'the place in which it finds itself is not reducible to the available co-ordinates of labour, life, language'. David Musselwhite is here referring to the Creature as an 'it' for important and fascinating reasons:

Anomolous and exorbitant with respect to all that would define it the Monster is the very figure of the unknown that haunts modern thought. This must be understood properly: the unthought is not something waiting in the shadows to be brought to light at some later date. The unthought that haunts the modern world is that which is the very condition of its knowledge. The basic paradigm of modern thought is not that of question and answer but the elaboration of 'problems' – the problem of gender, the problem of age, the problem of meaning.[17]

For Musselwhite the Creature is an 'it' because although assembled as a male, his identity is uncertain, conditioned as that 'free-floating' identity is by society's refusal to accept or even consider him. And yet that uncertainty need not be viewed negatively as a weakness and an evil. Instead, it could be considered, when experienced with an instinct for the affirmation of life, as a position of strength and exciting potential. The Creature of Mary Shelley's actual writing does in the end argue for such a view, and I shall now conclude by explaining this.

In Chapter 1 I started out by saying that *Frankenstein* deploys a range of underlying binary oppositions to make its way as a meaningful story with which we can connect, but that these are constantly undermined and fragmented as the telling of that story proceeds. Certainly it is the 'haunting' presence of the Creature in the novel that repeatedly threatens and undermines the security of the other characters, in particular his creator Frankenstein. And were we to remain on this plane in trying for an evaluatory 'overview' of the novel, we would no doubt be left sunk in gloom, full of regret and negative feelings for the Creature in his isolated predicament. Yet a close reading of the novel, curiously, stimulates in us at its end not a downward spiral of negativity, but an uplifting, anticipatory movement of affirmation. How can we account for this, when, much as in a Jacobean revenge tragedy, the 'stage' of *Frankenstein* is left littered with dead bodies, and we have a Creature announcing his intention to commit suicide? The difference is made apparent, for one thing, once we appreciate that it is not the resolution of the plot which suggests the kind of response we should have, but its *ir*resolution. The ending, carefully read, leaves things magnificently open. The Creature tells us of his *intention* to immolate himself on a 'funeral pile', and Walton tells us in the final sentence that the Creature was 'borne away by the waves, and lost in darkness and distance'. Yet we never witness, finally, the Creature's death, any more than we witness, or can envisage, the end of 'writing' itself. That is why I have been at such pains in this essay to close-read the text of *Frankenstein*. Mary Shelley's writing demands our close attention not only because all important literary works need to be explored in this way. It matters very much more so here because as a woman writing in the shadow of vain but mixed-up Promethean Romantic men, she exposes for us in this writing a 'fact of life' which cannot subsequently be ignored. That fact *is* the fact of 'life' itself. This is the major discovery that, as modern beings, we are above all to consider ourselves as creatures of desire who, having been given life, must explore and manage that life of desire in the best and most creative way we possibly can. The old certainties of divine guidance are no longer necessarily there for us. So we must nourish, satisfy, and negotiate the desires we find both within ourselves and between each other in the context of a world that will demand and have its satisfactions, but which, if it is to survive, must also *care* for itself. *Frankenstein* is all about how the urge to curiosity must be balanced by such care.

We have been able to trace all kinds of political, scientific and social ideas in *Frankenstein*, but finally we must recognize that Mary Shelley has written a novel 'that is, in many ways, a subversion of all ideology'.[18] Here is a passage partly illustrating this:

Soon a gentle light stole over the heavens, and gave me a sensation of pleasure. I started up and beheld a radiant form rise from among the trees. I gazed with a kind of wonder. It moved slowly, but it enlightened my path, and I again went out in search of berries. (99–100)

The moon, as we have seen, is symbolic of Mary Shelley's authorial presence in the text. But she makes it clear that this is a benevolent, caring presence whose 'enlightening' faculty is different in kind from that of the solipsistic Frankenstein. Absorbed as he has been by the abstract torment of wanting to real-ize the beautiful creature of his dreams, his success only results in imprisonment by the dreadful psychological traps of guilt, remorse and regret. But once created, his is a Creature of desire who proceeds to want to know, to enjoy, and to value life, and the buoyancy of this life-loving faculty is never finally, completely, lost. When his sexual desires are aroused, these are powerful and demanding, and because this is a female author writing, they carry the delirious, exorbitant and multifarious potential which the desires of women, above all, are capable of experiencing. Charlotte Brontë's *Jane Eyre* (1847) may indeed have introduced the 'madwoman in the attic' to nineteenth-century writing, but the wild and rebellious desires of Jane are also there to be read in a plenitude that is not to be denied, and as such I would argue that this reveals a literary debt to the energies and impulses generated thirty years earlier in Mary Shelley's Creature.

The Creature will not relinquish his natural impulses easily. That is why the final pages of *Frankenstein* are not depressing, but strangely uplifting. In his account of that which he would be relinquishing by committing suicide, the Creature in effect offers ironically but brilliantly reasons why *we* therefore should celebrate and value life:

'I shall die. I shall no longer feel the agonies which now consume me, or be the prey of feelings unsatisfied, yet unquenched . . . I shall no longer see the sun or stars, or feel the winds play on my cheeks. Light, feeling, and sense will pass away; and in this condition must I find my happiness. Some years ago, when the images which this world affords first opened upon me, when I felt the cheering warmth of summer and heard the rustling of the leaves and the warbling of the birds, and these were all to me, I should have wept to die; now it is my only consolation . . .

'. . . Soon these burning miseries will be extinct. I shall ascend my funeral pile triumphantly, and exult in the agony of the torturing flames. The light of that conflagration will fade away; my ashes will be swept into the sea by the winds. My spirit will sleep in peace; or if it thinks, it will not surely think thus. Farewell.' (214–15)

And like a heroic martyr of old, the Creature departs to his intended self-annihilation. But unlike such martyrs of old, his words and actions do not convey any obvious religious motivation or meaning; his triumph lies in the fact that, *despite* the miseries and disappointments of his existence, he is not rancorous. Bearing no ill-will towards anyone, he will have the satisfaction of ending the life of which he was once so enamoured, by his own hand and in his own time.

If, as has been said of them, stories are a metaphor for life, then Mary Shelley's *Frankenstein*, which shows that life is delicious and precious and should be properly nurtured for it to flourish, must rank as *the* story of modern times. For the Creature is here a metaphor for life itself, a complex of forces that we tamper with at our peril.

Notes

Full details of books referred to in abbreviated form will be found in 'Suggested Further Reading' on pages 195-6.

CHAPTER 1

1. Richard Holmes, *Coleridge: Early Visions* (London: Hodder & Stoughton, 1989), p. 173.
2. In his Introduction to *Three Gothic Novels*, ed. Peter Fairclough (Harmondsworth: Penguin, 1974), p. 20.
3. In her Preface to the edition of Shelley's poems she published in 1839, she described how 'The weight of thought and feeling burdened him heavily; you read his sufferings in his attenuated frame, while you perceived the mastery he held over them in his animated countenance and brilliant eyes.' See *The Poetical Works of Percy Bysshe Shelley*, ed. Mrs Shelley, I, p. xiv.
4. I wish to acknowledge here my debt to David Marshall, whose valuable chapter on Mary Shelley in his *The Surprising Effects of Sympathy* has been a valuable source of inspiration for my reading.

CHAPTER 2

1. Mary Wollstonecraft, *The Wrongs of Woman: or, Maria*, ed. Gary Kelly (Oxford: Oxford University Press, 1980), p. 89.
2. Marshall, op. cit., p. 183.
3. Carol Gilligan, *In a Different Voice – Psychological Theory and Women's Development* (Cambridge, Mass., and London: Harvard University Press, 1982), p. 174.
4. Quoted in Brian Easlea, *Fathering the Unthinkable: Masculinity, Scientists, and the Nuclear Arms Race*, p. 19.
5. Quoted in William St Clair, *The Godwins and the Shelleys: The Biography of a Family*, p. 317.
6. Anne K. Mellor, *Mary Shelley, Her Life, Her Fiction, Her Monsters*, p. 73.
7. *The Poetical Works of Percy Bysshe Shelley*, ed. Mrs Shelley, III, p. 72.

8. Holmes, op. cit., pp. 301–2.

9. In her editorial note to *Alastor*; see *Poetical Works*, op. cit., I, p. 142.

10. David E. Musselwhite, '*Frankenstein*: The Making of a Monster', in *Partings Welded Together: Politics and Desire in the Nineteenth-Century Novel*, p. 62.

11. Peter Conrad, *The Everyman History of English Literature* (London: Dent, 1987), p. 410.

12. William Veeder, *Mary Shelley and Frankenstein: The Fate of Androgyny*, pp. 56, 57.

13. John Milton, *Paradise Lost*, Book I, l. 229.

14. Edmund Burke, *Reflections on the Revolution in France*, ed. Conor Cruise O'Brien (Harmondsworth: Penguin, 1983), p. 248.

15. See Appendix A, pp. 223–4 of the Penguin Classics edition.

CHAPTER 3

1. St Clair, op. cit., p. 291n.

2. Frank Darvall, *Popular Disturbances and Public Order in Regency England* (London: Oxford University Press, 1934), p. 306.

CHAPTER 4

1. The psychologist William James would later characterize this new-born experience as a 'big blooming buzzing confusion'.

2. Claude Lévi-Strauss, *The Raw and the Cooked* (London: Jonathan Cape, 1970).

3. *Lives of the most Eminent Literary and Scientific Men of France*, for The Cabinet Cyclopaedia, conducted by Rev. Dionysius Lardner (London, Longman *et al.*, 1838–9), Vol. II, p. 157.

4. Peter France, in his Introduction to Jean-Jacques Rousseau, *Reveries of the Solitary Walker*, ed. and trans. Peter France (Harmondsworth: Penguin, 1979), p. 20.

5. John Locke, *An Essay Concerning Human Understanding* (Collins Fount paperback, Glasgow, 1984) III, 1, i, p. 256.

6. Jerome Bruner, *Acts of Meaning* (Cambridge, Mass., and London: Harvard University Press, 1990), p. 73.

7. Sir Walter Scott, *Blackwood's Edinburgh Magazine*, March 1818.

8. See Brian Rigby, 'Volney's Rationalist Apocalypse: "Les Ruines, ou Méditations sur les Révolutions des Empires"', in *1789: Reading Writing Revolution*, ed. Francis Barker *et al.* (University of Essex, 1982), pp. 22–37.

9. Peter Brooks, '"Godlike Science/Unhallowed Arts": Language

Nature, and Monstrosity', in *The Endurance of* Frankenstein: *Essays on Mary Shelley's Novel*, p. 210.

10. ibid., p. 210.

11. Michel Foucault, *The Order of Things: An Archaeology of the Human Sciences* (London: Tavistock Publications, 1985), p. 319.

12. A phrase used by Eric Hobsbawm in his *Industry and Empire* (Harmondsworth: Pelican, 1975).

CHAPTER 6

1. Cf. Rousseau's account of his time on the Lake of Bienne: 'I would make my escape and install myself all alone in a boat, which I would row out in to the middle of the lake when it was calm; and there, stretching out full-length in the boat and turning my eyes skyward, I let myself float and drift wherever the water took me, often for several hours on end, plunged in a host of vague yet delightful reveries . . .' Fifth walk, *Reveries of the Solitary Walker*, op. cit., p. 85.

2. This status is perpetuated, be it noted, in the 1931 James Whale film of Frankenstein, when, utilizing currently popular fringe-scientific theories of degeneracy, a 'criminal' brain is 'mistakenly' used by Colin Clive in building the Creature.

3. *The Letters of Mary Wollstonecraft Shelley*, ed. Betty T. Bennett, I, pp. 4–5.

4. Veeder, op. cit., pp. 7–8, 8.

5. ibid., pp. 9, 10.

6. Muriel Spark, for instance, in her book *Mary Shelley*, p. 164.

CHAPTER 7

1. 'Bastard/Masturbating a glitter,/He wants to be loved.' From 'Death & Co.'

2. We may here see a hint of Mary Shelley's feelings at the loss of her half-sister Fanny, who killed herself in October 1816, during the composition of *Frankenstein*.

3. René Girard, *Violence and the Sacred* (Baltimore and London: Johns Hopkins University Press, 1977), p. 26.

4. The title of the first chapter of Mellor's book, in which she argues for the plausible view that Mary Shelley's 'desperate desire for a loving and supportive parent defined her character, shaped her fantasies, and produced her fictional idealizations of the bourgeois family' (op. cit., p. 1).

5. 'Catastrophe': an older word for the resolution of a plot.

CHAPTER 8

1. *The Poetical Works of Percy Bysshe Shelley*. ed. Mrs Shelley, I, p. 375.
2. ibid., II, pp. 133–4.
3. ibid., p. 135.
4. Mary Louise Pratt, *Imperial Eyes: Travel Writing and Transculturation* (London and New York: Routledge, 1992), pp. 56–7.
5. Mellor, op. cit., pp. 41, 44.
6. ibid., pp. 42, 44.
7. Quoted by Peter H. Marshall in his *William Godwin* (New Haven and London: Yale University Press, 1984), p. 74.
8. Quoted by Mellor, op. cit., p. 5.
9. Quoted in David Marshall, *The Surprising Effects of Sympathy*, op. cit., p. 188.
10. ibid., p. 188.
11. Quoted in David Lodge, *After Bakhtin: Essays on Fiction and Criticism* (London and New York: Routledge, 1990), p. 90.
12. David Collings, 'The Monster and the Imaginary Mother: A Lacanian Reading of *Frankenstein*', in *Frankenstein*, ed. Joanna M. Smith, pp. 246, 247.
13. ibid., p. 246.
14. Anthony Wilden, in Notes to *The Language of the Self* by Jacques Lacan, trans. Anthony Wilden (New York: Delta, 1968), pp. 129, 130.
15. Lodge, op. cit., p. 90.

CHAPTER 9

1. Richard Holmes, *Shelley: the Pursuit*, p. 271.
2. See Glossary in Joanna M. Smith's edition of *Frankenstein*, op. cit., p. 349.
3. Christopher Small, *Ariel Like a Harpy: Shelley, Mary and Frankenstein* (London: Gollancz, 1972), p. 59.
4. George Levine, 'The Ambiguous Heritage of *Frankenstein*', in *The Endurance of* Frankenstein, op. cit., p. 7.
5. Paul A. Cantor, *Creature and Creator: Myth-making and English Romanticism* (Cambridge: Cambridge University Press, 1984), p. 105.
6. ibid., p. 105.
7. Chris Baldick, *In Frankenstein's Shadow: Myth, Monstrosity, and Nineteenth-century Writing*, p. 29.

8. William Godwin, *Caleb Williams*, ed. Maurice Hindle (Harmondsworth: Penguin Classics, 1988), p. 144.

CHAPTER 10

1. See Mellor, op. cit., p. 1.
2. See Richard Holmes's Introduction to his edition of Mary Wollstonecraft's *A Short Residence in Sweden* and William Godwin's *Memoirs of the Author of 'The Rights of Woman'* (Harmondsworth: Penguin Classics, 1987), p. 16.
3. See the Introduction to *The Mary Shelley Reader*, ed. Betty T. Bennett and Charles E. Robinson (New York and Oxford: Oxford University Press, 1990), p. 5.
4. I quote from *Burke, Paine, Godwin, and the Revolution Controversy*, ed. Marilyn Butler (Cambridge: Cambridge University Press, 1984), pp. 72, 73.
5. Holmes, Introduction to *A Short Residence in Sweden*, op. cit., p. 11.
6. ibid., p. 17.
7. Quoted in St Clair, op. cit., p. 161.
8. William Godwin, *Memoirs of the Author of 'The Rights of Woman'*, ed. Holmes, op. cit., p. 257.
9. ibid., p. 258.
10. St Clair, op. cit., p. 171.
11. See C. Kegan Paul, *William Godwin: His Friends and Contemporaries*, 2 vols. (London: 1876), I, p. 240.
12. William Godwin, *Deloraine*, ed. with an Introductory Note by Maurice Hindle (London: William Pickering, 1992), p. 26.
13. ibid., p. 36.
14. ibid., p. 36.
15. For both letters, see Muriel Spark, *Mary Shelley*, pp. 213–14.
16. Thomas Jefferson Hogg, *The Life of Shelley* (London: 1858), II, pp. 537–8.
17. Mary Poovey, *The Proper Lady and the Woman Writer* (Chicago and London: University of Chicago Press, 1984), p. 116.
18. The story of the trip is told in Richard Holmes, *Shelley: the Pursuit*, pp. 291–4.
19. Quoted in ibid., p. 291.
20. Quoted in ibid., p. 325.
21. Letter of 17 May 1816. See *The Letters of Mary Wollstonecraft Shelley*, I, pp. 17–18.

CHAPTER 11

1. Letter of 9 September 1823. See ibid., p. 378.

2. Franco Moretti, *Signs Taken for Wonders* (London: Verso Editions and New Left Books, 1983), p. 83.

3. E.P. Thompson, *The Making of the English Working Class*, p. 747.

4. David Musselwhite, *Partings Welded Together*, p. 66.

5. *The Letters of Mary Wollstonecraft Shelley*, 1, p. 29.

6. For a full discussion, see J.R. Dinwiddy, *From Luddism to the First Reform Bill: Reform in England 1810–1832* (Oxford: Blackwell, 1987), particularly Chapter 2.

7. Thompson, op. cit., p. 700.

8. ibid., p. 819.

9. Musselwhite, op. cit., p. 67.

10. Letter of 30 September 1817, in *The Letters of Mary Wollstonecraft Shelley*, op. cit., I, p. 49.

11. Monette Vacquin, *Frankenstein ou Les Délires de la Raison* (Paris: 1989), p. 151.

12. William St Clair, 'Her Father's Daughter', in *Frankenstein*, illustr. Barry Moser (West Hatfield: Pennyroyal, 1984), p. 253.

13. Musselwhite, op. cit., p. 67.

14. Mellor, op. cit., pp. 81, 82.

15. Burke, *Reflections*, op. cit., p. 333.

16. Quoted in Lee Sterrenburg's essay 'Mary Shelley's Monster', in *The Endurance of Frankenstein*, op. cit., p. 156.

17. Mellor, op. cit., p. 73.

18. Quoted by Mellor, ibid., p. 82.

19. Quoted in Maurice Hindle, 'Vital Matters: Mary Shelley's *Frankenstein* and Romantic science', *Critical Survey*, II, 2, June 1990, p. 30.

20. Hogg, *The Life of Shelley*, op. cit., I, p. 33.

21. David M. Knight, *Natural Science Books in English 1600–1900* (London: 1972), p. 128.

22. ibid., p. 128.

23. Mary Shelley, *Frankenstein*, ed. James Rieger (Chicago and London: University of Chicago Press, 1982), p. 36.

24. Humphry Davy, *A Discourse, Introductory to a Course of Lectures on Chemistry* (London: 1802), p. 16.

25. Quoted in *The Age of Enlightenment*, ed. Simon Eliot and Beverley Stern (Ward Lock Educational and the Open University Press, 1979, repr. 1989), II, p. 141, n. 13.

26. Easlea, op. cit., p. 19.

27. Carolyn Merchant, *The Death of Nature: Women, Ecology and the Scientific Revolution* (London: Wildwood House, 1982), p. 189.

28. Quoted by Easlea, op. cit., p. 28.

29. See Marie Mulvey Roberts, 'The Male Scientist and the Female Monster', in *A Question of Identity: Women, Science and Literature*, ed. Marina Benjamin (New Jersey: Rutgers University Press, 1993), p. 61.

30. Easlea, op. cit., pp. 110–11.

31. Quoted in ibid., p. 27.

32. See St Clair, op. cit., pp. 430–31.

33. I am indebted to Iwan Rhys Morus of Cambridge University for this information and much of what follows, taken from his (unpublished) conference paper, 'Making the Body Electric: Galvanizing Nature and Culture in the Early Nineteenth Century' (1992).

34. Quoted by Morus, p. 4.

35. Quoted in ibid., p. 5.

36. Quoted by Owsei Temkin in 'Basic Science, Medicine, and the Romantic Era', *Bulletin of the History of Medicine*, XXXVII, 2, March–April 1963. Lawrence is quoting from Alexander Pope's *Essay on Man*, I, 99–100.

37. Quoted in Peter Marshall, *William Godwin*, op. cit., pp. 238–9.

38. See Temkin, op. cit., p. 101.

39. See Introduction to *Frankenstein or The Modern Prometheus*, ed. Marilyn Butler (London: William Pickering, 1993), p. xvii.

40. ibid., pp. xix–xx.

41. ibid., p. xxi.

CHAPTER 12

1. See Judith N. Shklar, *Montesquieu* (Oxford: Oxford University Press 'Past Master', 1987), p. 67.

2. See Introduction to *The Enlightenment and its Shadows*, ed. Peter Hulme and Ludmilla Jordanova (London and New York: Routledge, 1990), p. 12.

3. Marie Mulvey Roberts discusses Godwin's 'faith in prolongevity' in her *Gothic Immortals: The Fiction of the Brotherhood of the Rosy Cross* (London and New York: Routledge, 1990), pp. 25–34.

4. *The Enlightenment and its Shadows*, op. cit., p. 12.

5. Roy Porter, *The Enlightenment* (London: Macmillan, 1990), p. 14.

6. ibid., pp. 15–16.

7. ibid., p. 18.

8. ibid., p. 12.

9. By Isaiah Berlin, in *The Age of Enlightenment: The Eighteenth Century Philosophers* (Oxford: Oxford University Press, 1978), p. 30.

10. Quoted in Lee Sterrenburg, 'Mary Shelley's Monster', in *The Endurance of* Frankenstein, op. cit., p. 146.

11. Edmund Burke, 'A Letter to a Noble Lord', in *Burke, Paine, Godwin, and the Revolution Controversy*, op. cit., pp. 51, 58.

12. Michel Foucault, *The Order of Things: An Archaeology of the Human Sciences* (London: Tavistock Publications, 1985), p. 308.

13. ibid., p. 312.

14. Godwin, *Caleb Williams*, op. cit., pp. 313–14.

15. Clement of Alexandria, *The Excerpta ex Theodoto*, ed, and trans. R.P. Casey (1934). Quoted in Hans Jonas, *The Gnostic Religion* (Boston, Mass.: Beacon Press, 1959), p. 45.

16. Foucault, op. cit., p. 319.

17. See Musselwhite, '*Frankenstein*: The Making of a Monster', p. 73.

18. Sterrenburg, 'Mary Shelley's Monster', op. cit., p. 144.

Suggested Further Reading

I give here a short reading list of writings on Mary Shelley and *Frankenstein*, as well as some works of related interest. For a much fuller bibliography, see the 'Suggested Further Reading' section of the Penguin Classics edition of *Frankenstein*, ed. Maurice Hindle (1992). If time or budget constraints mean students can only read one further text, that text should probably be Anne K. Mellor's provocative but comprehensive *Mary Shelley: Her Life, Her Fiction, Her Monsters*.

BIOGRAPHY

Mrs Shelley (ed.), *The Poetical Works of Percy Bysshe Shelley*, 4 vols. (London: Edward Moxon, 1839). The Preface and notes she wrote for this first full edition of P.B. Shelley's poetry are an invaluable biographical source for Mary Shelley's evaluation of his poetry and his personality.

Richard Holmes, *Shelley: the Pursuit* (London: Quartet Books, 1976).

Betty T. Bennett (ed.), *The Letters of Mary Wollstonecraft Shelley*, 3 vols. (Baltimore: Johns Hopkins University Press, Vol. 1, 1980; Vol. 2, 1983; Vol. 3, 1988).

Muriel Spark, *Mary Shelley* (London: Constable, 1988).

William St Clair, *The Godwins and the Shelleys: The Biography of a Family* (London and Boston, Mass.: Faber and Faber, 1989).

Emily W. Sunstein, *Mary Shelley: Romance and Reality* (Boston, Mass.: Little Brown, 1989).

CRITICISM

Christopher Small, *Ariel Like a Harpy: Shelley, Mary, and* Frankenstein (London: Gollancz, 1972).

Sandra M. Gilbert and Susan Gubar, *The Madwoman in the Attic: The Woman Writer and the Nineteenth Century Literary Imagination* (New Haven: Yale University Press, 1979).

George Levine, *The Realistic Imagination: English Fiction from Frankenstein to Lady Chatterley* (Chicago: University of Chicago Press, 1981).

195

Critical Studies: Frankenstein

George Levine and U.C. Knoepflmacher (eds.), *The Endurance of Frankenstein: Essays on Mary Shelley's Novel* (Berkeley: University of California Press, 1982).

William Veeder, *Mary Shelley and Frankenstein: The Fate of Androgyny* (London and Chicago: University of Chicago Press, 1986).

David E. Musselwhite, '*Frankenstein*: The Making of a Monster', in *Partings Welded Together: Politics and Desire in the Nineteenth-Century Novel* (London: Methuen, 1987).

David Marshall, *The Surprising Effects of Sympathy* (Chicago: University of Chicago Press, 1988).

Anne K. Mellor, *Mary Shelley: Her Life, Her Fiction, Her Monsters* (London and New York: Routledge, 1989).

Chris Baldick, *In Frankenstein's Shadow: Myth, Monstrosity, and Nineteenth-Century Writing* (Oxford: Clarendon Press, 1990).

Maurice Hindle, 'Vital Matters: Mary Shelley's *Frankenstein* and Romantic Science', in *Critical Survey*, Vol. II, no. 2, June 1990.

Mary Lowe-Evans,, 'Reading with a "Nicer Eye": Responding to *Frankenstein*', in Joanna M. Smith (ed.), *Frankenstein* by Mary Shelley (Boston, Mass.; Bedford Books, St Martin's Press, 1992), p. 217.

OTHER RELATED OR USEFUL WORKS

E.P. Thompson, *The Making of the English Working Class* (Harmondsworth: Penguin, 1970).

Marilyn Butler, *Romantics, Rebels, and Reactionaries: English Literature and its Background, 1760–1830*, (Oxford: Oxford University Press, 1981).

Brian Easlea, *Fathering the Unthinkable: Masculinity, Scientists, and the Nuclear Arms Race* (London: Pluto Press, 1983).

H.T. Dickenson, *British Radicalism and the French Revolution, 1789–1815* (Oxford: Blackwell, 1985).

Roy Porter, *The Enlightenment* (London: Macmillan, 1990).

A. Durant and N. Fabb, *Literary Studies in Action* (London and New York: Routledge, 1990).

Martin Montgomery, Alan Durant *et al*, *Ways of Reading: Advanced Reading Skills for Students of English Literature* (London and New York: Routledge, 1992).

(These last two titles are study guides highly recommended for students just embarking upon literary studies, and who recognize that Part Two of this Critical Study is only a starting-point for developing the skills needed for studying literature.)

READ MORE IN PENGUIN

In every corner of the world, on every subject under the sun, Penguin represents quality and variety – the very best in publishing today.

For complete information about books available from Penguin – including Puffins, Penguin Classics and Arkana – and how to order them, write to us at the appropriate address below. Please note that for copyright reasons the selection of books varies from country to country.

In the United Kingdom: Please write to *Dept. JC, Penguin Books Ltd, FREEPOST, West Drayton, Middlesex UB7 0BR*

If you have any difficulty in obtaining a title, please send your order with the correct money, plus ten per cent for postage and packaging, to *PO Box No. 11, West Drayton, Middlesex UB7 0BR*

In the United States: Please write to *Penguin USA Inc., 375 Hudson Street, New York, NY 10014*

In Canada: Please write to *Penguin Books Canada Ltd, 10 Alcorn Avenue, Suite 300, Toronto, Ontario M4V 3B2*

In Australia: Please write to *Penguin Books Australia Ltd, 487 Maroondah Highway, Ringwood, Victoria 3134*

In New Zealand: Please write to *Penguin Books (NZ) Ltd, 182–190 Wairau Road, Private Bag, Takapuna, Auckland 9*

In India: Please write to *Penguin Books India Pvt Ltd, 706 Eros Apartments, 56 Nehru Place, New Delhi 110 019*

In the Netherlands: Please write to *Penguin Books Netherlands B.V., Keizersgracht 231 NL–1016 DV Amsterdam*

In Germany: Please write to *Penguin Books Deutschland GmbH, Friedrichstrasse 10–12, W–6000 Frankfurt/Main 1*

In Spain: Please write to *Penguin Books S. A., C. San Bernardo 117–6° E–28015 Madrid*

In Italy: Please write to *Penguin Italia s.r.l., Via Felice Casati 20, I–20124 Milano*

In France: Please write to *Penguin France S. A., 17 rue Lejeune, F–31000 Toulouse*

In Japan: Please write to *Penguin Books Japan, Ishikiribashi Building, 2–5–4, Suido, Bunkyo-ku, Tokyo 112*

In Greece: Please write to *Penguin Hellas Ltd, Dimocritou 3, GR–106 71 Athens*

In South Africa: Please write to *Longman Penguin Southern Africa (Pty) Ltd, Private Bag X08, Bertsham 2013*

READ MORE IN PENGUIN

CRITICAL STUDIES

Described by *The Times Educational Supplement* as 'admirable' and 'superb', Penguin Critical Studies is a specially developed series of critical essays on the major works of literature for use by students in universities, colleges and schools.

Titles published or in preparation include:

William Blake
The Changeling
Doctor Faustus
Emma and Persuasion
Great Expectations
The Great Gatsby
Heart of Darkness
The Poetry of Gerard
  Manley Hopkins
Joseph Andrews
Mansfield Park
Middlemarch
The Mill on the Floss
Paradise Lost
The Poetry of Alexander
  Pope

The Portrait of a Lady
A Portrait of the Artist as a
  Young Man
The Return of the Native
Rosencrantz and Guildenstern
  are Dead
Sons and Lovers
Tennyson
Tess of the D'Urbervilles
To the Lighthouse
The Waste Land
Wordsworth
Wuthering Heights
Yeats